D0922707

bauhaus and bauhaus people

personal opinions and recollections of former Bauhaus members
and their contemporaries edited by Eckhard Neumann

 Van Nostrand Reinhold Company
New York   Cincinnati   Toronto   London   Melbourne

N
332
G33
B45

Translation by Eva Richter and Alba Lorman

Van Nostrand Reinhold Company Regional Offices:
New York   Cincinnati   Chicago   Millbrae   Dallas

Van Nostrand Reinhold Company Foreign Offices:
Toronto   London   Melbourne

Copyright © 1970 by Reinhold Book Corporation

All rights reserved. No part of this work covered by the copyrights hereon may be reproduced in any form or by any means—graphic, electronic, or mechanical, including photocopying, recording, taping, or information storage and retrieval systems—without written permission of the publishers. Manufactured in the United States of America.

Library of Congress Catalog Card Number: 66-22690

Published simultaneously in Canada by
D. Van Nostrand Company (Canada), Ltd.

Published by Van Nostrand Reinhold Company
450 West 33rd Street, New York, N. Y. 10001

10   9   8   7   6   5   4   3   2   1

Art
11/22/71
30850

Contents

Preface

In this collection of personal statements and remembrances, the Bauhaus is shown from a heretofore all but unknown human perspective. Through their various reports former masters, students, and friends permit here for the first time a look at the internal structure of the Bauhaus and point out both the uncertainty and the continuity of that turbulent era, in and from which the concept of the Bauhaus developed.

The idea to publish this book originated in an exhibition entitled "The Bauhaus — Idea, Form, Purpose, Time." Following Professor Teo Otto's plan, this exhibition took place at the "Göppinger Galerie" (no longer in existence) in the spring of 1964. The Bauhaus was to be presented in the framework of its epoch and was expected to stimulate the viewer to relate it to the political and sociological realities as well as the concurrent cultural trends of the 1920's. The thought of letting the participants themselves be heard emerged quite spontaneously.

Put recollections of the good old Bauhaus in writing! Is this in keeping with the spirit of the Bauhaus that always pointed to the future? Who will learn from it? the skeptics asked. And then — the Bauhaus had also many enemies, even among artists. And again — will the Bauhäusler (Bauhaus people) really want to write? Perseverance, however, and impelling curiosity to know what the Bauhäusler and their contemporaries thought today of "their" Bauhaus and its effect on the present resulted in an unexpectedly interesting collection of readings. They are supplementary to the history of culture and art, insofar as they are documents of the lively and effective discussions within the Bauhaus in those days. The book is about life at the Bauhaus and about daily living and the Bauhaus. In 1964 Walter Gropius wrote to the editor: "Yesterday I received your catalog of the Bauhaus exhibition, and I have been absorbed the whole evening reading the various contributions of former members of the Bauhaus. This is indeed an excellent publication, quite an important contribution to the Bauhaus history."

The texts in the original catalog of the exhibition were partly revised for this book, and their number was augmented by many contribu-

8	tions written by new authors, in order to present as many aspects of the Bauhaus as possible. An effort was made to arrange the texts so that their main topics would correspond to the chronology of Bauhaus events. For illustrations, mainly photographs of life at the Bauhaus were chosen, in order to show a great many unpublished and little-known pictures. In addition, the book contains a reduced reproduction of the Bauhaus manifesto of 1919, together with a complete translation. A biography of the author, prefaced to each contribution, preserves that contribution's separate and individual character, while it conveys something of the author's personality. It also shows his participation in the work of, and his relationship to, the Bauhaus, and reveals that the Bauhaus proved a stimulus that more or less decisively influenced his life later on. Moreover, the biographies answer in part that question of ever-topical interest: what has become of the Bauhäusler, what do they do, how do they think and work today?

The editor wishes, first of all, to thank the Bauhäusler and friends for their manuscripts, their advice, and their interest in the production of this book. He speaks for all when he expresses profound gratitude to Walter Gropius, who personally supported the plan from the time of its inception.

Thanks are also due to the team of the "Göppinger Galerie" under the leadership of Dr. Herbert Müller; to Professor Teo Otto and Wolfgang Schmidt for their cooperation when the idea of the exhibition was first conceived; and to Dr. Emil Rasch for his generous financial promotion of the catalog that was the basis for this book.

The editor wants to thank especially Mrs. Elisabeth Daume for her assistance with the extensive correspondence and the German text. He is equally grateful to Mrs. Eva Richter and Mrs. Alba Lorman for the difficult task of translating such a variety of texts, and to Miss Ilsemarie Gnielczyk for her help in examining the American manuscript.

Above all, thanks are expressed to Jean Koefoed for directing publication of the project; and last but not least the editor thanks his wife Christa Neumann for her patience and forbearance vis-à-vis such enthusiastic interest in the Bauhaus.

This book is dedicated to all Bauhäusler.

E. N.

The complete building is the final aim of the visual arts. Their noblest function was once the decoration of buildings. Today they exist in isolation, from which they can be rescued only through the conscious, cooperative effort of all craftsmen. Architects, painters, and sculptors must recognize anew the composite character of a building as an entity. Only then will their work be imbued with the architectonic spirit that it lost when it became a "salon art."

The old art schools were unable to achieve this unity and, after all, how could they, since art cannot be taught? They must be absorbed once more by the workshop. This world of designers and decorators, who only draw and paint, must finally become one of builders again. If the young person who feels within him the urge to create again, as in former times, begins his career by learning a handicraft, the unproductive artist will, in the future, no longer remain condemned to the creation of mediocre art, because his skill will redound the benefit of the handicrafts, in which he will be able to produce things of excellence.

Architects, sculptors, painters, we must all turn to the crafts! Art is not a *profession*. There is no essential difference between the artist and the craftsman. The artist is an exalted craftsman. In rare moments of inspiration, moments beyond the control of his will, the grace of heaven may cause his work to blossom into art. But proficiency in his craft is essential to every artist. Therein lies a source of creative imagination.

Let us create a new guild of craftsmen, without the class distinctions that raise an arrogant barrier between craftsman and artist. Together let us conceive and create the new building of the future, which will embrace architecture and sculpture and painting in one unity and which will rise one day toward heaven from the hands of a million workers, like the crystal symbol of a new faith.

WALTER GROPIUS

The National Bauhaus at Weimar grew out of the merger of the former Grandducal Saxonian School of Graphic Arts and the Grandducal Saxonian School of Arts and Crafts, with the addition of a new department for architecture.

Objectives of the Bauhaus.

The Bauhaus strives to reunite arts and crafts — sculpture, painting, applied art, and handicrafts — as the permanent elements of a new architecture. The ultimate, though distant aim of the Bauhaus is the Einheitskunstwerk (Uniform Work of Art) — the great construction that recognizes no boundaries between monumental and decorative art.

The Bauhaus wants to educate architects, painters and sculptors of all sorts to become qualified craftsmen or independent creative artists. It also aspires to establish a study group of leading artists who will be able to design buildings in their entirety — from rough brickwork to completion, including embellishments and furnishings that reflect a similar spirit and unity.

Principles of the Bauhaus.

Art in itself is beyond all methods; it cannot be taught. However, one can teach a trade. Architects, painters, sculptors are artisans in the true sense of the word, therefore the thorough mechanical training of all such students in workshops is an indispensable foundation for all creative activities. (Their own workshops should be completed gradually, and apprenticeships should be entered into with outside workshops.)

The school is the servant of the workshop. One day the two will merge into one. Therefore there are no teachers and pupils at the Bauhaus, but masters, journeymen, and apprentices.

Teaching Methods at the Bauhaus.

The manner of teaching arises from the nature of the workshop: organic form developed from mechanical knowledge; elimination of all rigidity; emphasis on creativity; freedom of individuality, but strict scholarship. Masters and journeymen are examined according to the regulations of the guilds by masters of the Bauhaus or outside masters from the trade guilds. Students participate in the projects of the masters. There is common planning of extensive building projects — popular and cultural buildings — with utopian aims. All masters and students collaborate on these projects, aiming for eventual harmony of all elements and parts pertaining to the construction. There is continuous contact with the country's leading experts on trade and industry, as well as with the public, through exhibitions and other events. New experiments are carried on to solve the problem of exhibiting two- and three-dimensional art in an architectonic frame. Finally, friendly relations are fostered between masters and students outside of the work by means of theater parties, lectures, poetry readings, concerts, and fancy-dress balls.

Scope of Instructions at the Bauhaus. Teaching at the Bauhaus embraces all practical and scientific fields of creative production: architecture, painting, sculpture, and related handicrafts. Students are taught a trade as well as drawing and painting, and also scientific theory.

1. *Workshops* — be it Bauhaus workshops or others, where students are obligated by contracts — comprise:

A. Sculptors, stonemasons, stucco workers, wood sculptors, potters, plasterers;
B. Blacksmiths, locksmiths, founders;
C. Carpenters;
D. Scene painters, glass painters, mosaic workers, enamel workers;
E. Etchers, wood engravers, lithographers, printers of fine art, engravers;
F. Weavers.

The foundation of the Bauhaus teaching is instruction in a trade. Each student has to learn a trade.

2. *Instructions in drawing and painting* include:

A. Free sketching from memory and imagination;
B. Drawing and painting of heads, life models, and animals;
C. Drawing and painting of landscapes, figures, plants, and still life;
D. Compositions;
E. Execution of mural paintings, plaques, and decorated chests;
F. Design of ornaments;

G. Lettering;
H. Construction and projection drawing;
I. Design of exteriors, gardens and interior architecture;
J. Design of furniture and commodities.

3. *Instructions in the scientific and theoretical arts* include:

A. Art history — emphasizing not a history of styles but the understanding of historical working methods and techniques;
B. Science of materials;
C. Anatomy — with live models;
D. Physical and chemical theory of colors;
E. Scientific methods of painting;
F. Fundamentals of bookkeeping, drawing-up of contracts, contracts for the building of houses;
G. Single lectures on subjects of general interest in the fields of art and science.

Work-distribution Plan

The teaching is divided into three sections: (1) instruction for apprentices; (2) instruction for journeymen; and (3) instruction for junior masters. The details of education within the framework of the general program and the work-distribution plan, which has to be newly set up for each semester, are left to the judgement of the individual masters.

In order to provide the students with the most multifaceted, extensive technical and artistic education, the work-distribution plan is so arranged that each prospective architect, painter, or sculptor may also participate in some of the other courses.

Enrollment and Tuition.

Space permitting, any person whose basic training is considered sufficient by the master counsel is admitted regardless of age or sex. The annual tuition fee is 180 marks (with the increased earnings of the Bauhaus, this should be gradually eliminated). In addition a single admission fee of twenty marks has to be paid. Foreigners pay double. Inquiries are to be made to the Secretariat of the National Bauhaus at Weimar.

April 1919.

The Administration of the
National Bauhaus at Weimar:
Walter Gropius.

Bauhaus and Bauhaus People

Bauhaus and Bauhäusler (Bauhaus people) are catchwords and concepts that symbolize, depending on the personal interest of the reader, the trends of New Architecture, New Art, functional design, and new art education. In the words Bauhaus and Bauhäusler is also expressed the great polarity between master and pupil, between the institution and the man working in it, between the idea and those who bring it to life.

Under the dictates of a politically and culturally active and strenuous period, the influence of which is evident in every phase of Bauhaus development, a Bauhäusler then was frequently considered a Tollhäusler (lunatic), while today, 50 years after the founding date, Bauhäusler is considered an honorary title. Yet the Bauhaus was, of course, a natural organism. In the very beginning (as can be read in this text and still more between the lines) the Bauhaus was more a state of being than a school. Nobody who has experienced that epoch will be surprised at this; and if one questions those who were at the Bauhaus — which means that they are, indeed, still Bauhäusler today — one gets comments that often are as romantic as they are emotional.

Three distinctly different stages of development can be connected to the three locations of the Bauhaus — Weimar, Dessau, and Berlin: the stormy developments in Weimar, the unfolding of an active, programmatic epoch in Dessau, and the cruel close in Berlin. But the Bauhaus was an idea that was readily carried forward, not only physically but mainly spiritually. It has freed itself from the era of its original action. As we celebrate its intellectual and material documents today, it assumes more significance and radiance than in its own era. This is because the Bauhaus had no dogmatic program but was an idea. "To build not only houses, but first and foremost a community, is the task — because great things are always carried forward by the community!" said Alfred Arndt, a representative of those studying at the Bauhaus when the Bauhaus building was opened in Dessau in 1926.

Opposition to the Bauhaus began virtually at the time of its founding. And at all times there were problems within the Bauhaus as it was the center of individual intellectuals, many of whom were seeking their own Bauhaus, but who were nevertheless agreed on the goal: Unity in Diversity, as Walter Gropius formulated it. In Weimar, as early as 1921, Paul Klee wrote about the coming together of the individualists: "I welcome the fact that so many divergent forces work together at our Bauhaus. I approve of the contest among those forces, if the effect is expressed in the achievement."

Many who were neither instructors nor matriculated students are part of the Bauhaus, simply because they cooperated as friends. There are the painters Walter Dexel, Robert Michel, and Johannes Molzahn, for example, who were in Weimar at the very beginning; or the critics and writers Bruno Adler, Siegfried Giedion, and Will Grohmann, who all their lives and in their works stood up for the Bauhaus. Then there is Alexander Bortniyk who lived in Weimar for a long time and who, after his return to Budapest, was the first to found a second Bauhaus, although for many reasons on a smaller scale. There are also Emil Rasch and Heinrich König, who gave economic support to the Bauhaus; and then there is the man who as communal politician held the most dominant position in the history of the Dessau Bauhaus: Fritz Hesse.

The deep interest in the idea determined the life at the Bauhaus for each participant, even after it had ceased to exist. The end of the Bauhaus in Berlin and the roads taken by the emigrants (most of whom found a new home in the United States and called into being a new phase of Bauhaus history) show a particular aspect of the Bauhaus — its vulnerability to the political influences of the times.

The Bauhaus as an idea lives on. There are new generations of Bauhäusler. Most of them never were at the Bauhaus, yet they think and work as if proceeding from the Bauhaus and from ideas that arose at the same time all over the world.

Eckhard Neumann

Karl Peter Rohl,
first seal for the
Staatliche Bauhaus Weimar,
contest design, 1919.

Oskar Schlemmer,
seal for the
Staatliche Bauhaus Weimar, 1923.

Walter Gropius:

Born in Berlin in 1883. In 1903 he began his architectural studies at the Technical University in Berlin and Munich, and in 1906–1907 he constructed the first buildings of his own design in Pomerania. Thereupon from 1908 to 1910 he became the chief assistant to Professor Peter Behrens in Berlin, where he met Ludwig Mies van der Rohe, who also worked with Behrens. In 1910 he established himself independently as an architect in Berlin and, together with Adolf Meyer, built the famous Fagus works, a shoelath factory in Alfeld on the Leine, and in 1914 the model factory for the Werkbund Exhibition in Cologne. He served as lieutenant of the Hussars during the First World War. During the Revolution, together with Feininger and Marcks, he was a member, and later chairman, of the Arbeitsrat für Kunst (Working Council for the Arts) in Berlin.

In 1918 Gropius was appointed director of the Grandducal School of Arts and Crafts and the Grandducal College of Fine Arts, which he unified under the name Staatliches Bauhaus Weimar in April, 1919. In 1923 Gropius was asked by the authorities to stage an exhibit that would render an account of the development of the institute up to that time. The Bauhaus weeks of the summer of 1923 documented the events of the previous five years and led to a renewal of the Bauhaus Idea, culminating finally in Gropius' proclamation: "Art and Technology — a New Unity." The Bauhaus in Weimar was dissolved because of well-known political difficulties.

Walter Gropius and most of the Bauhaus faculty and students went to Dessau in 1925, where, on the initiative of the Lord Mayor Fritz Hesse, and under the advice of Ludwig Grote, the Bauhaus was reopened as a city institute under the name Bauhaus Dessau Hochschule für Gestaltung. The festive opening of the Bauhaus building in December, 1926 became an event of international importance. Two years later Gropius trans-ferred the direction of the Bauhaus to the architect Hannes Meyer and established his own architectural office in Berlin. During his stay in Dessau, he designed and built, besides the Bauhaus building, the Bauhaus master houses, the housing development in Törten, and the labor-exchange building. These buildings are ranked among the most important architectural achievements of the early twentieth century.

In 1929 Gropius was awarded an honorary doctorate by the Hanover Institute of Technology. From 1929 to 1957 he was vice-president of the Congrès International d'Architecture Moderne (CIAM) in Zurich. In 1934 he gave up his practice in Berlin and emigrated to London, where he worked with Maxwell Fry. In 1937 he was appointed professor of architecture at the Graduate School of Design, Harvard University. A year later he was named chairman of the Department of Architecture and a fellow of the American Institute of Architects. In 1952 Gropius became professor emeritus at Harvard. Many international honors followed, among them an honorary membership in the Royal Institute of British Architects (1937), honorary membership in Phi Beta Kappa (Harvard center, 1942), membership in the American Academy of Arts and Sciences (1944), and an honorary degree of Royal Designer for Industry in London (1946). Gropius also received a number of honorary degrees.

After settling in the United States, Gropius, in conjunction with others in the Architects' Collaborative, which he established, built extensively in the United States, Germany, and the Middle East. Besides teaching at Harvard and lecturing at colleges here and abroad, he published widely on the ideas of the Bauhaus and on the education for design, which he subsumed in the concept of a New Optical Culture. In addition, he continued the work of the Bauhaus itself.

After the First World War Gropius joined the effort to reopen the Bauhaus in Dessau and supported the planned Bauhaus exhibition, which was to have been in Dessau, 1948. Gropius, together with his wife, Ise Gropius, and Herbert Bayer had arranged the exhibition on "Bauhaus 1919–1928" at the Museum of Modern Art in New York in 1938. The catalogue of this exhibition appeared as a book in Germany in 1955. Its publication gave the succeeding generation its first comprehensive information about his work and the idea of the Bauhaus.

Gropius promoted the founding of the Bauhaus Archive in Darmstadt and attended its opening in 1960. He granted the director of the Bauhaus Archive the rights to new editions and the extension of the series of books on the Bauhaus. Gropius also gave full support to the exhibit "Bauhaus — Idea, Form, Purpose, Time," arranged in 1964 at the Göp-

pinger Gallery in Frankfurt and he assisted the preparation of the current exhibition, "50 Years of the Bauhaus," which is now touring Europe, the United States, and Japan. At the opening of the show in Stuttgart in May, 1968, he collected all his thoughts on the Bauhaus Idea in a spontaneous and impressive speech that evaluated the Bauhaus as a contribution of understanding and communication in a new society.

Together with his team the Architects' Collaborative, Walter Gropius worked on international architectural and city-planning projects and he remained, until the time of his death, a major force in art and architecture. His own publications on architecture and design education are as numerous as the books written about his work. Gropius died on July 5, 1969, in Boston.

The idea of the Bauhaus— the battle for new educational foundations

Today, after the ups and downs, the victories and defeats accorded the Bauhaus Idea in the course of its growth, I can look back more objectively upon that idea.

Some time ago, among other papers pertaining to the Bauhaus period, I found a diary that my wife kept from 1923 to 1928 and that we had not looked at since. I began to read and the further I went the more depressed I became, for it became clear from the text that about ninety percent of the unprecedented efforts made by all participants in this undertaking went into countering national and local hostility, and only ten percent remained for actual creative work. You must understand that I did not then feel the depression this disproportion now arouses in me, or if I did, it was only momentary. Only in retrospect does the opposition to an institution proclaiming so unorthodox and revolutionary an education method appear in full measure. During the battle itself we were, of course, aware that we had to wrest our very existence from the lions' den, but at no instant did we doubt our ability to conquer obstacles. We were angry that people hindered us in our work, but we were not discouraged. We knew that we represented a new beginning and that we had taken only the first steps into a newly discovered world full of fascinating tasks.

If I had known then what I know now I would have had to tell myself that it was an impossible undertaking, that the intermezzo between the First World War and the Thousand Year Reich was far too short to create anything of lasting value, that the long winter's sleep imposed on all creative spirits during the Nazi period would destroy the carefully sown seed. But you must never believe an old man when he says something is impossible. For even with the best of wills he cannot put himself back into the frame of mind of a young man who, without the burden of experience, simply works and plans everything trustingly, as if he were going to live forever. Only by the strength of his imagination can he project his ideas so that they will last beyond his lifetime. I have observed that it takes at least a generation before a new idea can be diffused safely. Besides, the speed with which this process may be accomplished also depends on current social conditions. One could ask oneself what chance the Bauhaus Idea has to continue to operate when it is no longer dominated by the artist and does not even really reflect the wishes of the creators or consumers, but is merely governed by the might of advertisers or, as Toynbee calls them, the "great tempters." Under their domination it seems pointless to create buildings and monuments of good quality, which will endure for only a short time and soon give way to other products equally short-lived.

How can we escape this directionless whirlpool and give the younger generation the necessary elasticity, independent judgment, and moral resistance to enable them to withstand the avalanche of pseudoproducts that threatens to choke us?

One could rightly reproach me with being repetitious when I suggest increasingly intensified education as the only antidote. We cannot at this time hope to regain lost ground gradually through the slow, natural accommodation of human nature to the developments of the times. These developments deluge us so quickly today that we are hardly in a position to react properly to them. Rather, we must learn to broaden our education in such a way that it may sharpen not only our intellect but our perception and train both eye and hand. Such training has up to now been denied the artist.

But if we wish to bridge the abyss that yawns between the artist and the general public, we must determine to provide *everybody* with an education that will enable him to observe his environment with trained eyes. If today we are proud of the progress we have made in freeing the young artist from his dependence on the methods of his teacher, we must nevertheless remember that the greater part of our task still lies before us — that from the beginning of their schooling *all* young people should be given visual training based on objective principles. Given such a foundation, the talented being will always develop his own personal creative style, but if the artist is to be able to count on his employer's willing acceptance of his work, then both he and the public must start with the same general assumptions.

In this connection I should like to make one major statement: Today I feel sufficiently removed from the drama of the Bauhaus to be able to draw my own conclusions and evaluate what actually was novel in the Bauhaus' *method.* I can best illustrate this with reference to the methods of two such respected masters as Henry Van de Velde and Frank Lloyd Wright. Both of them conceived of the idea of the unity of the arts before me. How did they seek to accomplish this goal?

Van de Velde, the ingenious, imaginative artist with a world-wide reputation and inspiring *élan,* thought it was possible to establish the unity of the arts by means of his own formal vocabulary, his ''Line,'' as he called it. Almost without exception his students' work show Van de Velde's characteristics.

Some years ago I visited Frank Lloyd Wright's school at Taliesin, now being carried on by his widow. I saw the works of approximately sixty students and without exception they were pale copies of Frank Lloyd Wright's designs. I saw not a single independent experiment.

This shows that a great artist does not automatically develop a fruitful system of education. Assistants, not independent artists, were being developed in Van de Velde's artists' seminar in Weimar and at Taliesin. Certainly students' contact with a great, radiant personality is meaningful from a human standpoint, but I am concerned here with an educational *method* and its *goal.*

When the Bauhaus was founded I had already come to the conclusion that an autocratic, subjective learning process choked off the innate creative tendencies of talented students (when the teacher, even with the best of intentions, impressed on them his own thought and production results). In clear opposition to Van de Velde's method I concluded that the teacher must beware of passing on his own formal vocabulary to the students and that he must rather allow them to find *their own way*, even if they were detoured. If he comes up against independent thoughts and feelings in the student, he should encourage them, ruthlessly fighting imitation, or at least letting the student know that he was poaching on forbidden territory. The teacher must remain objective, using the study of natural phenomena to form the basis of the creative process, which can be gradually understood in terms of well-directed observations of their own biological and psychological development.

Artists at the Bauhaus attempted to find an objective common denominator of form — in a way to develop a science of design; this has since been expanded in countless schools in various countries. Such a foundation of general, superpersonal formal laws provides an organic and unifying background for various talents. Personal expression then has reference in each individual creation to the same, universally acknowledged basic concepts. In my opinion such education should begin in kindergarten. With such a foundation, if we can keep the hucksters at bay, we could gradually develop an art form that expresses the times, such as existed in strong cultures of the past.

Because the teacher's *method* is as important as his *power* — and this is so often misunderstood today — I want once again to analyze this educational problem, for I am convinced that the objective teaching method, which, it is true, must travel a much longer, thornier road than the autocratic one, nevertheless does not guarantee us against imitation and equalization. At the same time it preserves what is unique in each creative person and gives a common spiritual cohesion to the times.

The importance of the Bauhaus did not lie in the decree of a stylistic absolute, but in a new spiritual attitude intended to provide the art forms of our environment with an objective method of work and thought developed from elementary roots, whose spontaneous, artistic initiative was anchored in communal life to protect it from its own despotism.

The Bauhaus was and is a movement with dynamic momentum — its object, unity in diversity and conquest of the cult of personality.

Johannes Itten:

Born in the Berner Oberland in 1888. After attending the teachers college at Bern-Hofwil, he briefly attended the École des Beaux Arts, Geneva, and studied at the University of Bern, completing his studies as a secondary-school teacher. Then he turned to painting. From 1913 to 1916, Itten was student of Adolf Hölzel in Stuttgart, where he also made the acquaintance of others in the group, like Oskar Schlemmer, Willi Baumeister, and Ida Kerkovius. He began painting his first abstract works, which were exhibited by Herwarth Walden in his gallery, Der Sturm, as early as 1916. In 1919 in Vienna Adolf Loos gave the first exhibit of nonobjective art with a showing of Itten's abstract paintings.

In 1916 Itten moved to Vienna and taught. Through Alma Mahler he got to know Gropius in 1919 and was invited by him to join the newly founded Bauhaus in Weimar. A number of his Vienna students went with him. By the time he left the Bauhaus in 1923 he had developed a general course in design, which became known as the *Vorkurs* and later gained universal currency. In the beginning, until Klee and Kandinsky joined the Bauhaus, Itten was entrusted with developing the study program at the Bauhaus. His highly personal teaching method and his love of Mazdaznan greatly influenced Bauhaus activities in Weimar up to the exhibit of the summer of 1923. In 1921 he published his analyses of old masters in the *Utopia-Almanach* ("Utopia Almanac: Documents in Reality"), edited by Bruno Adler.

After leaving the Bauhaus, Itten immersed himself in Mazdaznan philosophy at Herrliberg, near Zurich. In 1926 he founded the Itten School of Painting, Graphics, Photography, and Architecture in Berlin. In 1932 he undertook the additional directorship of the State Flächenkunstschule in Krefeld. Two years later, however, the Itten school in Berlin was closed. Itten's first book, *Tagebücher* ("Diaries"), was published in 1930.

In 1938 Itten emigrated to Amsterdam, where he worked on commissions attained through Willem Sandberg for the Stedelijk Museum. In the same year Itten was elected director of the School and Museum of Arts and Crafts in Zurich. In 1943 he became director of the Textiles Trade School in Zurich. From 1952 to 1955 he was also director of the Rietberg Museum for Non-European Art, which he had begun to organize years before.

In the last few years before his death Itten was free to devote himself to his painting and he published two pedagogical works. In 1961 his book *Die Kunst der Farbe* ("The Art of Color") appeared and in 1963, *Mein Vorkurs am Bauhaus* ("My First-Course at the Bauhaus). In a large retrospective exhibit in 1964, his paintings were shown in the Kunsthaus in Zurich and in various European cities. He was further honored by a one-man show in the Swiss pavilion at the Venice Biennale in 1966. Works by Itten hang in many museums in Europe and the United States. He died in Zurich on March 25, 1967.

How the tremendous influence of the Bauhaus began

The general unrest, disorder, lack of direction, and uncertainty in the years after World War I fostered the establishment of institutions with new types of programs.

The Bauhaus in Weimar was both novel and unique because its art faculty consisted of persons who were among the leaders of modern art. Gropius allowed each of them a free hand in creating the curriculum.

The Bauhaus became known as the center of modern design, and progressive, talented students from all over the world came to take a decisive part in the construction of the program and the work. Many of these later became recognized artists and designers, and their achievement contributed toward the general outlook of the Bauhaus.

The Bauhaus was a center of activity for the problems of creation in art, architecture, design, technique, and sociology. But these were common problems for many progressive artists and technicians all over the world.

At the Bauhaus, artistic and technical media was taught systematically and thoroughly for the first time. The aim of my instruction in the Vorkurs (basic design course) was education to form the creative individual. This new method became famous throughout the world.

It is tendentious and absolutely false to describe the Weimar period at the Bauhaus (1919–1924) as unimportant and meaningless. The following facts are important: The art faculty in Weimar comprised Feininger, Marcks, Itten, Klee, Muche, Schlemmer, Schreyer, Kandinsky, and Moholy; Breuer, Scheper, Schmidt, Stölzl, Bayer, Albers were students at the Weimar Bauhaus during the second and third Vorkurs.

The first Bauhaus building was constructed in Weimar in 1923 by Muche and was furnished by the Bauhaus workshops.

Bruno Adler:

Born in Karlsbad in 1888. He studied art and literature in Vienna, Erlangen, and Munich, obtaining a doctoral degree. In 1919 he went to Weimar where he became closely connected with the artists of the Bauhaus. He founded the Utopia Press there and in 1921 published the famous *Utopia-Almanach,* with analyses of medieval paintings by Itten. Later he continued to publish in Berlin and Austria and in 1936 emigrated to England where he concerned himself with the interpretation of German art and literature. Since 1940 he has made frequent appearances on London radio. He has delivered lectures in England, the United States, Canada, and Germany on the history of the Bauhaus. At the time of his death he was working on a book about Hans von Marées, hoping to introduce this painter to the English-speaking art world. Under the pseudonym Urban Roedl he published books on Matthias Claudius and Adalbert Stifter, which have been widely circulated. Adler died in London on December 26, 1968.

Weimar in those days...

The Bauhaus — so one reads in books and magazines today — was an idea, a school of thought, a living organism. A description of the beginnings of these notions may not be out of place.

How can one get at the facts, looking at it from a chronological and geographical distance? Even those who were members of the Bauhaus are subject to illusions. In the first place the Weimar Bauhaus phase is characterized by a mixture of trends, which appear alien in contrast to literature, particularly foreign literature. This often leads historians and critics to risky judgments and interpretations.

The confusion is understandable: the Bauhaus began in a drastic period. Only one who was an observer, not a member, can recognize a historically determined and logical progress in the apparently contradictory development of the "crystalline symbol of a new creed" into a "machine for living," and of emotional expressionism into the integration of art and technology.

The movement, which did not erupt after the First World War but rather had its roots in it, and which one designates by the general term

"Expressionism," developed in two opposing directions. Janus-like it faced both forward and backward, dreaming of a romantic past and a utopian future. The young avant-garde German leaned toward mythologizing bygone eras, loved the medieval mystics and Far Eastern religions, and his artistic endeavors were influenced by the innocence of the primitives and the newly discovered world of the exotics. Thus there was a denial of everything merely rational, a distrust of industrialization and the masses. In other words, the movement was a flight from the brutal reality of a present that threatened to lead in a terrifying direction. But this visionary attitude was also connected with an optimistic belief in the renewal of mankind, in which mankind remained a pure abstraction. Individualists glowed with universal brotherhood, pacifists dramatized class hatred and parricide. Soul, regarded by others as the adversary of intellect, was done to death in manifestos and proclamations; and the kernel of truth hidden in all these postulations was stifled in a boundless enthusiasm.

No wonder the winged language of Gropius' first Bauhaus proclamation spoke directly to the hopes and quests of the young. Here they saw purpose, a new way of artistic thought, and more: a new way of life, founded on a real community of creators; new teaching methods in place of the old, worn-out conventions; a return to handicrafts; and above all the vision of a future creative unity.

Those who came to Weimar in 1919 to attend the laying of the cornerstone for this church of the future did not, however, have the impression that the young people were actively concerned with the theme of the new community that the unified work of art would build. They were concerned with matters of practice and method. More topical than theories concerning life was the actual establishment of the most basic conditions for a school and the clarification of questions of artistic education. Everything was lacking. There was not much more than Van de Velde's beautiful building, with its sorry neighbors; the old art academy was still organizationally connected with the new foundation, and at first Gropius had brought with him only Lyonel Feininger and Gerhard Marcks as new teachers. For the time being there could be no question of regular, systematic instruction.

Things changed only when Johannes Itten joined them. The strongest and most influential personality of the group, a teacher in the truest sense of the word, he laid the educational foundations for the first Bauhaus years in his Vorkurs, which — although much altered in form — was adopted by numerous art schools all over the world. Itten made unusual demands on the student. His theoretical and practical ideas were to include more than the basic teachings about figure and form; to comprehend all sensual, spiritual, and intellectual faculties — in short, the whole man, his very breathing, diet, and clothing. Itten's more immediate circle was for the most part composed of students who had come with him from Vienna, and actually constituted the only coherent group at the Bauhaus. Georg Muche, appointed to the faculty shortly after Itten (Oskar Schlemmer and Paul Klee were next, and after them, Kandinsky) called this group "the yeast which initiated the process of organic development in the Bauhaus. They replaced the initially somewhat crude spirit with relaxed composure and the grace of the free imagination. They were not what one generally calls *Bauhäusler*, for they would not lend themselves to simplification. They were and remain art enthusiasts."

There is an intimation here of the conflict that was coming to a head. There were frictions among the students and tensions among the faculty, not to mention endless attacks from outside. Oskar Schlemmer's diaries and letters movingly reflect the situation again and again. Basically it was the ideological and structural changes in society that led the participants to disagree despite themselves. Reorientation proved just as inopportune as an escape into an unreal image of the future. Gropius was the first to recognize the signs of the times and thought he must decide between the reforms offered: he chose the exoteric over the esoteric. Modern technology replaced handicrafts; contact with industry became more important than contact with an Oriental philosophy of life. Foreign influences fostered the change, especially the functionalist manifesto of the Dutchman Theo van Doesburg, the advocate of the De Stijl group. Itten withdrew and soon left. He was replaced by Laszlo Moholy-Nagy, who, more than the other masters, had real connections with technology and science. His teaching talent and his temperament soon assured him a leading place.

The fact that the pendulum did not swing to the other extreme was due to circumstances and the prudence of the director. Gropius imposed neither a style nor De Stijl principles upon his institute. But as little as he bowed to a new dogma, so little did he remain attached to an old one.

He was sufficiently unprejudiced to allow himself to be advised by his colleagues and to let the opposition respect what was worthy of respect. After all, the Bauhaus had been founded on the concept of cooperation with technology, and it needed only the ideological change to affirm its contact with industrial means of production. And had he not in his early structures anticipated much of what this new salvationism preached so vehemently? Functionalism was in the air, and sooner or later the Bauhaus had to follow the trend of the time.

Art and Technology — a New Unity, that was the watchword. Thus the difficulties of yesterday were replaced by a new one.

From the beginning the Bauhaus was not intended to be an art school. It was not to have been a sanctuary of nonfunctional art. For years, however, architecture was not taught. Paradoxically, while the construction of dwellings, the creation of functional objects, and technological processes occupied the foreground, in those years above all it was the important painters who lent luster to the Bauhaus. True, they did operate as artistic directors of the workshops, but what Feininger, Klee, Kandinsky, and the others created in their studios at the Bauhaus would probably have been no different in any other setting. Their works had hardly anything in common with the rational principles of the organization. Feininger would not hear of the unity of art and technology; Schlemmer, that man of utter integrity, faced the problem honestly and would have liked best to find some synthesis of the two opposing principles, had that been possible; Klee, of course, could not acknowledge anything less than free artistic creativity; and Muche explained lucidly the essential difference between art and technology. On the other side of the fence were the practitioners, with their engineers' aesthetics. The conflict was insoluble: only the director's intelligence could hold the opposing parts together. He could reconcile internal differences, but even he could not cope with external crises. Reactionary Weimar agitated and fought against the institute with the most incredible measures. Day-in, day-out Gropius had to fight lies and slander. And when a nationalist government took the reins of Thuringia, the Bauhaus's final hour had been tolled. The Weimar adventure foundered heroically on the political blindness and baseness that from the beginning had been, and would remain, their undoing.

Johannes Molzahn:

Born in Duisburg in 1892 and spent his youth in Weimar, where he attended the Grandducal College of Drawing. He studied photography, but was essentially self-taught as an artist. During a stay in Switzerland from 1909 to 1914, he became acquainted with painters Hermann Huber and Otto Meyer-Amden, who gave impetus to his artistic interests.

Molzahn began producing important paintings while still in the army, and in 1917 Walden exhibited them in his gallery, Der Sturm. In 1918 Molzahn returned to Weimar and took part in the founding and first phase of the Bauhaus there. Together with Karl Peter Röhl and Robert and Ella Michel, he was among the first artists with whom Gropius established contact after his arrival in Weimar. In 1919 in *Der Sturm* he published his "Manifesto of Absolute Expressionism," expressing strongly romantic objectives. As a result of the shock of the First World War, he began for a time to date his works from the year One.

In 1920 he moved to Soest. Besides continuing his painting, he began to work as a commercial artist in industry, for the Fagus works in Alfeld among others. In 1923 he was invited by Bruno Taut to conduct classes in advertising graphics, typography, printing, and lithography at the School of Arts and Crafts in Magdeburg. Working as a commercial artist, he designed all the visual effects for the "Mitteldeutsche Handwerks-Ausstellung" in Magdeburg in 1925 and "Wohnung und Werkraum" for the German Werkbund in Breslau in 1929.

In 1928 Molzahn was appointed professor of graphics at the art academy in Breslau, then recently revolutionized by Oskar Moll. Discharged in 1933, he returned to Berlin. After the interdiction on painting and exhibiting, he contributed six pictures to the exhibit of "Entartete Kunst" (Degenerate Art).

In 1938 Molzahn emigrated to the United States, where he was professor of art at the University of Washington in Seattle until 1941. Because of U.S. involvement in the Second World War, he had to give up his position and move to New York. In 1943 Laszlo Moholy-Nagy invited him to teach at the school of design in Chicago. In New York again from 1947 to 1952 he taught at the New School for Social Research.

In 1959 Molzahn went to Munich to work independently as a painter. His works are represented in many public and private collections in the United States and Germany. As one of the collaborators on *Der Sturm* he was represented in the retrospective exhibit at Schloss Charlottenburg in Berlin in 1961 and had several one-man shows in various cities in Germany. His most important one-man show was at the Wilhelm Lehmbruck Museum in Duisburg in 1964. He died in Munich on December 31, 1965.

From a letter

My attitude towards the Bauhaus has always been one of understanding rather than criticism. I have followed the work of the Bauhaus with the greatest interest and sympathy throughout the years, and I have always been conscious of the fact that it fulfilled a unique historical function in the world. If there were any criticism to be made, it would have to be directed not against the Bauhaus but against the modern world, which pulled the rug from under the Bauhaus and destroyed it, without even being aware of it.

It should therefore be the most natural and prime undertaking of our contemporary society, its institutions, and artistic education, to develop anew the educational foundations of the Bauhaus and related institutions of the twenties, such as, for instance, the Breslau Academy, which like the Bauhaus was sacrificed to the evil spirit of the thirties. It would thus fulfill a gaping hole in the development of our modern society. It is surprising that not even a beginning has been made in this.

Gerhard Marcks:

Born in Berlin in 1889. After his studies in 1907, he shared a studio with the sculptor Richard Scheibe. In 1914 he and Richard Scheibe were asked by Gropius to design the Werkbund Exhibit at Cologne.
Marcks was in the army from 1914 to 1918 and in 1918 he was appointed to the Staatliche Kunstgewerbeschule in Berlin as a teacher. In 1919 Gropius asked him to join the Weimar Bauhaus as one of its first masters, to take over the direction of the ceramics workshop at the Dornburg. In 1925, when the Bauhaus moved to Dessau, Marcks became a ceramics teacher at the Kunstgewerbeschule at Burg Giebichenstein in Halle on the Saale. In 1930 he became the director of the school. In 1933 the National Socialist party relieved him of his office and in 1937 they confiscated his works, (showing them in Munich at the exhibition "Entartete Kunst" (Degenerate Art). In 1939 Marcks built his own studio in Berlin, which was destroyed by bombs, together with a major part of his early works, in 1943.
In 1946 Marcks became professor at the Landeskunstschule in Hamburg. In 1950 he stopped teaching and settled in Cologne. Among his outstanding artistic achievements are six large figures for the facade of the Katharinen Church at Lübeck, completing a series started by Ernst Barlach. Marcks' work as sculptor and graphic artist has become well known internationally through many exhibits, and he is represented in many museums and collections in Europe and the United States. He is an honorary member of the Freie Akademie der Künste (Free Academy of the Arts) in Hamburg and a regular member of the Bayerische Akademie der Schönen Künste (Bavarian Academy of the Fine Arts) in Munich and also the Akademie der Künste in Berlin. In 1952 he received the order Pour le Merite for peace, science, and the arts.
Marcks has made numerous trips to Italy, Greece, the United States, Mexico, and South Africa. In 1969 he donated a great number of his paintings, drawings, and graphic art, as well as his own library and letters, to the Kunsthalle of the city of Bremen, for exhibition and research purposes. Marcks is living in Cologne.

My short stay in Weimar

I have been asked to write about my attitude to the Bauhaus, but I am so far removed from these problems.

I was invited there as an old friend of Walter Gropius, and I arrived there with the sole artistic purpose of uniting handicrafts with art as much as possible.

It was the romantic period, and the *clou* (Gropius' term) was Johannes Itten, who undoubtedly had magnificant teaching ability.

Very soon my instincts took me to Dornburg to the pottery workshop (Krehan was the last Thuringian potter). Soon we developed a sort of independence there that probably seemed reactionary.

Here I developed lifelong friendships with Feininger, Schlemmer, Gilles, and Johannes Driesch, who died before his time, and also with other students such as Mr. and Mrs. Wildenhain, who continued the Dornburg tradition in the United States.

The year 1923 marked a change: the poster at the train station, Art and Technology — a New Unity, was the signal. "Exactly what we didn't want," Feininger said to me. Now Moholy became the clou instead of Itten, besides of course the great masters Klee and Kandinsky, who preached the collective.

The year 1925 marked the refounding of the Bauhaus in Dessau; for Itten, Schlemmer, and myself, it meant our leaving. Since then I have had nothing more to do with the Bauhaus.

Walter Gropius, the
Founder of the Bauhaus
Weimar, 1924
Photo: unknown

The Office of the
Bauhaus Director
Weimar, 1923
Photo: unknown

Johannes Itten in his
Bauhaus dress
Weimar, 1921
Photo: unknown

32

Oskar Schlemmer and
Joseph Hartwig working
on a relief sculpture in
the entrance to the
Bauhaus workshops
Weimar, around 1922
Photo: unknown

Sculpture workshop at the
Bauhaus
Weimar, 1923
Photo: unknown

Dragon Festival of the
Bauhaus people
Weimar, 1922
Photo: Archive of
Tut Schlemmer

Dragon Festival of the
Bauhaus people
Weimar, 1922
Photo: Archive of
Tut Schlemmer

Theo van Doesburg during
his stay near the Bauhaus
Weimar, 1921
Photo: Herrmann Eckner

Born in Munich in 1907. He had very early contact through his father with the painters of Der Blaue Reiter (The Blue Rider), in particular with Kandinsky, whom he visited often when he was his neighbor on the Ainmillerstrasse in Munich. In 1917 Klee studied at the secondary school in Munich, and in the fall of 1921, after his father was appointed by Gropius to teach at the Bauhaus, he was accepted as its youngest member into the preliminary course of Johannes Itten. Later he worked in the Bauhaus carpentry workshop and graduated as a journeyman in 1925. When his parents went to Dessau with the Bauhaus, he stayed in Weimar to prepare for his theater career. From 1926 to 1928 he became production assistant at the Friedrich Theater in Dessau, at the suggestion of Georg Hartmann. Between 1929 and 1931 he made his first independent production experiments at the Stadttheater in Breslau, again under Hartmann, and he also renewed his friendship with Oskar Schlemmer, who was then professor at the Breslau Academy. In 1931 he went to the Stadttheater Basel as operatic producer and actor, under the leadership of Oskar Wälterlin. He married the Bulgarian singer Efrossina Greschowa during the same year. Klee continued his theatrical engagements in Düsseldorf, Ulm, Berlin, Wilhelmshafen, Göttingen, and Würzburg. At the end of 1944 he joined the army and was captured by the Russians in 1946.

Around 1948 Felix Klee began trying to improve the organization of the Klee Society at Bern, and in 1953 he purchased its estate. In addition to his own activities as a producer and actor in radio dramas at the Swiss Radiostation Beromünster, where he has been working since 1949, Klee has made it his duty to cultivate his father's estate. Cataloguing, sorting, and publishing, as well as editing, of the diaries, poems, and letters of Paul Klee, and also working on his own book are among the varied occupations of Klee since he became president of the Paul Klee Foundation in Bern in 1962. In 1955 he organized the first of many exhibitions on his family's work. Klee is living in Bern.

My memories of the Weimar Bauhaus

The beginning of October, 1921, when I was not quite fourteen years old, my Aunt Mathilde, the sister of my father, Paul Klee, took me from Bern to Basel in her carefree way and dutifully put me on the train to Frankfurt. We were going north into what was for me completely new territory. In vain I looked for the Black Forest highlands; thick fog allowed me to see only the telegraph wires dancing up and down. My father met me at the large train station in Frankfurt. There were a few hours between trains, during which we visited Zingler, the Kaiserstrasse, the Hauptwache, and the Goethe house. That night we traveled northeast again, the same direction young Goethe must have taken. In the morning around seven o'clock we arrived at our desired destination. A rural quietness surrounded the central station in Weimar. A little streetcar with an open platform and a gigantic, bent contact arm rising to the overhead wires waited for the sleepy guests. At every bump of the rails it swayed from side to side like a ship. It often had to wait on a siding for oncoming trams to pass.

Our four-room apartment at Horn 35 first seemed like a paradise to me. For the first time I had my own room. And it had a little balcony, too. The resident household genie was named Helene and came from "Affrt" — that was supposed to be Erfurt. We just couldn't get enough of the Thurinigian dialect. Our landlords were Count Kayserlingk and his family. He was from the Baltic and was a former Russian governor of vast territories. He had the habit of following every second sentence with "sososososo," which I coaxed from him again and again to the unspeakable delight of, above all, my father. Then there was the Countess, a lovely lady, always hospitable and patient, and her sensitive eleven-year-old only son, Hujo, who had the highest soprano voice. So the inhabitants of this house came from the four corners of the earth. There was my father's Bern German, or Alemanic-tinted high German, and my mother's and my Munich man-in-the-street speech, which we both jealously nurtured. Another sensation: in Weimar we had electricity for the first time! No gas-petroleum and carbide lamps or candlelight anymore. I could play with the light switch in my room for hours on end. But I mustn't forget our fellow lodger Fritzi, a half-wild, tiger-striped tom we had inherited five years before from Suzanne Schülein.

The curious reader is probably beginning to get impatient, wondering when the subject of the Bauhaus will finally come up. I want to point out that this preamble was necessary just to illustrate the situation and show how the Bauhaus struck me, a boy, at the time. On the basis of a few of my watercolors, my father had previously arranged for my immediate acceptance at the Bauhaus. Johannes Itten directed the Vorkurs. He looked like a priest to me, with his red-violet, high-buttoned uniform, his bald, shaven crown, and his gold-rimmed glasses. From the very first I was fascinated by his personality, his teaching ability, and his overwhelming imagination. The fact that he was also a fanatical Mazdaznan disciple and counted many of his students among his converts did not affect me in any way. We had composed among ourselves at the Bauhaus a "hymn," with the words "Itten, Muche, Mazdaznan" sung to the tune of the Bavarian jingle

"Und Dann Kommt der Prinzregen mit der Kerzen in die Händ." ("Now Here Comes the Prince Regent, with His Candle in His Hand").

A balanced diet was a basic concern of my adolescent years. What bad times those were! Inflation swelled apace, and we were all filled with concern for our daily bread. In addition, all the teachers and students were generally in financial straits. But these circumstances only made the Bauhaus community close its ranks more tightly.

But back to Itten: He gave lectures three times a week. Once a week there were those marvelous exercises, which especially relaxed the cramped, tense students. Here we also presented the work we had done during the week, both on assignment and on our own. There were studies of materials that we could fool around with in our own studios. These were necessary in order to familiarize us with the materials of any one of the Bauhaus workshops, for after the Vorkurs it was mandatory that we learn a handicraft. What magnificent creations were produced by the Bauhaus in 1923! The whole development of modern art — its attempt to create something new at any price — was anticipated by us forty-five years ago, without any particular ax to grind and with a light touch. One colleague, for example, by the name of Pascha, had a long mane that came down all the way to his shoulders, like the Beatles today. One day, in full public view, he was shorn of his adornment. But more important, Pascha artfully made this hair the central point of one of his studies of materials.

Itten delivered a second course of lectures devoted to the analysis of old masters. What an eye opener for us all, and how significant for me even today, was the world of the old masters! For example, how marvelous is the structure of Franke's "Birth of Christ" or Simone Martini's "Captain on Horseback," in the town hall in Siena. Itten had these pictures projected on the walls, took them away, and had us draw our impressions of them in charcoal on great sheets of paper. Then he started his correction, set to work here and there, brought the pictures out again, and drew the world of forms in the masterpieces on the board himself. When I later saw these works in the original, this eye-opening training helped me to fully appreciate their power. Once, everyone was allowed to pick a photograph of an old master, take it home, and try to copy it. I got a reproduction of a Badenian Souvereign by Baldung Grien. The task at first seemed insolvable to me, but slowly I worked my way into the world of that period. How one could relax over such a task! Itten was often merciless and unbending in his judgments, but never unfair.

Itten gave a third series of lectures on life drawing. What a revelation — the encounter with and analysis of the nude body. I am still fascinated by the beauty of the human body. Through it I was able to understand the classical ideal. I never saw my studies as academic exercises imitating nature, but rather as analogous to analyses of the old masters.

In the second story of the Bauhaus, Van de Velde's great building that we had to share with the Academy of Art, my father had two rooms allotted to him as a studio. Every morning father and son took the road to the Bauhaus back and forth, through the Weimar Park from our apartment on the Horn, across the Ilm bridge, and past the Dessauer-Stein and the Liszt memorial. Our conversations on these daily walks were very important to the development of my personality. No creature and no plant was hidden from my father's eagle eye. In summer we watched the nightingales, in winter the ptarmigans skidding about on the ice of the frozen Ilm. If we took the road separately, my father would draw hieroglyphics on the ground with his walking stick so that I would know he had passed here before me.

For the first year my father was very concerned that I not participate at the school parties. I only was allowed to appear at important festivals. That was hard but right. Every weekend at the Bauhaus there was a small party. And every month there was a great costume ball on some delightful theme. How right this form of self-expression was for us! There were never any sort of excesses. How clean and normal were the relationships between the girls and boys. For financial reasons all such festivities were held in the little village inns of neighboring Oberweimar. I remember the Ilmschlösschen (Golden Swan) there. Hirschfeld played his concertina, Andor, the piano, and Schmidtchen played his only piece on the violin. And we did our Bauhaus dance. There were exact rules: it was a passionate stamping, for which we needed much space. We danced in couples, not embracing but separated — today's dances often remind me of it.

Four festivals, one for each season of the year, were distinct high points. Everyone worked for them with great enthusiasm. Oskar

Schlemmer prepared his theater especially for them. On May 18 of every year we celebrated Walter Gropius' birthday with the traditional Festival of Lanterns. On the stage at the Ilmschlösschen Schlemmer had set up two sets featuring headless characters. The boys took the women's parts and vice versa. An improvised orchestra with imaginary instruments was directed by Oskar Schlemmer, in tails and a long black wig, and the choir sang, also improvising, "Hang It!" (first section) and "The Laurel Wreath!" (second section). Before the festival we gathered at the Bauhaus where we lit our selfmade lanterns at twilight. Then we competed with the glowworms, going through the park to the Horn, visiting Klee and Börner, the mistress of weaving; then Gropius; and finally the prince of poets, Johannes Schlaf.

One month later we celebrated the pagan Midsummer-night Festival. Once it was held halfway to Belvedere in the little coffee valley. Hirschfeld and Schwerdtfeger presented their reflecting light play *The Story of Creation.* I contributed to the festivities with a puppet show in which Emmy Galka Scheyer tries to talk my father into buying a Jawlensky. My father, however, doesn't want to, and Emmy breaks the Jawlensky on his head. The real Emmy and Klee arrived at the festival just as the performance was over, and the audience welcomed the originals, both unaware of the show, with applause. Later the bonfire was lit, and we jumped bravely and daringly over the flames.

In October, after the holidays, we celebrated the Dragon Festival. For this we made elaborate preparations with the most daring constructions. We went up to one of the neighboring hillocks, like the Gehäderich, where we let our abstract dragons sail in the wind, much to the surprise of the inhabitants below.

The fourth festival took place in the Bauhaus — the Christmas celebration in the sunlit room on the second floor, next to Klee's and Itten's studio. Of course we designated this festival by its pagan name — Yuletide — just as we greeted each other with raised hand, in the Roman style. A stepladder lent by the wall-painting workshop, with candles on cross-battens, served as a pseudo-Christmas tree. With great hue and cry a student dressed as an angel dragged a closed wash basket to the door, tore it open, and practically threw presents into our midst. There were large and small packages with names on them. We unwrapped one in high expectation, and there was another, a smaller package, with another name on it. Each package was handed around until finally the very last one produced the gift itself. Gertrud Grunow, the good spirit of the Bauhaus, got a pot with the inscription "If you think yellow she'll make tea; If you think brown there'll be coffee." The Schlemmers had just had two daughters, Karin and Jaina, born in the coachhouse of the Belvedere Palace. That night Oskar received thirteen more daughters with marvelous imaginery names. My father got a "Papal edict" from the Thuringian state government, accusing him of having hung monarchist pictures in his apartment — like "The Great Emperor Rides to War" — pictures incompatible with his position as a republican official. The edict was signed by Graupe, Kantinsky, Leinöl, Einfinger, and so on.

And now I can just see the reader becoming impatient, asking himself whether festivities are all the man has to say of the Bauhaus. I can only answer: My dear friend, you have no idea how important festivals were at the Bauhaus — often far more important than the classes. They made the contact between master, journeyman, and apprentice far closer. Weighty books have been written by important people about the Bauhaus itself, and in them one can learn all about the important manifestos that were published. But let us go back to personal contact: The masters radiated their influence on the students in the most positive way. They could develop all the more freely because they had enough time and were not hindered in their personal development by an overly rigid schedule. And there was a reciprocal action by the students on the teachers. One could call it all a "living give-and-take" such as I have never again come across to such an extent. That is the unique contribution of the Bauhaus' founder, Walter Gropius. Incidentally, my father, after first meeting him in 1920, called him "the Silver Prince."

From 1922 to 1925 I learned carpentry at the Bauhaus. Since I was not very well developed physically, this occupation did me a great deal of good in my youth. The comradeship of the handicrafters and their mutual dependence was of great value during my later life. But even there I allowed myself time for my new occupation. I started at eight in the morning and ended at two in the afternoon. I remember fondly today an inlaid chest and the bookcase that qualified me as journeyman. I built both for my father. In the afternoon I got further instruction in French and English by Tony Fiegles, and Bruno Adler enthusiastically guided me into the beauties of German literature, while my mother continued to teach me the piano. In addition there was my passion for painting and the completion of the Punch and Judy theater. My father made all fifty figures, beginning when I was nine years old. And then there were the important features of Weimar's classical past: the Goethe house on the Frauenplan, the castle museum, and other interesting points nearby. Ernst Hardt, the director of the National Theater, was closely connected with the masters of the Bauhaus. He often invited us to his private box, so we were able to attend many good productions. Thus my interest in the theater and especially in opera grew enormously, and when the Bauhaus closed in 1925 I chose to become a producer.

Otherwise we had a very isolated life in Weimar. We were often thoroughly boycotted by the townspeople. That was caused by the early rise of National Socialism. We all have a gloomy memory of the uproar created by the Reichparteitag (Reich-party day) in Weimar in 1925 and the related closing of the Bauhaus just before that. And so after four years we took our leave from a city that gave us a most lively time, but with which we never, or at least seldom, were able to establish any internal contact.

Perhaps the reader is disappointed to find that this is the end of my report. Certainly I have omitted much that is important and much that is unimportant. A great period like that could fill volumes. I could go on and on and on about the capricious Nina Kandinsky; the magnificent Schlemmer; the spiritualist Schreyer; the elegant Muche; the scurrilous Moholy; and "Our dear Lord," as they used jokingly to call my father at the Bauhaus. The continuing contact among the Bauhaus members who are still alive, watched over by our Bauhaus mother, Tut Schlemmer, is proof of how strong an influence this school had on all of us. Though everyone of us went a different way, each built his life on the soil of this outstanding education in humanity and handicrafts.

In the meantime we have become an older generation. Youngsters gaze at us in wonder. "What!" they say, "you were at the Bauhaus? Lucky you!"

What I have preserved for our time is not an animal earnestness, not agony over insoluble problems, but rather a relaxation of all inner doubts, and with that a liberating, though not intrusive, cheerfulness.

Paul Citroen:

Born in Berlin in 1896, of Dutch parents. He spent his youth in Germany. At the age of fourteen he left school to become a painter. He became the student of Martin Brandenburg and studied with him for several years at the private Studienateliers für Malerei and Plastik (Studios for Painting and Sculpture) in Berlin-Charlottenburg. There he met Georg Muche, who introduced him to the circle of Walden's gallery, Der Sturm. A qualified book dealer, Citroen organized the Sturm Bookstore in 1915. After the First World War he joined the Weimar Bauhaus as a student, upon Muche's suggestion. He was strongly influenced as a painter by Itten's preliminary course and his doctrine that the "work arises from the material." Citroen reached international fame through his photomontage "Metropolis," first shown at the Bauhaus exhibition in Weimar in 1923. He was the first artist to use the new technique of photomontage for complete compositions. After the Bauhaus moved to Dessau in 1925, Citroen went to Berlin as an independent painter.

In 1927 Citroen settled permanently in Holland. He founded the De nieuwe Kunstschool in Amsterdam in 1933, where the principles of the Bauhaus are being taught. From 1935 to 1960, interrupted by the war, he lectured at the Royal Kunstakademie (Academy of Art), The Hague. Since then he is painting and drawing extensively, mostly portraits and landscape studies. His paintings have been exhibited in group and one-man exhibits in Europe and the United States. Citroen has also published essays and books on art and literature. He is living at Wassenaar.

Mazdaznan at the Bauhaus

At that time I was, like all the new entrants, a pupil in the Vorkurs, which Itten taught. But at the time Itten was so full of Mazdaznan, expected so much from a deep immersion in its teachings, that soon after the beginning of the course he took several months' leave in order to become fully initiated into this doctrine at Herrliberg on Lake Zurich, the European seat and center of the Mazdaznan. Muche substituted for him, so that I actually sat at the feet of my friend as his pupil and had the opportunity to admire his modesty as a teacher and the security of his delivery. Muche maintained a certain cool distance, while Itten knew how to inflame us, shake us up, break down all the dikes and plunge us into a veritable frenzy of production, and still become one of us. We had the greatest respect for him.

There was something demonic about Itten. As a master he was either ardently admired or just as ardently hated by his opponents, of whom there were many. At all events, it was impossible to ignore him. For those of us who belonged to the Mazdaznan group — a unique community within the student body — Itten exuded a special radiance. One could almost call it holiness. We were inclined to approach him only in whispers; our reverence was overwhelming, and we were completely enchanted and happy when he associated with us pleasantly and without restraint.

When he returned from Herrliberg we Mazdaznan boys reached the zenith of fulfilment. There were all sorts of gatherings — lectures, exercises, religious services, councils, meals — all unbelievably enthusiastic work over the common goal of perfection, of the sovereign idea. A jealous community was simply unthinkable. And Itten, entrusted with the mysteries of reincarnation and other secrets of the doctrine, by virtue of his weeks in Herrliberg, was our undisputed master and leader. Muche and his wife, also connected with our group, took part in everything, and here, too, even more than in lectures, it was a matter of course that Muche substituted for Itten when the latter was prevented from being present at gatherings.

Now Itten had brought a young lady back from Switzerland with him, entrusted by her parents to take his courses at the Bauhaus. She was a Mazdaznan too, and such a happy example as we had never seen among our own neighbors.

Health and everything connected with it, such as breathing, movement, and nutrition, played an important role in Mazdaznan — it might even be called the cornerstone of the doctrine. And so it naturally attracted all sorts of people with physical defects or maladies that could not be relieved by ordinary medical means. The Weimar circle was conducted from a more spiritual standpoint, but nevertheless we delighted in relative health on the whole. Still, most of us did not look blooming. This must be ascribed to the fact that in Germany, disintegrating in economic inflation, sufficient and decent food was available only at great cost. The Bauhaus kitchen was conducted according to Mazdaznan principles, so we did get food that was unspoiled, though, because of a lack of money, not as nutritious as we needed. A general undernourishment was the result, stomach and intestinal trouble the rule, and our appearance what one might expect. For example, I, who was naturally sallow, could look green and gray whenever my innards were upset, which was often enough. However, Muche, who had a bright, rosy complexion, and Itten, too, stayed healthy. They did their own housekeeping and knew all sorts of vegetarian cooking secrets, so that for us bachelors it was a celebration everytime we were invited there for a meal. Marvelous and delicate meals put together of the purest ingredients were set before us. But for the poorer and less talented cooks among the Mazdaznans, it was a really difficult time. For while ordinary mortals could consume anything they could get hold of, we who were contemplating a higher plane of existence had to select among the few things available, and this selected diet must be prepared in a special way and enjoyed in proper sequence and with proper concentration. Great demands were made on our self-denial, and if we occasionally sinned when conditions were too hard or hunger or thirst too great, on the whole we felt happy and privileged to have the firm support of our doctrine, to know the right way so that we did not, like the others, collapse in the general chaos. Despite all difficulties we did not allow ourselves to be completely governed by the circumstances, but followed our own views, or rather the precepts of our doctrine, as faithfully as possible. And this lent us an exalted sense of self-knowledge.

Yes, the strength of this doctrine was so great that the other students refrained from making the crudest jokes in our presence and in general did not behave as impudently and vulgarly as was usual among many of them. While they sometimes ridiculed us, we did inspire some respect in them.

So, as I said, we all had a more or less vegetarian, that is to say, a wretched look. And there was Lotti Weiss, the Swiss girl, actually radiant and bright, and not because she was on a meat diet; she was a shining example of a natural, clean life. She was living proof of the rightness of the doctrine that she had known and accurately followed far longer and better than any of us, and that her family had been practicing for twelve years. She came, one might say, from the very center, had greeted the master and founder of Mazdaznan, the sage Dr. Zaraduscht Hanish, on his first visit to Europe; he had initiated her, and her adherence dated from that time. We were all the merest beginners compared with this girl, who had spent the greater part of her life in the state we were striving for and who now appeared before us like blooming life itself. Yes, Mazdaznan was Truth — one had only to look at that girl to be convinced.

Whenever we had some question or other, some doubt concerning something in our belief, or needed some practical hint, we turned, since we did not want to annoy Itten with trivia, to Lotti Weiss, who always knew the answers. She was an artist in the kitchen, and in fact up on everything and everyone — how one should conduct himself according to the rules, what one should do in any dubious matter. She answered so prudently that it was a delight to ask her questions. She would instruct us impartially, and it was quite stirring to hear this lovely young child speak so earnestly and with such conviction. Yet she never forgot to laugh, in accordance with our rule that we must wear a friendly, composed, "relaxed" smile. While most of us got no further than a distorted, sweet-sour grin, a convulsive pulling at the corners of the mouth, Lotti radiated true serenity; her eyes shone out at the world in happiness and calm. I felt blissful just looking at her and would no doubt have fallen in love with her had the admiration she inspired in me not driven away any thought of a more personal relationship. And then in spite of all her friendliness she was actually a private person; one felt that quite apart from her unique, cheerful manner with the friends of the community, she nursed a special inner life, which she would allow no one to glimpse. We respected this unique, most personal, secret life. In general we did not communicate with one another with complete openness, but allowed and did not begrudge one another his own secrets, for the ultimate was inexpressible anyway. We practiced aloofness.

I remember meeting a disagreeable person. Muche introduced him to me, and I started the appropriate breathing exercises immediately to make any contact with him impossible, to undercut any influence he might possibly have on me. The fellow noticed nothing of this, but Muche, who saw my nostrils flaring, was amused.

When we shook someone's hand we could tell more about him from the handshake, the dryness or dampness of his skin, and other signs, than he would find comfortable. His vocal pitch, his complexion, his walk, every one of his involuntary gestures gave him away. We thought we could see through any person, because our method gave us an advantage over the unsuspecting.

These little games or bits of nonsense — for it was not much more than that, since we did all this in a dilettantish, not to say superstitious,

SAN JOAQUIN DELTA COLLEGE LIBRARY

way, taking everything we read literally and on faith — these tricks we played had dangerous repercussions: they made us arrogant and made us despise the uninitiated. We became more and more sectarian. It is unbelievable what sheer madness we fabricated or took up from our reading, together with the certainly excellent and worthwhile precepts. The guest I brought along to one of our exercise hours, in which we dislocated ourselves, singing all the while, must really have thought us mad. Group singing is certainly a beautiful thing, and when rhythmical movements are added it can only be good for one, even if it seems grotesque to an outsider. But the immeasurably deep meaning we ascribed to everything, far too deep for the natural bent of most of us, was destructive. Easy contact with fellow human beings was difficult, and finally any ingenuousness, even among ourselves, was impossible.

One of the girls in our group once dressed up for fun as a grotesque. "Ida looks like a dev . . .," Lotti Weiss began, but interrupted herself, finishing with "angel," remembering that one must never say anything bad about a fellow human being. We all burst out laughing at this innocent example of the self-control we all practiced.

On Itten's birthday the whole group went to the master's house very early and serenaded him at his door. Itten, still in his bathrobe, soon appeared and thanked us, quite touched. The fact that he was not yet dressed and ready for work disappointed us a bit, for early rising was a much exalted precept; but even on this occasion he was able to deliver himself of a weighty, instructive speech that impressed itself on us.

Easter was celebrated in a unique way. At dawn we were to bathe in well water, dry ourselves vigorously, dress, enjoy a glass of wine, and go for a long walk. On our return we were allowed our first eggs, forbidden during the preceding fast.

I did without the more rigorous parts of the procedure, like dawn and well water, but I did get up early, drank a glass of sweet red wine, which warmed me internally, and marched off. It was rainy, windy weather, not the sort one would wish for the resurrection of the Lord. The sun remained hidden. When I got to the country road outside Weimar, I saw a phenomenon ill-suited to the significance of the day. The whole road was covered with long worms that, encouraged by the dampness, seemed to creep out of all the pores of the earth. I could not reconcile these horrors wriggling out from the underworld with the serene, holy thoughts to which I would gladly have dedicated myself. Nature seemed to have her own conception of the significance of the date, and I soon turned home again.

Fasts were the high point of our training, and spring and autumn were the seasons designated for this. We attempted and actually attained a thoroughgoing, internal physical cleansing, provided we kept strictly to the instructions and above all broke the fast in a wise manner, returning to normal daily rations very slowly and by degrees. This return to normality was most difficult of all, for after a period of fasting we were often overwhelmed by a ravenous hunger.

We began our fast by taking a strong laxative, after which, for a week, or two, or even three, depending on what we had decided, we neither ate nor drank, except perhaps some hot fruit juices. We communed with nature frequently, took hot baths, read spiritual works, sang, and communicated only with understanding friends. Since we owned a garden on a hillock near Weimar, with several hundred raspberry bushes, fruit trees, and so on, we couldn't spend our fast any better place than there, weeding — one of our favorite pastimes, since we were dedicated to rooting out the weeds of the whole world, the enemies of creativity — and practicing other useful tasks. And no one disturbed our pious singing there.

After a hot bath in one of the cubicles at the public bath house I intended to rub myself, according to the precepts, with ashes or charcoal. This, too, was part of the process of purification, this time of the skin. But when I got up from my bath, I lost my senses and fell unconscious beside the bathtub — lucky thing, too — spilling the black powder, while a fine rain sprayed over me from the shower. When I came to I was lying right in the middle of a graying puddle.

There were more such unpleasant side effects for the beginner in fasting. There was, among other things, a little needle machine with which we were to puncture our skins. Then the body would be rubbed with the same sharp oil which had served as a laxative. A few days later all the pinpoints would break out in scabs and pustules — the oil had drawn the wastes and impurities out of the deeper skin layers to the surface. Now we were ready to be bandaged. But we must work hard, sweat, and then, with continued fasting, the ulcerations would dry out. At any rate, so the book said. In actuality the puncturing didn't go according to plan or desire, and for months afterward we would be tormented with itching.

But I must admit that these inconveniences meant nothing at all beside the unique, unforgettable experience we had during and because of the fasting. The bodily changes and transformations gave rise to unexpected moods, opened unknown regions of feeling. I would never have thought it possible to attain such "transparency," to become so receptive to otherwise hardly noticeable spiritual vibrations. In the end it was a pity to have to leave this exalted, almost unearthly state.

And then the gradual resumption of familiar habits began with the first day's ration of a handful of popcorn. Six days later we were back to normality, but I felt the effects of the regimen throughout the whole year; I was spared even a single cold, something which had never before happened to me.

After his return from Herrliberg, Itten never again felt quite at home at the Bauhaus. He felt that what was being done there was not worth the effort, compared with what was taking place at Herrliberg. Only there could he see any chance of growth and spiritual enrichment for himself. And so he said farewell and left for Switzerland. The loss to us was great, but became even more pronounced when Lotti Weiss followed him there.

During her last days in Weimar I painted her portrait, helped arrange to have her luggage sent, and all in all spent more time in her presence. So it came about that, unconstrained with one another in the knowledge of our imminent parting, we gave free rein to our feelings and became aware of a mutual sympathy. Even though it was never expressed concretely, my love for Lotti became an open secret. Our little community was now robbed of her pre-eminent strength. Even though Muche took over, no matter how hard he tried it wasn't the old life of fulfillment. We all felt it. The meetings were attended more sparsely; we went our separate ways. And finally our group was absorbed into the great mass of the student body. Mazdaznan was no longer a problem for the Bauhaus.

Born in Kiel in 1890. He received his first education at the Städtische Handwerksschule in Kiel. From 1909 to 1911 he studied at the Royal Museum of Arts and Crafts in Berlin. There he made his first acquaintance with Chinese and Japanese art — the art of the Zen priests and woodcut masters. Next he studied with Professors Egger-Lienz and Klemm at the Grandducal College of Fine Arts in Weimar. In 1913 he became a master student. During a brief leave in Berlin, while he was still serving in the First World War, he met Herwarth Walden and visited his gallery, *Der Sturm*. He was also introduced to a number of leading personalities of that period, among them Leo Kestenberg, Emil Maetzel, and Emil Rudolf Weiss, who had great influence on his development. In 1919 Röhl returned to Weimar where he was one of the painters with whom Gropius established contact during his early exploratory visits to Weimar. Röhl witnessed the transformation of the Weimar college and school of arts and crafts into the Staatliches Bauhau Weimar and became an enthusiastic member. When, in 1921, Theo van Doesburg came to Weimar, Röhl became a member of the De Stijl group. His Constructivist tendencies were also re-alized in his colorful designs for the rebuilt theater in Weimar and in the building of an old-age home and a children's home in Stelzen-Voigtland. During this time he published in the magazines *De Stijl* and *Mecano*.

In 1926 Röhl was appointed to the Städel-schule in Frankfurt to teach fundamental principles. During his seventeen-year tenure there he developed a special method for an elementary course in art. In connection with the city-planning commission under the direction of Ernst May and Adolf Meyer, he took part in color-design projects. In 1926 his "Abstract Series" for music notation was exhibited, and the following year he designed the first purely abstract stained-glass windows. Independently, he designed a system of signs for all the medical institutions in Frankfurt, which was published in the magazine *Das Neue Frankfurt.*

In 1946 Röhl returned to his birthplace to become a free-lance painter again. Exhibits of his abstract paintings in Kiel in 1947 provided material for discussions of new directions in painting, and their influence was widely felt. In 1949, together with his daughter, he founded a children's art circle for preschool children. Röhl lives in Kiel.

The idea, form, and times of the State Bauhaus in Weimar

The Bauhaus is part of the past. Many of its members have died, but their power lives on. The springtime of the Bauhaus has been transformed into a colorful autumn. The bright leaves of the Bauhaus members whirl throughout the whole world for its joy and contemplation. Through the architect Walter Gropius the idea of the Bauhaus was born, and he gave his new school its name. He was a medium of the times. An invisible power directed his generosity and his spontaneous perception. In fair weather or foul he always fostered the freedom and liveliness of the Bauhaus. Nowhere outside of the Bauhaus in Weimar was there a comparably free and creative art education. The Grossherzoglicher Hochschule für Bildende Kunst (The Grandducal College of Visual Arts) bequeathed this freedom to the Bauhaus. The enthusiasm and passion for the Bauhaus activated the students, who were open-minded about the new foundation.

I myself was a master student at the Grandducal College of Visual Arts and was an initiator and founder of the Weimar Bauhaus, to which I belonged until 1922. By 1914 Gropius with Adolf Meyer had already created the modern buildings in Alfeld and Cologne. After the First World War this unity had to be renewed, and that meant a delay because of the take-over of the existing college. Perhaps this even determined the other obstacle to the development of the Bauhaus, namely the fact that the integration Gropius envisioned between the architecture and engineering school, with their workshops and the experimental master studios with scientists and technicians, could not be achieved. Because of this situation Walter Gropius had to call in new teachers, those who would or already had undertaken to find new paths in art. These became the new Bauhaus masters: Feininger, Klee, Itten, Kandinsky, Schlemmer, Muche, and later Moholy-Nagy, who gave it the power of their personalities and their creative abilities. Soon the Bauhaus became known throughout the whole world, and thus artists and others came to the Bauhaus to experience it, to enliven it anew through their own work.

Thus Theo van Doesburg, editor of *De Stijl*, came to Weimar from Paris in 1921. He was enraptured by the existence of such a school and said: "There is no government in the whole world which would finance such an institution and foster such a creative education. As a Dutchman van Doesburg identified with Modernism in Holland, and now he could put his principles to effect in Weimar. The results can be found in his Bauhaus book. My enthusiasm for van Doesburg and *De Stijl* resulted in my joining his De Stijl movement in Germany, and I still use De Stijl theories in my teaching today.

The great influence of the Bauhaus was possible because the students, whom we called journeymen and apprentices, dedicated themselves with liveliness, ability, and great enthusiasm to the notion that the Bauhaus Idea could and would be fulfilled. The Bauhaus festivals were conceived and successfully carried out in lively cooperation with the Bauhaus masters. The Dragon Festival and the Lantern Festival, too, developed basically at my suggestion and were based on my adventures in Schleswig-Holstein, my home. The Lantern Festival was first celebrated in honor of the sixtieth birthday of the poet Johannes Schlaf in Weimar on June 21, 1920.

The Bauhaus is unique, and its influence remains enormous and undisputed today. The great battle it had to fight has been forgotten.

Alfred Arndt:

Born in Elbing in 1898. He began his education as engineering and architectural draftsman. In 1919 he attended a course for arts and crafts at the trade school in Elbing, and from 1920 to 1921 he studied at the Akademie der Bildenden Künste in Königsberg, Prussia (today Kaliningrad, U.S.S.R.). As an ardent supporter of the German Wandervogel movement, he passed through Weimar in 1921, became acquainted with the Bauhaus, and enlisted as an apprentice during the same year. After completion of service as a journeyman (mural painting), he opened an architectural office in Probstzella in 1925, where among other works, the *Haus des Volkes* originated. He also did publicity work in graphics. In 1927 he married Gertrude Hantsch, a Bauhaus member.

In 1929 Arndt was hired as a teacher at the Bauhaus in Dessau by Hannes Meyer. There he was responsible for the so-called "completion" department and he also tutored in construction, draftsmanship, and perspective. In 1930, he supervised the architectural design of a touring Bauhaus exhibition and the special exhibit at the Kunsthalle Mannheim. After closing down of the Bauhaus in Dessau, Arndt worked again in Probstzella as an architect, and after the Nazis prohibited any further building work, he returned to advertising graphics. As a free-lance assistant to the Allgemeine Elektrizitäts-Gesellschaft (electric company) of Berlin, he developed the first Norm-Küche (standard kitchen) and he wrote a number of technical publications for the AEG during the thirties. After 1936 he again increased his activities as an architect, working mainly on industrial projects.

Before the end of the war, in the spring of 1945 when there was no doubt about its outcome, he and the former Bauhaus members Joost Schmidt (then still a soldier near Saalfeld) and Georg Neidenberger, as well as the architect Wassily Luckhardt from Jena, tried to revive the Bauhaus Idea in Weimar. In 1945 Arndt became director of the Office for Building and Planning in Jena. Under the new political regime he tried to enforce the plans for reviving the Bauhaus by a memorandum to the National Office for Popular Education in Weimar. Since Mayor Fritz Hesse and Hubert Hoffmann were also working toward a revival of the Bauhaus, both efforts were coordinated. Owing to the political situation in East Germany, however, this plan was never realized. Later the idea for the Hochschule für Gestaltung (Ulm Design School) grew out of these plans. From 1945 to 1948 Arndt was director of the Department for Building and Planning of the city of Jena. In 1948 he fled to West Germany and settled down as architect and painter in Darmstadt. Since its beginning, Arndt has been acting as adviser and member of the governing body of the Bauhaus Archives. His output as an architect, painter, and designer has been presented in every exhibition of the Bauhaus. In 1968, on his seventieth birthday, his lifework was honored by a one-man show at the Bauhaus Archives. Alfred Arndt lives in Darmstadt.

how i got to the bauhaus in weimar...

it was 1921, just before noon, a warm may day in weimar. my back was in a sweat from my heavy rucksack, and besides i was weighed down by a heavy, homemade portfolio that hung about me. thank god both arms and legs were quite bare: that was cooling. i'd tramped from hamburg across the moors, through the thuringian forest, through the beautiful park around goethe's garden house, past the liszt monument with a few marble figures stuck on it, and landed on the belvedere alley, right in front of a house that looked completely different from any other weimar house. i turned to see if there was anyone around i could ask about it. there was someone! he had a strange rig on: a brown jacket with a low collar, belted with the same material; the trousers were very wide above and very narrow below. "funnel trousers," i thought to myself. i asked him politely what sort of building that was, and he answered: "man, man you're from elbing!" of course i hadn't expected to be recognized as being from elbing by my dialect, which i thought i'd overcome. the man was kube. he told me this was the art school built by the famous architect van de velde. now it was the bauhaus, directed by the architect walter gropius. i couldn't make much of that. who was van de velde? who was gropius? what did he mean — bauhaus? kube invited me to dinner with him at the bauhaus canteen, which made me very happy.

as i entered the canteen with kube there was a hullabaloo about tramping and long hair. suddenly i was bear hugged from behind: "man, emir," (my tramping name) "how did you get here?" it was kurt schwerdt-feger, the pomeranian i had met during the war as a soldier at a youth movement meeting. schwerdtfeger said: 'man, you're going to stay right here. this is where we belong. this is the place — you'll see!"

that afternoon i was received at the main office of the bauhaus by a tall secretary — sister von hirschfeld — who asked me what i wanted. "i'd like to speak to the director." i must have sounded a bit shy, for miss hirschfeld said that the director was a friendly, approachable man. i was announced and immediately admitted. with a bow i gave my name and explained that i had eaten in the canteen and that an acquaintance of mine had invited me to stay. "well, now," he mused, pressing me into a fantastically overstuffed chair — square and yellow, "you can't stay here just like that. you'll have to show what you've learned up to this point; in other words, send in some drawings or photos with a curriculum vita. the masters' committee will judge and then decide whether you have enough talent." "what is the masters' committee?" i wondered silently and then told him that i was tramping and had no work with me outside of the sketches i had made on the road. but i would write my mother and ask her to send a portfolio with sketches, life drawings, line cuts, and my records and so on to the bauhaus. i myself was thinking of wandering down into the bavarian, or rather bohemian, forest (my interest had been fired by adalbert stifter) and in about two months, *poste restante passau*, would expect the decision of the masters' committee as to whether or not i could come. gropius agreed, shook my hand, and wished me a good trip.

quite excited by the bauhaus experience i went off to the youth hostel, lay down on the straw ticking, and let all that i had seen and heard pass through my mind again. next day i went to jena and then via kahala to the leuchtenberg to visit mucklamberty, who was trying to improve the world through handicrafts. then on through the fichtel mountains into the bavarian forest to find a letter from the bauhaus in passau two months later. it said that i had been accepted into the vorkurs, or orientation, semester. so, on to weimar!

i finally arrived after many detours, on september 30, 1921, by slow train. i'd slept on a hard bench in the waiting room — and that's how my studies began. on the first of october i begged and begged to be allowed to sleep at the youth hostel for a couple of days because i was going to study at the bauhaus. they weren't very friendly, but in my need i explained that i'd be happy to help clean. so the first few days of my bauhaus adventure were assured. after a week i had hunted down a room, without bed, without furniture. the door had no handle, but there was a sword — i'm not kidding, a real sword — which i could use to open the door. during the day it had to stay open, of course, or i wouldn't have been able to get in myself. i borrowed a bed with a straw mattress and so on from the youth hostel, and it was more comfortable. things were looking up. so much for my accommodations, and now for the courses at the bauhaus.

the vorkurs was conducted by a certain master itten, who was dressed in the same gear as the good master kube, the first bauhaus man i had met. i still remember exactly what happened that first day, and because i once told the story about master itten at a festival in the new ulm institute, it has remained relatively fresh in my memory.

there were about twenty of us, predominently men, with very few women. the door opened. itten came in and said, "good morning." we stood and in chorus said, "good morning." thereupon itten said, "that isn't a good morning!" went out again, came back in, and said, "good morning!" the same from us, only louder this time. but itten wasn't satisfied. he felt we hadn't woken up yet; we were still cramped. "please stand up. you have to be loose, completely loose, or you won't be able to work. turn your heads. that's it! more! you've still got sleep in your necks!"

i was more than curious to see what the work would be like after all this head turning. an old man we were to draw was asked in. itten left, returned after two hours, and just said, "continue." and so the life drawing continued for awhile — the old man, an old women, then something quite different. itten had ordered everyone to get a large pad of newsprint, charcoal, chalk, and soft pencil. one day he said, "today we're going to draw the war." everyone was to make a drawing of his experiences in the war or his impressions of the war. we drew. dieckmann, who had been through the war and had a shot-up hand, sat next to me. he leaned on his shattered arm and sketched, with great concentration i must say, trenches with barbed wire, guns, and soldiers. behind me was menzel, the youngest member of the vorkurs, who had not been in the war. he was in a turmoil of work; his chalk broke constantly. after less than five minutes he said, "i'm through," and left. when itten returned after several hours we had to put all the sheets on the floor and pick the one that best carried out the assignment. the choice fell on menzel, who had rushed the chalk back and forth with his fist, break-it several times, making sharp points and zigzags, hammering it down upon the paper. itten said, "here you see very clearly this was done by a man who really experienced the war in all its relentlessness and harsh reality. it's all sharp points and harsh resistance; in contrast look at this sheet," (the one by dieckmann). "this artist did not experience the war; this is a romantic picture in which even the landscape and all the details, so to speak, play soldier."

i thought to myself, "so menzel, who was too young to be drafted, experienced the war, and dieckmann, who was in the war and was wounded, didn't experience it?" I was nonplussed. itten had brought along some reproductions of old masters whose pictures had to do with war, and the best of these showed predominantly harsh, pointed forms. suddenly it hit me that our common choice — menzel's sheet with only pointed forms and traces of broken chalk — was the right one.

we also had to copy reproductions of old masters for itten — that is, copy accurately in black and white, exactly reproducing the model. itten brought in a bunch of photos and said, "today we're going to empha-size." each of us was to copy accurately a section of the plate he was given. he would first look at the student, leaf through the pile of illustrations, and then hand out a sheet. i got "john on patmos," which i liked very much; my friend gebhart, an illustration he liked too. that's what i call "recognition of individual tendencies." each student copied with love and reverence be-cause he got a work he could relate to. that was itten's strength.

around the middle of the semester we were concerned with studies of texture: rough-smooth, pointed-blunt, soft-hard, and so on. the last stage was more or less the high point. itten urged us to be on the look out on our walks for materials in refuse dumps, junk piles, garbage cans, and scrap heaps. with these materials we were to create something that would clearly represent the essential nature of and contrast between the individual materials.

"you have a week to practice in peace; then you are to bring in the study you think best in terms of the assignment."

on the appointed day everyone brought in his construction. the works were quite characteristic. the girls brought little, dainty works, about as big as a hand. several fellows had constructions a foot high. often they were real scraps, rusted and corroded. several dragged in individual pieces, like sticks of wood, stovepipes, wire, glass, and so on, and knocked them together in class. as always, itten allowed the students themselves to decide which were the best works. unanimously we decided that mirkin, a pole, was the winner. i can still see that "horse" today. it was a wooden plank, partly smooth and partly knotted, with an old kerosene lamp cylinder anchored down with a rusty saw through it, ending in a spiral. the sculptured texture studies were then sketched, and intensified contrasts of material and movement emphasized. everyone was free to create such sculptural forms graphically.

i shall not speak of life drawing with schlemmer and analytical drawing with kandinsky — it would lead me too far afield. but even here everything was quite different from the academies. my impression of the overall course of study i went through was, "they're knocking everything we know and consider right and good out of our heads, with the idea that a full pot can hold no more."

the first semester was over. each student had to prepare an exhibit of his works. it is a pity that a collected exhibit like that (it contained over twenty booths) could not have been immortalized in a single picture. what a fabulous portrayal of multiplicity and of curiosities.

one day while waiting for the judgment of the masters' committee i went down to ettersberg with my friend pascha. weimar lay before us all lit up. we spoke of our future, reviewed the previous exciting, stimulating half a year, and concluded that everyone spins at the bauhaus. we had joined in with dedication and industry — but we were not quite sure whether this was right for us. we went on, and suddenly i stopped, tapped my friend on the shoulder, and said, "man, pascha, just imagine if that town down there were rome!" "let's go to rome," he said.

the masters' committee found us both worthy — we could stay; but we didn't. we took a semester's vacation and went down to italy. it was 1922 and spring.

and now i come to the end. in rome, lying on a bench, hour after hour, in the sistine chapel (that sort of undisturbed artistic life was still possible then, i made my decision. pointing to the last judgment of michelangelo i asked my friend, "do you think anyone today could manage to produce a thing like that? and is it really today's task to create things like that? isn't the expression of our times completely different?" the answer came, "let us affirm today!" back to weimar! back to the bauhaus!

Robert Michel:

Born in Vockenhausen, a town near Frankfort, in 1897. During the First World War, while on leave from the army, he studied at the Grandducal School of Arts and Crafts in Weimar, He and Ella Bergmann, whom he later married, both students under Professor Walter Klemm, soon joined forces in strenuously opposing the "antiquated" drawing methods taught at the school, and in 1918 Michel was summarily dismissed by the director, Fritz Mackensen. Michel remained in Weimar, however, doing free-lance work. Closely associated with former students of the Van de Velde workshops, and such others as Johannes Molzahn and Karl Peter Röhl, Michel witnessed the founding in 1919 of the Weimar Bauhaus from the "house next door." Gropius, who had remained in close contact with these painters from his first visit to their studios, prominently displayed their work at Bauhaus receptions. Michel's future mastery was only now developing and not yet fully evident. Between 1917 and 1921, working in a medium now known as collage, Michel documented the entire history of the Dada revolution to that time. In the twenties, he worked in Frankfort as an architect, typographer, and painter. In addition he worked with Ella Bergmann in an *Arbeitsgemeinschaft* Film and with members of *Das Neue Frank*furt group, he took part in the project *Die Neue Stadt* (The New City). After the "Art Council 1928" in New York, he participated in the "Société Anonyme" exhibition, which traveled all over the United States. Through this exhibition he made important new contacts with many like-minded artists and architects and he began his long and enduring friendships with Kurt Schwitters and Adolph Meyer. As a commercial artist, Michel was a member of the avant-garde *Ring Neuer Werbegestalter* (Circle of New Advertising Designers). He participated in their exhibition tours as well as in the "Internationale Kunst der Werbung" (International Advertising Art Exhibition), organized in 1931 in Essen, by Max Burchartz. Until 1933 Michel maintained his membership as an architect in the German Werkbund and the Bund Deutscher Architekten (Association of German Architects). The art work of both Michel and his wife was last shown in "Pioneers of Collage," an exhibition held at Leverkusen in 1963. His work is represented in the Yale University Art Gallery in New Haven, among others, and in private collections.

In his home in the Schmelzmühle at Eppstein/Taunus, Michel has recorded his experiences and gathered together his own works and those of others, with the intention of creating a native modern art museum there.

Like many other ideas, those of the Bauhaus in the beginning were strongly or completely humanistic. Even the conversations in 1915–1916 at the offices of the Hofmarschall were friendly and pleasant. It was the only attitude known at the court of Weimar — and a memorandum would follow. The topic was way off the problems of the war, but serious concerns allowed war to be forgotten.

Suddenly the revolutionary winter of 1918–1919 was in full swing, new jokes went around the city, all of them having to do with a certain "fiacre" — a new word given currency by a lady from Vienna. And lo and behold there *was* a new carriage going about the city paying innumerable calls on studio after studio. In it, a couple with their little daughter. And the news traveled through the city. New phrases — "In the spirit of the great German art reformation," "German Werkbund," "Arbeiterrat for Art" — all brought from Berlin and supposedly being distributed by the carriage. All sorts of humanitarian concerns, but the word "Bauhaus" never cropped up in the local gossip. Everyone had his hands full with yesterday's revolution.

But the interests of yesterday's art and education, in the studios and in the colleges, lay elsewhere — more deeply enmeshed in the human impulses than would show in hastily thrown together contemporary publications. Since Henry Van de Velde, as a Belgian, had been a civilian intern in Weimar since August, 1914, and could not teach architecture, and since most of the other faculty members of the colleges around had been drafted, only the Personals columns could be counted on for help. So Klopfer, the director of the Baugewerkschule, taught at the art school and the Henry Van de Velde workshops, then being dissolved and corresponding roughly to a school of arts and crafts.

Klopfer had some graduate students in the architecture seminars at his polytechnic institute. There was even some teaching contact with Erfurt — through Edvin Redslob in art history and Jena in anatomy. They would have to obey the Saxonian Grandducal emergency war decrees concerning education. There would have to be short cuts and combinations serious students never dreamed of — some of them made in the middle of the war. The director of the art school, F. Mackensen, became Weimar city commander. And these were the educational conditions that continued throughout the war. Later, on April 23, 1919, it was Klopfer who for the first time publicly supported Walter Gropius and the Bauhaus, and in a lengthy introduction to it announced the first courses in the daily papers. It was to be the preface to the new curriculum at the College of Fine Arts in Weimar, henceforward to be known as the Staatliches Bauhaus. And in the field of art, Expressionism was being hotly debated.

There were no foreign contacts during the war and few publications. But after the revolution some foreign magazines filtered into Weimar. We were delighted to be able finally to study their counter isms. It was amazing and comforting to find that there were at the same time so many international parallels, independent of one another, deriving from and continuing different movements.

In the wake of the merciless winter of the revolution came the general elections, and in Weimar Germany became a republic. Let us not forget one thing: the Bauhaus was born and had its early beginnings in April, 1919, in the middle of this radical change, both before and during the establishment of the Weimar Constitution for the German Republic. Suddenly Weimar became the center of important events, a national and international crossroad; half of Berlin even came to town. Politically as well as legally it was an open question *what* State Bauhaus lay in the cradle. The interregnum was godfather to the state and the Bauhaus. But note: without the ruling sovereign — never the point of discussion in the city anyway — there was only one criterion for this sponsorship: revolution!

Because the more recent literature often heedlessly speaks of the Bauhaus in the same breath with the landed aristocracy of the times . . . "in the spirit of the great German art reformation," let us clear this matter up too, once and for all. So much for the foundation and the first piece of early Bauhaus history. It continues, interwoven with the people of the time.

The carriage has long since gone elsewhere. The Staatliches Bauhaus, finally put under the authority of the Thuringian government, is known simply as the art school, or even the Van de Velde school. For, little by little, more and more old Weimaraners return from the war and from prison camps, going back, of course, to their old educational haunts and filling up the new provincial administration. Since Parliament and the government of the new German republic already have their seat in Berlin, and the second semester has begun in Weimar, we meet Van de Velde again, both in the city and for the first time in the press. Not yet objective enough is the Bauhaus history written here, which highhandedly dismisses everything outside the Bauhaus as philistine. (Intellectual battles of 1913–1914 flare up again, the Werkbund Exhibit, yes, even the memorandum of 1915–1916 are among these.)

By 1920 Weimar is full of internal conflicts among the artists, in Weimar as well as in Berlin, as to what — all joking aside — can help its Bauhaus now. At the same time there are the squabbles among the citizens, again going beyond the confines of the city. At the State Bauhaus there are also differences of opinion, beginning in 1918 and going through to 1920 and beyond. The results may be found in Oskar Schlemmer's *Briefe und Tagebücher.*

Neither in its publications nor in its numbers did the Bauhaus in its fourteen years actually recognize the high percentage of people engaged in art who would today be permanently indebted to it. If one now adds to these the increased number of people in the field of art (not only creative artists) between the period of the Bauhaus, 1919 to 1933, and 1963, then many contemporary matters become more humanly understandable, especially the fact that aesthetic achievements must grow steadily, side by side with failures. "Of course," we say, even though aesthetic failures may be very painful to others.

Living space, tides, and the amount of water in the world have remained constant as ever. And experimental failures — even blunders — of an elementary nature are difficult, if not possible to balance out. Probably not at all though — in the most modern instances they simply remain today's misfortunes. Cultural analyses come to the same grief, omitting to point out the consequences of experimental failures, to point at the bier. It is just as real a topic as the one to which we address ourselves here: to seek out ideas and faces. And those who "experienced the development" (which, after all, is the basis for this book), think of its small toe hold before 1919 and in their daily life continue to work in fields foreign to art. The last chance for Culture lies perhaps in the future.

Herta Wescher:

Born Herda Kauert in Krefeld and studied art history at the universities of Munich and Freiburg. In 1923 she graduated from Freiburg, where she presented a dissertation on German painting of the sixteenth century. That same year she married art historian Paul Wescher. In 1924 she went to Berlin where she worked without remuneration in the municipal museums, first for Max I. Friedlander in copperplating and later as personal assistant to Ludwig Burchard, a Rubens specialist. Her association with modern art arose through personal contacts in the circle of Curt Glaser and Hans Curjel, who was dramatic producer at the Kroll Opera. In 1928 she became friendly with Laszlo and Lucia Moholy-Nagy. In 1933 Herta Wescher immigrated to France, and her interests turned more and more toward contemporary art. During the years 1936 and 1937 she wrote art reviews from Paris for the English art magazine *Axis*. During 1942 to 1945 she lived in Basel. In 1946 she returned to France, becoming correspondent for the *National Zeitung* in Basel. On occasion she also wrote articles for the *Frankfurter Allgemeine Zeitung*. At the beginning of 1950 she became a regular contributor to the magazine *Art d'Aujourd'-hui* and in 1953 founder and member of the editorial staff of the magazine *Cimaise*, which aimed to promote rising young artists. For the past fifteen years she has been particularly interested in the development of collage and has written its first historical survey in a double issue of *Art d'Aujourd'hui* (March/April, 1954). She organized exhibitions of collage in Paris and Brussels and participated in organizing the historical exhibitions at the Galerie Rose Fried in New York and at the Musée d'Art et d'Industrie in Saint-Étienne.

Mrs. Wescher has written many essays on topics of modern art for European magazines, among them *Quadrum*, *XXième Siècle*, *Das Kunstwerk*, *Werk*, and *La Biennale*. She has summarized her studies of the technique and effect of collage in her vast work *Collage, History of an Artistic Means of Expression* (Cologne, 1968). She lives in Paris.

Weimar painters in the pre - and early Bauhaus era

The fame that has gathered around the Bauhaus over the years should not allow one to forget that Weimar was certainly not a dead or sleeping town before the Bauhaus was founded there in 1919. New artistic impulses were felt when Henry Van de Velde was invited there at the end of 1901 by the archduke of Saxony-Weimar to serve as artistic adviser for industry, arts, and crafts, and to modernize these by developing new designs in contemporary materials and techniques. In 1906 he opened a new Kunstgewerbeschule (School of Arts and Crafts), together with studios in which Van de Velde introduced new methods of relevant and craftsmanlike teaching. In the educational program of the Bauhaus they found consequent continuation.

A new spirit also arose toward the end of the war at the Grandducal College of Fine Arts. Students like Robert Michel and Ella Bergmann, who met in Walter Klemm's drawing class in 1917, and Karl Peter Röhl, who was later to go on to the Bauhaus, blazed new and independent trails in opposition to the all too academic school exercises. They were joined by Johannes Molzahn, who had been a student at the college before the war and returned to Weimar after his discharge from the army in 1918 to take up a friendship with Robert Michel and Ella Bergmann. In the search for new, unacademic solutions, the young painters found partitions among the circle of students and architects about Van de Velde, who as a Belgian in 1914 was forced to give up teaching at the College of Arts and Crafts, but who, until his emigration to Switzerland in 1917, still continued as artist and author, lending practical and theoretical stimulus to his admirers.

When Walter Gropius came to Weimar as director of the Bauhaus in 1919, he contacted the resident painters Michel, Bergmann, Röhl, and Molzahn, and, as Michel reports, borrowed their pictures to hang them on the still empty walls of the Bauhaus at its first public viewing. These pictures assumed a special place in the development of the art of the time. About this it is necessary to make a detailed analysis.

Robert Michel's drawings of the years 1917 to 1919 were clearly determined by the experiences of the war, during which he was a pilot at the front and was severely wounded in a crash in 1916. They bear titles like "Between Heaven and Earth" or "Between Earth and Heaven" and show line projections striking through space, filled with propellers, wheels, and screws. Regular collages are attached to these, for which Michel used cutout technical illustrations, airplane blueprints, etc. As long as usable paints were not available before and just after the end of the war, these had to serve as color values in his drawings. Into the compositions made of great, rotating sprocket wheels interlocking into a complex mechanism he also stuck strips of lined paper and notes, interjected names and fragments of words, and gave them such titles as "Neuste Schule der Geläufigkeit" (Newest School of Fluency) and "Mann-es-Mann-Bild" (Man-like-Man Picture). In "Die grosse Uhr" (The Great Clock) of February, 1919, he mounted a real airplane tachometer, a memento of his plane crash, and he decorated the picture with little metal wheels, brass wires, wooden rings, buttons, and colored cockades of the bygone imperial era. He had even intended at first to hang his pocket watch in it, feeling that its audible ticking strengthened the picture for him. Numbers, clocks, and dials in woodcuts like "MEZ" (1919–1920) reflect a unique middle-European time.

Artistic interest in the machine and its function in modern life was already evident since the Futurist manifestos. By 1913 in Paris Marcel Duchamp had started with mechanical drawing and pictures like his "Chocolate Grater," inspiring with it the pro-Dadaist group of Man Ray, Picabia, and Crotti, among others, who revolved about him. But while Picabia especially found pleasure in the invention of completely fantastic machines, the personal experiences at the base of Robert Michel's artistic creations gave rise to works of a different spirit. They are possessed of the experienced dynamics of functioning machines and engines, and he attempted to translate these into abstract rhythms. The concrete materials and rags of words that he interjected nevertheless lend these works an ironic note, which Michel in his own way owed to Dada and which often continued to appear in his later works.

The equal mixture of strict formal elements and gay, anecdotal ones can also be found in the works of Ella Bergmann, who married Michel in 1919. Even before the Weimar period in 1917 in Paderborn this artist created a material painting entitled "Sonntag für Jedermann" (Sunday for Everyman), using old materials from the Libori Market there. Bits of colored paper stuck onto the composition give it a cheerful coloring, and old wooden lattices are nailed over the spinning circles, out of which eyes peer everywhere. At one time there was even a bit of rabbit fur in the picture, but the moths got at it, and since then it has been represented in paint. In the winter of 1918–1919 Ella Bergmann did a collage in Weimar, entitled "Menschen mit Kopf sind Selten" (People with Heads Are Rare), in which she stuck different cutouts with ironic references to the events of the day. Among old maps and pages of calendars there are strips of text providing a glossary of the pathetic phraseology of such critics of the day as Adolf Behne. The words "That is the duty of Cubism, thus we shall change the European," perhaps indicate where one may find the roots of the distinct form sense that holds together the disparate elements of the composition.

In Ella Bergmann this sense of form is combined with a unique poetry especially expressed in the collage "Fische" (Fishes) of 1919. Strips of silver paper and dancing fishes cut out of color illustrations introduce subtle color accents into the finely hatched drawing. After a period of transition that gave rise to all sorts of drawings with fantastic and seemingly Surrealistic images in which the playful, inventive side of her artistic talents was expressed, her interest in new, objective means of expression reawakened and in 1923 led to the "prism pictures," abstract collages in which she used the color tables of an old physics book.

Molzahn, a few years older than Michel, already possessed (when he landed in Weimar in 1918) a personal, distinctive style. Its individuality lies in the fact that he constructed Expressionistic forms in space — constructions made of lines and planes. The surfaces soon become cubes and bodies, colliding with one another in dynamic tension. The human figures disappear, and abstract compositions appear, reflecting cosmic phenomena and processes. Molzahn participated in Der Sturm exhibits in Berlin in 1918, 1919, and 1920. In the *Der Sturm* magazine of 1919 he published "The Manifesto of Absolute Expressionism," an ecstatic pronouncement whose proclamations, like "Battling forward we shall drive our way into the stars," find their reflections in his pictures.

During the Weimar period Molzahn introduced new structural values into his painting. He scratched lines, spirals, and signs into the colored surface, imprinted lace into it, and stuck paper onto the oil paintings and water colors. In his "Zeittaster" (Time Calipers) opposite calendar pages of modern computation there are maps and pages from an old farmer's almanac with the signs of the zodiac, star charts, and phases of the moon used to predict the weather, while all around the picture are distributed little wheels demonstrating the passage of time. Among the abstract forms machine parts, axles, spokes, and belts running over coils appear.

In the oil painting "Neue Länder" (New Countries, 1920), Molzahn mounted a plastic cog wheel on a world map and represented the distant countries by an American match box and the top of a cigar box showing two Brazilians smoking. While in this picture the warm colors of the paints play over the picturesque elements, in other paintings, such as "Mit wertvollen Glühstoff" (With Valuable Incandescence), printed matter such as the advertisement for Dali lightbulbs are pasted onto the oil painting, or in the case of "Vorschlag politischer Trauerfeste" (Suggestions for a Political Wake), directions for the use of a crystalline sweetener are included in the water color. Dada thoughts that became clear in these works may have had their origin in his association with the Michels.

It is worth noting that this group of Weimar painters produced unique results. Dadaist components, machines, aesthetics, and abstract Constructivist forms work together and bring out in each one his own personal style. In 1920, when the Bauhaus in Weimar took over the cultural leadership, this group dissolved. The Michels retired to their "smelting mill" in the Taunus hills. From 1922 on Robert Michel worked successfully in Frankfurt am Main in advertising and also made a name for himself as an architect with his modern gas stations and all-glass stores. After a stay in Soest in 1923, Molzahn was invited to the school of arts and crafts in Magdeburg, and in 1928 to the academy in Breslau, to which the old Bauhaus members Schlemmer (1929) and Muche (1931) followed him.

Hans Haffenrichter:

Born in Würzburg in 1897. He started his studies at the art school in Nuremberg. At Burg Lauenstein he met Wilhelm Uhde, upon whose urging he went to the Bauhaus in Weimar. Haffenrichter studied painting and sculpture at the Bauhaus from 1921 to 1924, taking special part in the stage design work of Lothar Schreyer. After that he was the guest of the Royal Academy of Art in Copenhagen for two years, working in the studio of Professor Uzon Frank.

In 1927 Haffenrichter took over the direction of the art school *Der Weg* in Berlin. In 1931 he became professor of art and professional education at the Pedagogical Academy in Elbing, East Prussia. Discharged by the state in 1933, he worked as a free-lance painter and sculptor until the end of the war and also designed industrial exhibits.

In conjunction with several scientists at the Kaiser Wilhelm Institute for Physical Chemistry, Haffenrichter designed a model of atomic and molecular structure. After 1945 he established himself in Heidelberg and from 1949 to 1952 he directed the mural painting department of the Werkkunstschule in Wiesbaden. His works have been widely shown in museums and galleries in the United States and Europe, among them the Prussian Academy of Art and Der Sturm in Berlin. Besides painting and plastics, he works in mosaics and designs stained-glass windows. Since 1961 Haffenrichter has lived in Hittenkirchen, Chiemgau.

Lothar Schreyer and the Bauhaus stage

Everyone who came to the Bauhaus in Weimar in 1921 immediately felt the unique, even enchanted world of the new art. A visit to Lothar Schreyer's studio strengthened this impression to an extreme degree. Here stood the master's costumes, sculptures, and pictures, surrounded by mysterious South Seas statues, masks, and Negro idols, a leopard throne, and among these Schreyer's portrait in death of a man, and also a beautiful, large painting by Léger. In conversation one immediately felt that one was seated across from a trail blazer in poetry and stagecraft. He radiated the clear insights of a knowledgeable and experienced master of his art. His knowledge embraced all previous and contemporary forms of theater and poetry. There were memorable conversations with him, filled with a personal warmth, gaiety, and occasional sharply pointed criticism.

Lothar Schreyer, like almost all the masters of the early Bauhaus, came from Herwarth Walden's gallery, Der Sturm, in Berlin. He brought with him to Weimar the deep experience and practical knowledge gained from his own experiments and productions. He had built and managed Der Sturm's stage in Berlin and Hamburg from 1918 to 1921, presenting the poetry of August Stramm, Hölderlin, Herwarth Walden, and his own verse plays.

Hugely impressed since my childhood by Punch and Judy and other puppet shows (at the age of eight I built myself a little theater) and generally stage struck, I was so fascinated by all the things I learned from Lothar Schreyer in the fall of 1921 that I accepted delightedly when he invited me to join his theater workshop. The same was true for the dancer Eva Weidemann, whom I had assisted. Lothar became teacher and master to us.

First we worked under his direction on dances and movement, with costumes and instruments. We developed a "Song to Mary," danced in front of a large tapestry painted by Schreyer, a "Dance of the Wind Spirits," with rhythms played on an African calabash xylophone, and a "Trooper's Dance" in full costume, which we designed ourselves. At the same time in many conversations Schreyer explained the connection between what we were doing and his stage plays — their meaning and significance; thus we came closer to the man himself. Finally Schreyer composed and developed his *Moon Play* for us. The "Spielgang," as he named his specific scores, made his intentions clear in every detail. The long daily training stood us in particularly good stead for the *Klangsprechen* (speaking on a particular pitch) of the poetry. The player had first to find his own *Grundton* (base note), and from this find his own *inneren Klang* (internal sound). The words of the poem were strictly rehearsed in the rhythm and bar of the "Spielgang" and in the pitch and intensity of the *Klangsprechen* until the "spiritual dimension" became actuality. The movements of the players derived from the tone of the words. Thus every individual movement and our paths across the stage were accurately rehearsed in costume and with dance props. The dance shield was very hard to master in the beginning, especially when it had to be moved in close time with the speech. Gertrud Grunow often helped us here with her harmonizing exercises.

In addition to this intensive training, under Schreyer's direction and together with other Bauhaus members, we built in the studio the large, over six-foot-high figure "Maria," designed by him, and the great dance shields that completely enveloped the players. But work on the play always remained the main thing, and the meaning of this artistic creation became ever clearer to us. We recognized with Schreyer that the new way must lead away from the theater of style and illusion and its pseudo-Expressionism, and that we would rediscover the origin of the theater and the birth of tragedy. Schreyer often showed us his new paintings, his many balancing exercises, and his writing pictures. He helped us in our work in painting and sculpture with his criticism and inspiration. And new ideas were developed, experiments and designs for the stage and for masks.

Outside of our work we attended many performances of new theater and dance works, above all Alexander Tairoff's exciting *Unchained*

Theater. Of course we also took part in the work of Oskar Schlemmer in the room next to ours. Schreyer and Schlemmer shared the directorship of the Bauhaus' theater workshop. With great enthusiasm we went through the production of Schlemmer's *Triadic Ballet* in Stuttgart in 1922. At that time, too, Kurt Schwerdtfeger, the sculptor, invented his reflecting-light play; his presentation of the Story of Creation was unforgettable. We were delighted by this new light play and took part in several experiments, sometimes with colored lights. Once we presented our dance pieces, and later, when it seemed ready, we did the *Moon Play* for a small group.

Besides our stage work each of us worked in a studio — I in sculpture. We heard important lectures and discussions, unforgettable seminars by Paul Klee and Wassily Kandinsky, and enjoyed the overwhelming Bauhaus festivals.

The exciting magnetism of the Bauhaus drew many friends from far away — poets, musicians, and artists. There were confrontations with De Stijl, with Arnold Schönberg's music; Kurt Schwitters read his poetry. It was a life filled with work and companionship, serious and earnest, full of gaiety and fun. But the discussions concerning the Bauhaus, the attacks of the uncomprehending Weimar public, and the misery of the inflation distressed us more and more. So that the stage work could continue Schreyer sold his large painting by Léger. In the Bauhaus itself the change of direction from Expressionism and Cubism to Constructivism and functionalism was ever more clearly to be felt, as was the conversion from handicrafts to machine and industrial production. There were heated discussions and intellectual battles among those of different persuasions who were nevertheless still held together by Walter Gropius and some of the other masters.

When the Bauhaus moved from Weimar to Dessau, and Gropius was able to build anew under very favorable conditions, the objective, Constructivist trend dominated. As the Institute of Design the Bauhaus had cooperation from industry. From 1923 to 1924 Johannes Itten, Gerhard Marcks, and Lothar Schreyer, together with a number of their students and coworkers, withdrew in a friendly fashion to pursue their own work. After some years Johannes Itten and Georg Muche founded the Itten School in Berlin. Lothar Schreyer and I continued our work in the studios of Der Weg in Berlin. In connection with Der Sturm we exhibited and conducted some art soirées. On one occasion I presented among other things a light play for which Lothar Schreyer provided the text *The Birth of the Flower* — an echo of the work at Weimar — and a reflected-light play by Kurt Schwerdtfeger.

Later Schreyer wrote: "Looking back on the many Bauhaus experiments: we were attempting to find a new connection with the metaphysical . . . we know that we gave the contemporary world and the world of the future a new view of reality. . . . We are concerned with the internal picture of mankind, that which cannot be lost, which is hidden, which gives us art, the certainty of spiritual reality."

To conclude, one more word by Lothar Schreyer, which has been with me throughout my life and work: "The word *Kunst* [art], which derives from the old high German *kunnan*, not only subsumes *Können* [ability] but also *künden* [annunciation] — spiritual mastery. Thus have I understood it and tried to realize it in my work: the artist does not only represent and interpret his time, but he must also be conscious of his responsibility to find new paths which will lead man to a higher spiritual level."

Lothar Schreyer:

Born in Blasewitz near Dresden in 1886. He studied art history and law at the universities of Heidelberg, Berlin, and Leipzig. In 1910 he graduated from Leipzig as a lawyer. However, very early in his life he got involved with art and the theater and started to paint. Between 1911 and 1918 he worked as producer and assistant stage manager at the German Schauspielhaus in Hamburg. Around 1914 Schreyer visited Herwarth Walden in Berlin. As a result of this meeting an intensive collaboration developed. First Walden published Schreyer's poems, and then he became editor of the magazine *Der Sturm* from 1916 to 1928. In 1918 Schreyer founded the Sturm-Bühne in Berlin, with its first production a drama by August Stramm. Schreyer moved the Sturm-Bühne to Hamburg in 1919, where it was continued as Expressionistic experimental theater under the name *"Kampfbühne."*
In 1921 Schreyer was invited to the Weimar Bauhaus to teach in the stage workshop. There he turned toward Christian mysticism and art, which at one time was practiced by a small group of people at the Bauhaus. He left the Bauhaus after an unsuccessful performance of the *Mondspiel* in March, 1923, which he had produced, and Oskar Schlemmer became director of the stage workshop. From 1924 to 1927 Schreyer was teacher and occasional director of the art school *Der Weg* in Berlin. After this, he became chief editor for a Hamburg publisher. In 1933 Schreyer converted to Catholicism and kept busy as a free-lance writer in Hamburg, mostly dealing with Christian art. He wrote *Erinnerungen an Sturm und Bauhaus* ("Memories of Sturm and Bauhaus," Munich, 1956). Schreyer died in Hamburg on June 18, 1966.

Hope for a new world

We got into the spiritual adventure during a difficult time. The Bauhaus became the bastion of Expressionism, which those about us took as the sign of the world's decline. In our artistic work, we were hardly depressed by the various views that shook the Bauhaus. For example, Häuser, an apostle of the youth movement, exposing the vagabond life; the Mazdaznan teachings that Johannes Itten brought with him (the Bauhaus kitchen cooked in keeping with this doctrine); anthroposophy; theosophy; Catholicism; spiritualism — all these were founded on the hope for a new world. We were ironical about everything, particularly about ourselves, and thus were freed to revere all mankind and life. The Bauhaus years in Weimar were a time of fiery purgation and bound our little lost group into a unit. Many Weimaraners called us Bauhäusler, and it sounded like convict — it had the taste of horror and fear. But many were indulgent toward us and did us good turns that we never forgot. We needed indulgence. We had invented a costume that we and the masters, too, if they wished, wore openly. I still have and use my old Bauhaus suit. When one day Itten declared that hair was a sign of sin, his most enthusiastic disciples shaved their heads completely. And thus we went around Weimar.

We loved Weimar, especially the park and Tiefurt and Belvedere, the Goethe house in the park, and the Tempelherrenhaus in which Itten had his studio.

Despite all outward signs of poverty, these were festive years. We celebrated the Dragon Feast, and for weeks in the workshops we constructed dragons, imaginary birds, and flying fishes. We flew them in the autumn skies of Weimar.

What did we experience in Weimar? Love of art's creativity. Love of the reality of the spirit. Love of art's unceasing transformations. Love of the laws of nature, our ancient teachers. Love of mankind in his fragility. Love of community despite all man's differences. And love of resignation, born of knowledge: anything we do is temporary — no more.

This love unites all Bauhaus people, whether they worked in Weimar or in Dessau or carry on their work today on this or the other side

of the ocean. When we meet under the sign of the Bauhaus or see each
other for the first time we are one — we agree. Then reality becomes truth.
And the legend that began in Weimar becomes present life.

Werner Graeff:

Born in Wuppertal in 1901. He
began his art studies while still in school
and in 1921 came to the Bauhaus in Weimar.
After Theo van Doesburg had established his
studio and started lectures, Graeff continued
his studies there. From 1922 to 1930 he was
a member of De Stijl group. In 1922 he participated in the so-called "Constructivist Congress" in Weimar, together with Dadaists
Tzara, Arp, Schwitters, Richter and Constructivists van Doesburg, van Easteren, Lissitzky, and Moholy-Nagy.
Besides his work as a Constructivist, Graeff
wrote scripts for abstract films and invented
an international traffic-sign language. From
1922 to 1923 he was a guest participant in
the exhibits of the November Group in Berlin
and in 1923, together with Hans Richter, he
founded the magazine G (for Gestaltung),
whose editorial board later also included
Lissitzky and Mies van der Rohe. During
that time he produced new designs for auto-
mobiles and motorcycles — designs which
were, unfortunately, never used in industry.
In 1925 Graeff became a member of the German Werkbund, whose vice-president, Mies
van der Rohe, appointed him press and public relations manager for the Werkbund exhibit "Die Wohnung" (Weissenhof Settlement)
in Stuttgart in 1926–1927. The Werkbund
then commissioned him to publish the books
Bau, Wohnung, and Innenräume, dealing
with the exhibit. Subsequently Graeff returned to films and wrote scenarios for avant-
garde movies. From 1931 to 1933 he taught
at the Reimann School in Berlin. In 1934 he
emigrated to Spain and by the end of the
thirties had settled in Switzerland, where he
again worked in films. On a federal commission there, from 1942 to 1945, he conducted
an orientation course for refugees. After the
war he lived in Paris for a short time and
then went to Essen, where the Folkwang-
schule für Gestaltung appointed him to their
faculty in 1951. Since leaving teaching in
1959, he has devoted himself wholly to painting. Several one-man shows have made his
work well known in Germany. Graeff now
lives in Essen.

The Bauhaus, the De Stijl Group in Weimar, and the Constructivist Congress of 1922

At the beginning of the twenties little Weimar was one of the
most important centers of artistic life in Europe. For the Bauhaus attracted
extraordinary personalities. Never before and never since the Bauhaus has
any director of an academy been able to gather together such extraordinary

artistic talents into one teaching body as Walter Gropius did. In those years Kandinsky, Klee, Feininger, Schlemmer, Marcks, and finally Moholy came to Gropius. These seven names alone indicate an incomparable plane. Among the other teachers I shall name only Itten who, as founder of the orientation course at the Bauhaus that contained the Vorkurs and the constructions classes, created a highly original thing. Even today his influence is felt in every progressive art school the world over.

It is generally agreed that the original program of the Bauhaus, besides having a strongly practical orientation, also produced some rather fantastic, romantic flights of fancy. These derived from the high estimate placed on the quality of medieval and perhaps even Far Eastern handicrafts, and on the fact that they were part of the past. One recognizes the heritage of John Ruskin here, and one may also see a glimmer of Bruno Taut's Expressionistic, fantastic "dawn light"; one might blame it on Itten's religio-mystic tendencies — at all events romanticism and mysticism rated highly at the Bauhaus in 1921–1922. Nevertheless, schisms gradually developed among teachers as well as pupils and in 1923 led to an open break between Itten and Gropius and to a new conception of the Bauhaus.

Without a doubt one man who himself had originally wanted to become a teacher at the Bauhaus (and probably should have) contributed to the development of these things. He was Theo van Doesburg, the Dutch painter and editor of the Dutch magazine *De Stijl* ("The Style"). From 1921 to 1923 he lived in Weimar. Perhaps Gropius himself had once given van Doesburg hopes of being appointed to the faculty; certainly that would have corresponded to the wishes of one of Gropius' closest collaborators, Adolf Meyer, who valued van Doesburg and the goals of De Stijl most highly. But Gropius had recognized that van Doesburg, despite all his outstanding pedagogical and propagandistic talent, despite all his ability and vision, was a rather difficult man, sensitive and extremely aggressive. Van Doesburg would almost certainly have drawn blood from at least half the Bauhaus faculty in those days. His only purpose in staying in Weimar was to do battle from outside. He could not understand why Gropius, who as early as 1911 (in Alfeld) and 1914 (in Cologne) had given bold proof of his Constructivist spirit and variety, could as director of the Bauhaus in the beginning have produced or even merely countenanced a backsliding into

Expressionism and romantic rapture. In contrast to the medieval-handicraft ideal of the original Bauhaus program, van Doesburg promoted the machine and the mass production of well-designed goods. By 1922 he was already anticipating part of the later Bauhaus program. He gave many lectures on typography and for students of the Bauhaus and other interested people instituted a design course of his own. Nevertheless, this was the beginning of the Weimar De Stijl group to which, besides Theo and Nelly van Doesburg, such people as Peter Röhl, Harry Scheibe, Max Burchartz, Walter Dexel, and the author of these lines belonged.

In spring of 1922 a monster congress was organized in Düsseldorf by a group of artists from the Rhineland. Calling itself the First International Congress of Progressive Art, it had almost six hundred participants. In our view it offered little that was satisfactory, and when on the second day an incredible number of dull constitutional paragraphs were read to us (I seem to remember it was far over a hundred), we made a fuss. The rest of the Constructivists and the Dadaists, together with those members of the De Stijl still present, left the hall. And so van Doesburg conceived the plan of calling together a smaller congress of Constructivists and Dadaists, that is to say a congress of those outspokenly opposed to ecstatic Expressionism, which was so offensive to us and also seemed an anachronism, since it appeared to have reached its zenith before 1911.

It fitted van Doesburg's plan of battle that the congress could be called in Weimar; here and in Jena he and Walter Dexel organized propaganda lectures on Constructivism and Dadaist productions. A manifesto was drawn up, and De Stijl and Suprematism and its variations throughout the whole world (including for instance its Hungarian descendant) were gathered together (quite correctly) under the collective concept of Constructivism.

From van Doesburg's point of view the congress was a new blow at Expressionism and romanticism at the Bauhaus. Secretly, however, Gropius had by then already decided to change the course given at the school and to concentrate on his own original, that is Constructive, line. In 1923 he hired the Constructivist Moholy-Nagy. As Itten had championed the old course with great intensity, so now Moholy pursued Gropius' new motto with fiery zeal: Art and Technology — a New Unity!

Sigfried Giedion:

Born in Lengnau near Zurich in 1888. He first studied mechanical engineering at the Technical Highschool in Vienna, where he graduated as an engineer. From 1917 to 1922 he studied art history at the universities of Zurich, Berlin, and Munich, receiving his degree under Heinrich Wölfflin. In 1923 he met Walter Gropius in Weimar and became a fighter for the Bauhaus Idea. Among his personal friends were Walter Gropius, Laszlo Moholy-Nagy, Herbert Bayer, and Marcel Breuer. In 1928 Giedion was one of the founders of CIAM at the Castle of La Sarraz near Lausanne, and he remained its general manager until 1956. Giedion occupied himself extensively with questions of modern architecture in essays and publications. His book *Bauen in Frankreich: Eisen, Eisenbeton* ("Building in France: Steel and Reinforced Concrete," Berlin, 1928) became quite well known.

In 1938 Giedion was invited to Harvard University, Cambridge, as professor of art and art history. The results of his findings about the development of architecture were condensed in his famous book *Space, Time and Architecture* (Cambridge, Mass., 1941). This standard work on the history of architecture had sixteen reprints in the United States alone, and translations have been published in many European countries and Japan. Other definitive publications by Giedion are: *Mecanisation Takes Command,* (Oxford, 1948), *The Eternal Present: The Beginnings of Art,* volume I (New York, 1955), and *The Beginning of Architecture,* volume II (New York, 1957).

After 1946 Giedion taught at the Eidgenössischen Technischen Hochschule in Zurich. By 1937 he had already been appointed honorary member of the Royal Institute of British Architects; in 1952 he became a member of the Belgian and American Academies of Science; in 1960 he became officer of the Order of the White Rose of Finland, and in 1963 he received the Gold Medal of the Mexican Institute of Architects.

Among Giedion's publications dedicated to the Bauhaus and its personalities is a monograph on Walter Gropius, which appeared in 1954. The last book before his death was "Architecture and the Phenomenon of Transition," which will appear in the U.S. in 1969. Giedion died in Zurich on April 9, 1968.

Bauhaus week in Weimar, August 1923

I no longer know how I heard of it, but it drew me there. And so I took the night train from Munich to Weimar. I gazed into a world newly forming. Those who took part in that event carry the impression of it all their lives; at least, that was how it struck me.

For the first time I got a universal insight into the cosmos of contemporary art. At the Weimar theater Hermann Scherchen directed one of the first performances of Stravinsky's *Histoire du Soldat.* In the theater at Jena, recently transformed by Gropius' renovations, we saw the *Triadic*

Ballet by Schlemmer. And besides this there was an experiment in completely abstract forms: a red and a blue square glided past one another against a black background and in the closing act they stood up on the stage. This was a ballet by Kandinsky.

Giula Pap:

Born in Oroshaza, Hungary in 1899. He studied at the Graphischen Lehr — und Versuchsanstalt in Vienna and at the School of Arts and Crafts in Budapest. From 1920 to 1924 he continued his studies at the Bauhaus in Weimar. Johannes Itten's teaching methods appealed to Pap, and he later adopted them in his own teaching. Besides studying painting, Pap also worked in the metal workshop at the Bauhaus.
From 1926 to 1933 he was engaged by Itten to teach creative design in Berlin.
After his return to Hungary, Pap opened his own private school in Budapest, where he was joined by the art historian Ernst Kállai, among others. At the end of the war, in 1947, he founded a school of painting for talented children of destitute workers and farmers, in one of the most beautiful parts of Hungary — the artist colony of Nagymaros at Danube-Knie. It was attempted to apply the theories of art education in the twenties to the new socialist conditions in Hungary. After two years, most of his students had transferred to the College of Fine Arts in Budapest, where Pap became professor of painting. Pap's paintings and metal designs have been shown internationally.

Liberal Weimar

When I visited the Bauhaus again in Dessau I was greeted as a member of the institution's great historical era. In the history of the Bauhaus, Weimar was the period in which the clear ideas of Gropius gradually took visible shape, developing through many transformations out of the dust and fog. Yes, it was an exciting period of groping and seeking, of error and recognition, of painful doubt and flaming enlightenment. Crazy actions and fun took turns with contemplation and devotion, with feverish search and creative impulse. We knew that only the first steps had been taken, but this started the basis for the great common goal.

I had just had my first one-man exhibit in Vienna at the Haus der jungen Künstlerschaft when I heard of Gropius' manifesto: "The goal of all creative work is building. . . . Architects, sculptors, painters — we all must return to handicraft.''

One could not remain indifferent or inactive. I knew that Johannes Itten, too, in whose much discussed course I hoped to find answers to many questions, was at the Bauhaus. This fact made me decide, at any cost, to go to the Bauhaus in Weimar.

At this time the Bauhaus was not a college and not simply a collective community, but both. Above all it was a working team of distinguished, independent individuals.

In the first years Gropius left the pedagogical and artistic direction of the teaching entirely to Johannes Itten. The Vorkurs, which was entirely different from academic dogma and teaching methods, was preserved in its basic principles after Itten left the Bauhaus, even though it was complemented by newer technological requirements and the individual convictions of the teacher.

Itten had the ability to recognize the tendencies and talents of each individual and thus to help their creative strengths toward real, independent work, freed of all convention. He revealed the basic laws of visual creativity, the laws of form and color, including the grammar of visual expression.

He was a fascinating, influential phenomenon: his personal remarks were pointed; in his analyses he continually amazed us with new insights. The thoughts and ideas that he called forth in us were all embracing, inexhaustible, and work on us still, like chain reactions. The encounter with Gropius and the Bauhaus was most fortunate for us all. Great problems give wings to and broaden the creative personality, especially in a harmonious community.

So it was in the year 1922 that the decision was made to build an experimental house on a beautiful hill called Am Horn. Everybody could enter his design in independent competition. The designs were discussed in a working seminar and finally judged in common. Gropius, too, submitted a design and left the final judgment completely to the Bauhaus collective.

The design of the master Georg Muche was accepted. The individual workshops of the Bauhaus produced all the furniture of the house. Is it conceivable that in such a comparatively short time the hoped-for unit could have been achieved, without the belief of Gropius in the collective work of the youth and the masters?

But there were times, I felt, when there was much too much theorizing. Above all I did not care for the ideas of van Doesburg, who wished to replace everything, also intuition, with numbers.

Several times I heard that one working seminar had for some time been busy determining which colors correspond to the rules of the circle, the square, and the triangle. I was curious and once joined in.

Besides Klee and Kandinsky, Schlemmer and other senior students also participated. They were just discussing yellow. Someone said it reminded him of the high twittering of the blackbird, and yellow paint seemed close to the triangle. Klee replied that the yolk of an egg was yellow, too, but still circular. After a while I piped up with the arrogance of which only the young are capable. I asked how one could discuss things that were so obvious. Let us examine the internal characteristics of metals (I was working in the metal workshop at the time): when I work with silver it seems to me the most supple metal; thus it corresponds to the circle and to blue. In contrast, brass is hard and its splinters most damagingly sharp; thus it corresponds to the triangle and to yellow. Copper, bulky and heavy, not too soft and not too hard, corresponds to the square and to red. My analysis was unexpected; no one contradicted me, and if I remember correctly, herewith the seminar was finished.

Alexander Bortnyik:

Born in Marosvasarhely (Siebenburgen) in 1893. He studied at the Budapest Academy of Art, where he was a master student under Karl Kernstok and Josef Rippl-Rónai. After 1917 he began to take part in the avant-garde exhibits in Buadpest and Vienna and turned toward Constructivism. After the fall of the Räte Republic he emigrated to Vienna; from 1922 to 1926 lived mainly in Weimar. He exhibited at Der Sturm.

In 1921 in Vienna he published a portfolio of his Constructivist paintings entitled *Bild Architekturen* ("Picture Architecture").

From 1928 to 1938 Bortnyik conducted a school of graphics in Budapest, the Mühely (Workshop), which became known as the Bauhaus of Budapest. Bortnyik's most prominent student at the school was Victor Vasarely.

Besides teaching before the war, Bortnyik worked extensively as a commercial artist, producing above all posters, notably the one for Modiano cigarette papers. In 1943, together with Ivan Hevésy and Marius Rabinowsky, he published a book entitled *Two Thousand Years of Painting* and edited the magazines *Neue Erde* ("New Earth"), *Plakat* (Poster), and *Freie Kunst* ("Free Art"). After the war Bortnyik adopted a partly Surrealistic art style that has become known as Satirical Realism. From 1948 to 1949 he taught at the School of Arts and Crafts in Budapest and from 1949 to 1956 he was director of the College of Fine Arts in Budapest. Bortnyik has been awarded several national prizes. He now lives in Budapest.

Something on the Bauhaus

In the spring of 1922 in Vienna I met a young Hungarian countryman, Farkas Molnàr. He was studying architecture at the Bauhaus and told me about the aims and the life at the Bauhaus. He also portrayed Weimar as a center of contemporary art movements in Europe. In the beginning of September, 1922 I went to Weimar. I did not intend to study at the Bauhaus, but merely to look around. Everything I found there really was new, interesting, and educational, and I stayed there for some time. Besides the many other masters of the Bauhaus and its many guests who came to Weimar, I remember above all my Hungarian comrades who were members of the Bauhaus: Laszlo Moholy-Nagy, Farkas Molnàr, Marcel Breuer, Andreas Weininger, Gulia Pap.

Above all I was interested in the question of what sort of ideological and aesthetic conditions, relationships, and interrelations there were at the Bauhaus between architecture on the one hand and painting and sculpture on the other. My interest was not confined merely to canvas painting, but on the contrary I meant particularly that type of work that, so to speak, grows into architecture: mural painting with all its special techniques — fresco, sgraffito, mosaic, relief, and full-scale sculpture. I questioned Gropius at our first meeting, but his answer was disappointing. There were painting classes and technical workshops at the Bauhaus, but there was no internal ideological and aesthetic collaboration with architecture. Nevertheless, a flyer on the Bauhaus read: "The goal of all creative endeavor is construction. . . . Architects, painters and sculptors must learn to recognize and understand the many-limbed form of the construction in its unity and in its parts. Then their works will of themselves be filled with the architectural spirit lost in salon art.''*

To found an institute that was to strive toward a ''unity of the arts'' and that, to this end, wanted systematically and generously to educate young artists was a brilliant idea. It was timely and completely new. Gropius could not completely realize the program quoted above, and whatever did not succeed — could not succeed — cannot be regarded as Gropius' fault. What was lacking for a real, internal unity of architecture with painting and sculpture, in fact with all the arts, was a unity in human society. Nevertheless, the Bauhaus was and remains a significant factor not only in German art but in the whole world.

Not least among the contributions of the Bauhaus, one must remember that it helped to develop Oskar Schlemmer's new and valuable works for the stage. Despite the differences between architects and Bauhaus painters, I believe that the art of Klee, Kandinsky, and Feininger helped to lighten the threat of standardization and monotony of construction. These limitations often occur today, too, and the answer to them is the search, the powerful search, for originality through subjectivity. The lively, imaginative, and individual art of the Bauhaus masters prevented such inflexibility and fostered variety.

Another thing that created opposition within the Bauhaus was the hypothesis generally accepted in architectural circles that ''we must free ourselves of everything decorative. A building needs no embellishment of painting or sculpture, no pictures in interior space. Constructively organized space, colorful walls and furniture replace pictures. An object if it functions well and its form follows its function also exercises such aesthetic effect.'' Developments since then have shown that this was a hastily formed idea, which remained unrealized because it did not correspond to human, spiritual, and aesthetic needs. It was a mistaken oversimplification, based on too narrow a point. And after all, there were paintings on the masters' walls, and the students painted, too.

* Walter Gropius in the *Bauhaus Manifesto* of 1919.

Perhaps it is superfluous to wonder who was the originator of the new architecture — Frank Lloyd Wright? Le Corbusier? Walter Gropius? The Dutch? It seems to me that the engine driver who took the train onto new rails was Frank Lloyd Wright. But the others created new cars, new wheels, new roads, and perhaps instead of the old steam they adopted electricity for power. One could say that an artist, out of economic need and because of competition, must discover in a restless, changing environment new materials and a rational method befitting the express tempo of the times. These must reform residential buildings from the ground up and lead from a relatively monumental size and shape to functional and proportioned construction. On this basis the Europeans created a civilized work embracing all the arts.

A few words about Theo van Doesburg. He played a not insignificant role in Weimar at that time. His lectures also influenced the Bauhaus and many of its members. But it is remarkable that his theories and their realization in his paintings are closer to Gropius' ideas as expressed in Art and Technology — a New Unity than those of many Bauhaus masters. He should have been a master — I think that was why he came to Weimar. What probably put Gropius and the younger generation off was a distinct dullness and the narrow, too dogmatic ideology in the composition of his pictures, in which there remained very little play of the imagination.

Finally, what did the Bauhaus and indeed the atmosphere at the time in Weimar give me? What did I experience and learn there? Above all there was the experience of a new art and style that sought consciously to unite all fields, with the exception of architecture and painting; there were the fruitful discussions of the most widely varied subjects between those of like minds; and there were the seeds of the development of a collective, creative spirit. There was the experience of the beginnings of co-operation among the arts, the consciousness and energy of the students, and the generosity of the masters' leadership. But I also became aware that one must pursue the questions of decorativeness and subjectivity. The search for a new order in the chaotic profusion of art movements existing even then was impressive. Confusion reigned over all of Europe, but at the Bauhaus one could sense the still faint lines of a beginning order in art. Yet for the realization of the Bauhaus Idea a healthy social basis was necessary. The experience taught me that there were many live and constructive elements in the idea of the Bauhaus and in the principles of the "new creativity" worked out by Mondrian and van Doesburg. But art lives through man; it exists with and for men. Its boundaries must be broadened and expanded.

When I returned from Germany to my native Budapest in 1925 I tried (of course in a smaller way) to establish an artists' workshop based in general on the principles of the Bauhaus. I wanted to stress painting, including free-hand drawing, mural painting, graphics, and commercial art. But the realization was impossible because the officials of that time were not interested in it. They were against progress in art. There was no private interest either, because no material results could be expected from such an undertaking. And so my plan had to remain limited to one area: graphics and commercial art, with emphasis on Constructive tendencies. We called this school *Mühely*, or workshop. After twelve years I had to give up this work because of a serious illness. At that time the Mühely had about 120 students. Many of them work in Budapest and still more work abroad. And through them, too, the impulses of the Bauhaus are carried on.

Georg Muche:

SEE BIOGRAPHY, PAGE 201

Speech on the seventy-fifth birthday of Johannes Itten

My Dear Friend:

When in this serene hour of your life I entwine your figure with anecdotes then I must unbutton my mantle of discretion. Yet I think you would rather have that than have me crown your head with laurels and sing you a hymn of praise.

In 1920 we were bored at the art academy in Düsseldorf. The studio hummed with empty chatter. Then a girl from Cologne said: "You talk of the wonder of Weimar! I keep hearing Bauhaus, Bauhaus, Bauhaus, but none of you knows what it really is. I'm packing my bag and leaving for Weimar." When the girl talked to Gropius she heard him say: "No, we can't accept you in the middle of the semester!"

"Then it's no different at the Bauhaus than at the academy in Düsseldorf!"

"Well, try it. Go to Professor — that is Master — Itten, at the Tempelherrhaus and ask him if he'll let you into his Vorkurs."

Itten said: "Yes. Go to studio 21. Watch carefully and start working. Right now!"

In the studio the girl lowered herself onto a footstool. She watched . . . and everything she saw made her doubt her sanity. She did not understand why her neighbor was reducing a bit of bark to pulp and why everyone had a little heap of rubbish next to him — all sorts of useless things — bits of glass, crunched-up paper, rusty scraps of iron, feathers large and small, pebbles, wood, buttons, and anything else. Most of all she was amazed at the attention people bestowed upon all these things, combining them, taking them apart, eying them, and touching them dreamily or critically, according to invisible criteria, and finally somehow making them fast.

A girl who looked like the witch of Westerwald grown young and beautiful again — yellow hair, cinnabar red cheeks, green eyes, and on the pale lips of those starvation years an always ready smile — went from place to place helpfully bringing this and that, and she brought the girl from Cologne the petal of a red rose. Wonderingly she took it in her hand, and the thought went through her head that this strange creature was being unselfish and helpful in a foolish but beautiful way. And so she asked her neighbor: "What shall I do with it?" The answer came: "You can't do anything with it. That's not the sort of material you can do anything with. It's far too impermanent. Its structure will change between today and tomorrow, and the day after that you'll be holding in your hand something that will look as though it had never belonged to a rose. Its dusky quality will be transformed, and this red will finally become black. One might use something like that as a contrast, a sort of antiform for permanence. But that is too difficult for you. You must have materials that keep their shape and retain their superficial structure. Instead of a rose she ought to bring you something that will last — best of all would be a piece of railroad track."

Now the girl from Cologne was no longer in doubt. People were either crazy here or played dumb — or smart — whichever. Then she noticed a young man busy with a bunch of old tin cans. With a pair of pliers he was trying to pry off the rusty, dented top of a large tin, which had once held Bismark herring. When he succeeded he filed the sharp edges down and rubbed the spots of rust off. She could understand that. When she saw how he piled the cans on top of one another and secured them with holes and wire, it occurred to her to sit down next to him and help him get the rust off. But then the boy stood up, went to a jacket hanging on the wall, reached into a pocket, took out a piece of paper in which something was wrapped, went back to his seat, and opened the package. He pulled out a fish bone, complete with head and tail. He held it over the end of his tin-can tower, which was about four feet high, carefully and deliberately increasing and decreasing the distance between the fish bone and the tower, tore the head off the skeleton, fixed the rest onto the point of a knitting needle, poked a hole with the needle into the top of the smallest can, and wedged the needle into it. "Master Klee would say: 'A spirit hovers over the whole!'" a gay wag called out. Again this was completely incomprehensible to the young girl. Then the boy got two colored bird feathers — down feathers — out of a small junk pile and stuck them onto the fish bone where the head had been. Well, now, he was clearly crazy, too! Fortunately they all went home because the clock had struck twelve.

Next day was judgment day. Itten came, went over to the tin-can tower, looked it over from all sides, and finally said: "What are those feathers doing up there? Take them right down. They have no connection with the rest and as contrast are far too minute." "Itten agrees with me," thought the girl, and gave him all her trust. Then the boy said: "I didn't want to give up all color."

"Then you must treat the sculptural body in a colorful manner. Paint it!"

"I don't want to. It must stay metallic. I'd rather give up the colored feathers."

"And then," said Itten, "that relief up there — the bone — it stands up there far too abruptly over the whole. You have to find a connecting shape." And with that he left the boy alone.

The latter ran out the door, and the girl from Cologne thought: "He won't come back again. Too bad!" But he was back already with a piece of barbed wire in his hand. He spiraled it around the tin cans, and she understood immediately that he was trying to solve the problem Itten had just set him. By means of the thorny wire the bones were being brought into a better relationship with the sculptural metallic shapes.

The next day the girl heard Itten analyze paintings for the first time — [that day] Cézanne's "Murder." Itten spoke passionately and vehemently of the impact of the picture's decisive, expressive form. Everyone copied Cézanne's rapid brush strokes, first in the air and then, charcoal in hand, on paper. The girl thought of the sharp points of the barbed wire and the fish bone. When she met the boy one day soon after in one of the studios she asked him to set the little feathers back on his construction, because it was as aggressive as a minister of war and needed battle decorations. "Well, good," said the boy. "Master Itten will be pleased. But we must color the lower section to match. Write down on a piece of paper: 'The Minister of War.' Don't write straight and stiff as you learned to do in Düsseldorf, but pointed, slanting, and in black on yellow. That will be the minister of war's standard."

I have remembered all this because in later years the girl from Cologne told me the story and because I had to defend this "Minister of War" and finally sacrifice him. For at the end of the semester this work and others done in the Vorkurs was exhibited in the skylight room of the Bauhaus to give the Thuringian ministers and other officials the opportunity to judge the Bauhaus and finally appropriate the budget for another year. I had to lead the gentlemen through the rooms and finally stand next to the

"Minister of War," because they asked me what it meant. I explained the background of Itten's educational ideas, hoping to convince them. But when I saw their disgruntled faces I suddenly understood that I wouldn't succeed that way. I was afraid they would withhold the grant and that I would come to grief and endanger the Bauhaus if I failed to change their aversion into assent. So I shifted ground — though no one noticed — and said: "This work shows that not everyone who thinks his talents lie in a particular direction necessarily has the proper ability. This example shows that it would have been a waste of money had the candidate been accepted into the metal workshop. He has no talent for handicraft. Perhaps some day he will be an imaginative sculptor or painter, but he will never be a good artisan. These works done in the Vorkurs quickly uncover such facts, and that is their purpose." The ministers and the officials nodded their heads, and the Bauhaus was granted the means to continue for another year.

Now I am going to speak of the angry young men of the twenties. Three Bauhäusler on whom Itten could rely if others failed him wanted to break away from his influences. They were afraid they would lose themselves if they continued to follow him. One was very robust. I shall call him X, because he had grown to look robustly like a capital X, and besides, he was a puzzling man. I shall call the other Z because he seemed to move in the rhythm of a Z and was aggressive. The third I shall equate with Y, written with a soft pencil. He was a dreamer. He seemed entranced when one day in the rain he placed himself under the eaves of the Tempelherrenhaus, Itten's studio, right where the gutter leaked. Great drops fell onto his neck. Absorbed in looking at the clouds he just stood there.

This Y came to Itten's apartment one evening shortly after ten during the last days of 1921 and said: "X and Z have prepared a New Year's Eve celebration in their studio. We should like to have you with us, Master Itten, at the beginning of the New Year."

"I can't," said Itten. "I have a guest. May I bring him along?"

"I don't know. X and Z said nothing about that," answered Y.

"If Muche will come along I will come. I think it will be all right with you!"

Shortly before twelve midnight we appeared in the studio. It was empty and desolate, but in one corner a small room had been partitioned off and shimmered in a deep purple light with glimmering red and green specks. The mood was uneasy. We soon realized that we were to be the participants in a happening, which was to transform Itten's doctrine of color into its gloomy contrast. The actors were silent. X had bared the upper part of his body and smeared it with a wild confusion of colors. His skull was so made up that it looked split apart. I said to Itten: "They're going to do the guinea-hen dance."

"What did you say? . . . What is that?"

"I don't know either. Y is standing out there. He's covered his stomach and chest with little colored squiggles. He looks like a guinea hen."

First X slid across the room, moving clumsily and vulgarly. Itten: "Well, that's pretty!" Then Z crept in like the smoke of a sputtering candle and swept out again like a whirlwind. Itten: "Pretty!" Then Y came through the door, upright, dancing lasciviously. Itten: "Well . . . yes, pretty."

For a short time we were alone, then all three came back, gestured dumbly with their mouths wide open and spat out blasphemous phrases poking fun and making nonsense of Itten's teachings. The bells tolled from the steeples. Firecrackers exploded on the street. The screams and good wishes of strangers floated through the window. Itten: "That was pretty — yes, yes! But now I need some fresh air. I wish you much joy in the New Year."

What had happened! They had expected Itten to get angry. They had anticipated some shattering explosion. Then it would all be over, even if it brought the whole Bauhaus crashing down, too. But now it was as if nothing had happened. As once Orpheus' gentle melodies subdued wild beasts, so the irony of an assumed cheerfulness tamed the annoyance of these young men. When next he saw them in class Itten said to X, Y, and Z: "Draw an apple." And when they looked around in wonderment, he added: "It doesn't have to be a wormy one."

Paul Klee
Weimar, around 1923
Photo: unknown

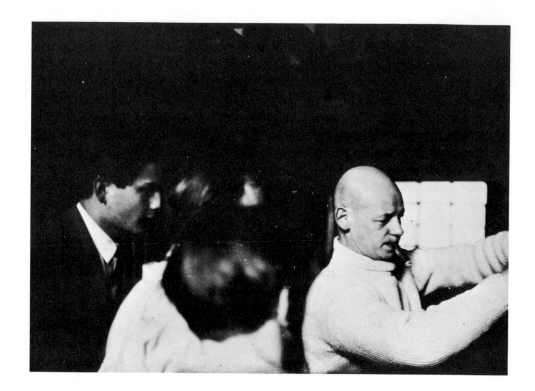

Oskar Schlemmer with
some of his students
Dessau, 1927
Photo: T. Lux Feininger

Oskar Schlemmer in a
performance on the
Bauhaus stage as a
musical clown
Dessau, 1928
Photo: unknown

Scene from "Feminine
Repetition" by Xanti
Schawinsky
Weimar/Dessau,
circa 1925-26
Photo: unknown

Scene from *"Treppenwitz"*
(Staircase joke)
by Xanti Schawinsky
Dessau, 1925
Photo: unknown

Andor Weininger in a
Performance on the
Bauhaus stage in the role
of the musical clown
Dessau, around 1927
Photo: unknown

Scene from "Olga—Olga"
by Xanti Schawinsky
Dessau, 1927
Photo: Erich Consemüller (?)

The Bauhaus Ballet on the
roof of the new building,
arranged and designed by
Oskar Schlemmer
Dessau, 1927
Photo: Erich Consemüller (?)

Born in Chemnitz in 1893. After 1911 she studied art and sculpture at the Grandducal College of Fine Arts in Weimar. In 1919 she married in Norway and then went to Paris, where she studied for a year. In January, 1924, she went to the Bauhaus in Weimar, completed the Vorkurs, and then worked in the metal workshop, under the direction of Moholy-Nagy. In Weimar and Dessau she developed her famous Kandem lamps as well as tableware, which were both manufactured under a Bauhaus license. Despite their revolutionary use of metals and glass, her designs, especially the lamps, quickly gained public acceptance and won the Bauhaus a leading role in the area of industrial design. After Moholy-Nagy left the faculty of the Bauhaus, she was commissioned to take over direction of the metal workshop in Dessau for one year.

In 1929 Mrs. Brandt left the Bauhaus and worked temporarily in Walter Gropius' studio in Berlin. From 1929 to 1932 she worked as a designer for the metal factory of Ruppelwerk in Gotha/Thuringia. Out of work in 1932 she withdrew to familiar surroundings in Chemnitz and continued her art projects. Mrs. Brandt was appointed in 1949 to the faculty of the College of Fine Arts in Dresden, as instructor in wood, metal, and ceramics. From 1951 to 1954 she worked at the Institute for Applied Art in Berlin, traveling to China with their exhibit in 1953–1954. Thereafter she worked as an independent industrial designer. In 1955, for reasons of health, she again returned to her birthplace, where she has devoted herself to painting and sculpture.
Marianne Brandt lives in Chemnitz, now Karl-Marx-Stadt, East Germany.

Letter to the younger generation

Dear Bauhaus Friend:

I am sending you what I have written down. It was difficult for me, and I crossed out most of it, for I am no theoretician, and whatever there is to be said about the Bauhaus has long since been said by professional critics. I would not be at all hurt if you would rather forgo my analyses.

In 1924, when on the advice of Moholy-Nagy I transferred from the Vorkurs to the metal workshop, they had just begun to produce objects capable of being mass-produced though still fully handicrafted. The task was to shape these things in such a way that even if they were to be produced in numbers, making the work lighter, they would satisfy all aesthetic and practical criteria and still be far less expensive than any singly produced item.

At first I was not accepted with pleasure — there was no place for a woman in a metal workshop, they felt. They admitted this to me later on and meanwhile expressed their displeasure by giving me all sorts of dull, dreary work. How many little hemispheres did I most patiently hammer out of brittle new silver, thinking that was the way it had to be and all beginnings are hard. Later things settled down, and we got along well together.

Gradually, through visits to the industry and inspections and interviews on the spot, we came to our main concern — industrial design. Moholy-Nagy fostered this with stubborn energy. Two lighting firms seemed particularly interested in our aims. Körting and Matthiessen (Kandem) and Leipzig Leutzsch helped us enormously with a practical introduction into the laws of lighting technique and the production methods, which not only helped us in designing, but also helped the firms. We also tried to create a functional but aesthetic assembly line, small facilities for garbage disposal, and so forth, considerations which in retrospect seem to me no longer prerequisites for a first-class lamp. We went to the fair at Leipzig, with some student grub as our only food, and returned dead tired but full of new impressions and a thousand plans, our bags stuffed with pamphlets. If we had even dreamed at that time of plexiglass and the other plastics, I don't know to what utopian heights we would have aspired. But good enough: those who come after us must have something to do, too!

Far more difficult than electric lamps was the problem of industrially producing our silverware and other tableware. Not many such things were being produced. So to a certain extent we were branded as a lighting department. We furnished whole buildings with our industrially produced lamps and only rarely designed and produced special pieces in our workshop for particular rooms or showrooms. At the time I was convinced that an object had to be functional and beautiful because of its material. But I later came to the conclusion that the artist provides the final effect. My error probably resulted from the fact that we lived in a community primarily composed of such persons, and that the high quality of their work was taken for granted.

In our workshop we always had a master craftsman at our side and didn't fare too badly with this division — here design and there handicrafts — even though changes became necessary from time to time. We had all our tools — presses and lathes, drills and large shears, etc. Even in Weimar an apprentice was attuned to mass production along the lines of handicrafts. Later he would become one of us, after he had participated in the Bauhaus Vorkurs.

The camaraderie in our workshop was in general good, although as is only natural an arrival or a departure brought with it new impulses and thus also new difficulties. Of the commissions that we got for our models, the Bauhaus, as far as I can remember, got half; the rest was divided equally among master, designer, and workshop. We also got part of the proceeds of our Sunday guided tours through the house. So I was generally quite flush, but also, to my sorrow, generally envied. But that didn't stop people at the end of the month from making lots of little loans from me.

I was not allowed a long period of instruction in handicrafts. Very soon I was told to help design, produce, get busy, and finally — on the urgent request of Gropius and Moholy when they both left the Bauhaus at the same time and I wanted to quit, too — I was offered the provisional directorship of the workshop for one year.

Even though I was made a tempting offer to continue the work with Kandem and simultaneously learn photography from the ground up at Peterhans, I did finally have to leave, however painful this was. But shortly afterward I had the pleasure of joining Gropius in his studio in Berlin. That, too, was a happy, if all too brief, time.

"I remember" and "Do you remember?"

When Gropius went (we assume with pleasure) to see his work, the newly established Bauhaus in Dessau, he got no little shock when he found that his students were using its flat roof and studio front for balancing exercises and as a cat burglar. Later he probably got used to it — there are some beautiful photographs of it. At least I managed to sit freely on the railing of my balcony, though at first I had attacks of dizziness when others did it. How well we lived in those studios, and how pleasant were the conversations back and forth from one balcony to another!

On the basement floor was the gymnasium. There was a large, soft carpet there, and though it was strictly forbidden, several people who couldn't afford anything else slept there. Showers, baths — all very convenient. Not bad. From down there *Päpchen* often appeared with his beautiful shepherd bitch. (But all that is strictly top secret!)

The tours of visitors through the studios didn't make me very happy. For two years it went on every Sunday morning — lots of questions, several annoyances, even though there were some compensations. I was especially impressed by a special tour of two hundred book printers. They were furious when I talked of writing without using capital letters and the saving this would mean in time and labor. A miniature rebellion! They even threatened me with canes!

Satisfying the appetite of the largely penniless "boys" was often a problem. At first, when we were still in the Seiler factory and had no canteen, we were allowed to eat in the soup kitchen for ten pfennig. It was dreadful! Then we bought two pitchers and earthenware pots and took turns by twos getting buttermilk and bread. So the studio had breakfast after all, cheap and modest. In the new building things were much better. There was a canteen and proper meals.

I wasn't around for the Mazdaznan period in Weimar, but only because Gropius took part in it did the Bauhaus members endure it. It can't have been too great — it was a bad time all around as far as that goes.

But there were still enough pleasures of a different sort. In Weimar I heard Klee play his violin, but unfortunately only once. Then there was Kurt Schwitters in Weimar and in Dessau, with his pointed wit and punning comments. Who remembers? Palucca enchanted us when she presented her newest dance. And Bela Bartok. It would be impossible to count it all up.

And now I come to the birthday of our revered Pius (Gro-*pius)*. Once he had to climb over a mountain of chairs and tables to get to his rose-strewn throne, which hung fairly high. He overcame all difficulties and dangers smilingly. Another time he was to have been carried around the room, but unfortunately the four bearers couldn't decide on the direction. Calmly he smoked his cigar despite his precarious situation.

It was marvelous at Seiler's. Not that Gropius really enjoyed being celebrated, but on insistent requests he did finally come down to the basement where the stage was housed. A decorated throne for him, as usual a place for Pia at his feet. For his cactus collection he was given many artful artificial pieces, the most beautiful of these a green cucumber with carved radishes as blossoms. Wolf was allowed to fire several shots, and of course there was dancing. The Charleston was coming up then — a real piece of contortionism. But I want to remember the dances in the great hall in Weimar: a bit affected, freely inventive, swinging and leaping. And that, too, did us good.

Last I dedicated a thankful thought to the indefatigable ones who played for us: Hirschfeld, Andi, Xanti, Paris, and all those whose names I have forgotten. And may this be a greeting to all who still remember.

Erich Lissner:

Born in Chemnitz in 1902. He graduated from the Vitzthumsche Highschool in Dresden. In 1922 23 he studied with Richard Dreher at the Kunstakademie in Dresden. When still young, he was greatly influenced by meetings with Otto Dix, Oskar Kokoschka, Walter Hasenclever, Carl Sternheim, and Kurt Schwitters, and also by a very close association with Jakob Hegner at the Künstlersiedlung Dresden-Hellerau and at the school of dancing of Mary Wigmans. In 1923 he visited the first Bauhaus exhibition in Weimar, which left a strong impression.

During the inflation Lissner worked in the book trade. In 1925 he started his studies at the universities of Berlin, Cologne, and Munich, specializing in archaeology, ethnology, philosophy, and art history. During his midterm vacations he worked in a Dresden shop specializing in East Asian art. He also worked without pay for daily papers and magazines. After 1933, however, the National Socialist regime made it impossible to work as a teacher or at a museum without making compromises, so Lissner accepted a job in the neutral field of industrial advertising. He worked first as a copy writer with Werner & Mertz in Mainz and after 1938 as artistic advisor in the promotion department of Kalle AG in Wiesbaden, where he later became an assistant to their general manager. He published an extensive study of the history of the sausage. From 1943 to 1945 he was in the army medical service.

In the spring of 1946 Golo Mann appointed him editor-in-chief of the literary department of the Hessischer Rundfunk in Frankfort. Since 1948 Lissner has been cultural editor of the Frankfurter Rundschau. He is living in Frankfurt on the Main.

It is now exactly forty-six years ago. I was a nothing at the time. After my final exam, when the rector asked me what I wanted to be, I laconically answered "an artist." And to his amazed question of what I thought that involved I answered simply "living."

Then I took my paint box and went to Goppeln and the Moritzburg lakes, as did the Bridge painters in the early years, stole glances at Otto Dixen's studio on the Antonsplatz, and shared the same model with him for life drawing. I tried my first abstractions with my younger colleague Hans Hartung. It was the wild time, sparklingly happy and shatteringly sad, for the twilight of mankind was always imminent.

The trip from Dresden to the first retrospective exhibit at the State Bauhaus at Weimar four years after it was founded seemed a great adventure. It was late summer, 1923. "Gold mark times code number" gave you the exchange rate for your money, and we had to figure on it literally changing every hour as a result of the inflation. I was able to make the trip only because I had earned a few kroner from a Swede in exchange for German lessons. I exchanged these piece by piece everyday for astronomical sums in paper money.

Several of the famous special-issue publicity postcards of the Bauhaus have come down to me from this period. They were lithographed in the graphics workshops after designs by the masters: Feininger's "City" and "Church," Kandinsky's "Composition," Klee's "Abstraction," Moholy-Nagy's "Geometrical Forms," Schlemmer's "Abstracted Profile"; also a two-page flyer with Feininger's woodcut of "The Cathedral of Socialism," with programmatic lines by Walter Gropius. Such souvenirs of bygone times are first-class rarities today.

In those late summer days Weimar was not Goethe but Bauhaus. It was the goal of thousands. I felt far removed yet comfortable. I belonged, for many of the Bauhaus members — apprentices and journeymen

— like me wore a sort of Russian smock and sandals. It was a protest against middle-class conventions. In Weimar, as Lothar Schreyer later wrote, we placed our trust in being able "to be allowed to cooperate in constructing a new world, in the consciousness of an actual world change in which, as the fateful hour of history struck, the creative forces would push directly out of the depths of life into the light." Today one may smile at such pronouncements.

I don't remember anymore how I came to live with the poet Bernhard Bernson. It was an early-Victorian house on the Herderplatz above a bakery, from which the smell of fresh rolls wafted up. He gave me his drama *The Plague* and his *Legend of the Son's Sunday* with his autograph. Displaced from Lemberg to Weimar, he was then thirty-five — still young — and in my eyes certainly a mature, stable man. He and his wife, a cheerful woman from Alsace, came with me to the pseudo-Renaissance building that housed the Weimar provincial museum and contrasted so heavily with the free designs the Bauhaus people were exhibiting.

They led me into studios and workshops, to Muche's model house, which was to have been only the first of a planned but never realized Bauhaus colony on the Horn, to Schlemmer's murals and reliefs in the hallway and gatehouse of the workshop building, that example of art in construction that was later demolished by the National Socialists. It could be there were some things I did not immediately understand, but I was very much impressed by Gropius' magazine rack, Wagenfeld's Bauhaus lamp, the Marcel Breuer chair, Bogler's pottery, and Hartwig's chessmen — in short, all the clean, pure forms of everyday household articles.

I remember fondly fabric studies from Josef Albers' class in the riding school on the Ilm, the products of Kandinsky's seminar on color, Moholy-Nagy's kinetic sculpture, and a patchwork rug by Ida Kerkovius. And the tearoom, too, in which we sat on tubular chairs in front of batik wall hangings with other dedicated Bauhaus members, enthusiastically debating the teachings of the masters and the possibility of mass-producing unique pieces. In the end we did after all revert to Goethe and his ideas on the connection between art and science, and Novalis' synesthesic thought fragments.

The Weimar Bauhaus days ended with a most remarkable meeting. The Bernsons had to leave on a trip and sent me off toward Tiefurt. There I would see a little garden house in a broad poppy field. I was to ask for accommodations there. It was dusk, and a woman greeted me; a child, six years old, was with her; he was called Michael. She took me in quite as a matter of course, as if she had long been expecting me.

The three of us ate fruit-flavored blancmange together out of a great earthenware pot. She seemed tired as a result of doing heavy spade work. I did not know who she was — she remained sparing of words. I was able only to find out that she made a living from her poppy plants, selling the buds to an oil mill in Erfurt. Soon she fixed a bed for me against a book-lined wall. Before going to sleep I pulled out one and another of them — all of them Rilke and in every volume a very personal, handwritten dedication from him. The next morning questions seemed indiscreet. Years later I was to discover from a little book put out by the Insel Press whom I had spent the night with. It was the "Young Woman" to whom Rainer Maria Rilke had addressed his letters from Muzot.

This, too, is bound up with my Bauhaus days of 1923. For me it was the beginning of many things that have determined the rest of my life.

Walter Dexel:

Born in Munich in 1890 and studied art history at the universities of Munich and Jena. In 1916 he received his doctorate from Jena, under Botho Gräf, and on his recommendation undertook the direction of the exhibits of Jena's Art Union (until 1928). During those years he arranged many exhibits for the artists of Die Brücke, Der blaue Reiter, Der Sturm, and, of course, the neighboring Bauhaus, including ones for Kandinsky, Schlemmer, and Klee, who, at the invitation of Dexel, gave his famous lecture "On Modern Art" on January 26, 1924.

In addition, under the direction of Dexel, the Art Union organized exhibits entitled "New German Architecture" (1924) and "New Advertising" (1927), in which the Bauhaus members, along with other avant-garde groups, were represented. As a Constructivist painter, Dexel exhibited in Der Sturm in 1918, 1920, and 1925. He also took part in the international exhibits in Moscow and Paris.
In Weimar from 1921 to 1923 Dexel was especially close to Theo van Doesburg while the latter was attempting to found a De

Stijl group. During this time Dexel was especially concerned with commercial art and typography and in 1925 was invited to come to Frankfurt by Adolf Meyer and Ernst May as *Berater für Reklame in Stadtbild* (advertising consultant).

In 1928 Wilhelm Deffke transferred the direction of the professional course in commercial art at the School of Arts and Crafts in Magdeburg to Dexel, but in 1935 he was discharged as a Decadent artist. Two years later his paintings were displayed in Munich as part of the exhibit 'Entartete Kunst' (Degenerate Art). From 1936 to 1942 Dexel was professor of form studies at the State College of Art Education in Berlin and thereafter, until 1955, built up the renowned and unique 'Formsammlung der Stadt Braunschweig'. After his participation in the retrospective exhibit of Der Sturm in the National Gallery in Berlin in 1961, his painting was rediscovered. Since then it has been displayed in several one-man exhibits throughout West Germany. Dexel lives in Braunschweig.

The Bauhaus style—a myth

I do not think the Bauhaus in its time produced all the ideas that today are conveniently lumped together as the "Bauhaus style." People mistakingly use the term for everything that was produced in the twenties. Actually it is far more likely that the Bauhaus, which began the period under a completely different sign and with completely different goals (one need only read through the founding proclamation of 1919 carefully), was carried along by the broad current of the times. It did not bring about and certainly did not link itself with the architectural and formative developments that almost simultaneously set in in many European countries. Far rather it was seized by this development until in these last Weimar years and the first Dessau years it finally won its own face.

Then, of course, the Bauhaus share — I stress "share" — soon became considerable because, considering the poverty of the times, it could develop a sizable thrust, having at its command quite abundant means, buildings, and workshops, a concentration of excellent energies, and a never-failing flow of publicity. It had far more force, for example, than the earlier De Stijl movement in Holland, which for years under Theo van Doesburg fought an almost futile war against the romantic ideas about handicrafts existing at the Bauhaus in its founding years, and against the doctrines of Johannes Itten, which rested on anthroposophical Mazdaznan concepts. It was a most important war, considering what later came to be called industrial design.

It can be firmly established that the ideas that developed in the twenties were not born at the Bauhaus. When I say that, I say it as one of the closest observers and an intimate acquaintance of both its many participants and its many critics, even in friendly camps.

If one thinks back on the important events of that decade the Weissenhof colony, the principal item in the exhibit "The Dwelling" in 1927 in Stuttgart, must be named above all. And the loudest trumpet call was sounded by the German pavilion in Barcelona by Mies van der Rohe. The Bauhaus had nothing to do with this and little to do with the Weissenhof colony. In no way did it appear even as *primus inter pares*, but simply took a respectacle, though in no way towering, part, as critics and discussions clearly attest. And its director was in no way set above others in the Architects' Circle, but was accepted into it (the Circle was an association of some twenty of the most important architects in Germany).

The modern art of construction, which manifested itself so superbly in the Weissenhof colony, was the authentic international style of the day. The idea that people would in those days have talked of a Bauhaus style is absurd and even laughable. The direction of the Weissenhof colony was in the hands of Mies van der Rohe, who was considered the most prominent German architect. The largest and most important block of buildings was his work, as was the over-all organization of the buildings in this first-rate example of town planning and also the selection of architects from home and abroad. The most interesting and novel houses were those of Le Corbusier — there can be no doubt of that. Further, Hans Schauon was much discussed because of his then unusual, rounded building shapes; J. J. P. Oud of Rotterdam, who had had long experience in building such colonies; and because of their especially practical floor plans, the German Hilberseimer and the Dutchman Mart Stam. All other buildings, among them the Bauhaus entry, no matter how interesting and beautiful they may have been, stood back before those named above.

The Bauhaus' part in commerical advertising design in those years was similarly adequate though not outstanding, as the exhibit "Advertising Graphics, 1920–1930" in the Göppinger Gallery in Frankfurt conclusively demonstrated. The Bauhaus did not even take part in porcelain design, so important in the twenties. It developed out of the industry itself, which knew how to pick the right people, like Trude Petri and Herman Gretsch. The situation was similar in glass (Bruno Mauder). In steel furniture and lighting fixtures, thanks to its experimental workshops, the share of the Bauhaus was greater (Marcel Breuer, Wilhelm Wagenfeld). But again the very best steel furniture of this time was not indebted to the Bauhaus, but like the Barcelona pavilion to the genius of Mies van der Rohe. His steel chairs still exist unchanged and even today have not been surpassed, which is certainly saying something.

And the great masters of the Bauhaus who gave it legendary fame — Feininger, Kandinsky, and Klee, — even stood somewhat apart from what today goes by the name of Bauhaus style. It was Oskar Schlemmer who made the main contribution to the Bauhaus week of 1923 with his murals and above all his *Triadic Ballet*. The later Bauhaus festivals in Weimar and Dessau, which became so famous, were also imprinted with his ingenuity. Incidentally, his letters and diaries provide a highly informative illustration of my theme.

After 1945 an all-too-convenient journalism did not take the trouble to really study the history of the twenties, neither in architecture nor in so-called industrial design. It is high time that we stop using the cliché "Bauhaus style," which only ignorance of the most elementary facts of the twenties could have allowed to become current. Far more important than the endless repetition of this phrase would be finally a historical enumeration and specification of the thoughts and principles of design that come from almost all of Europe. One can no longer simply cover over a broad range of phenomena that grew from many roots with the catchword "Bauhaus style." That phrase fosters a myth: it is an inadmissible oversimplification and unfairly conceals the many significant forces that worked to create the style of the twenties.

Walter Mehring:

Born in Berlin in 1896. He studied art history at the universities of Berlin and Munich from 1915 to 1916. He then joined the artillery during the First World War. After 1915 he came in contact with Herwarth Walden and his circle at Der Sturm, and also with the Berlin and Paris Dadaist movements. In 1918 his first drama, *Die Frühe der Städte,* was published in *Der Sturm.* During that time he contributed to independent political magazines, among them *Der Blutige Ernst*; *Die Pleite*; *Der Dada*; *Der Einzige*; *Zukunft,* published by Maximilian Harden; and *Weltbühne.* He was also a playwright and dramatic director at Max Reinhardt's little theater, Schall und Raisch. In 1927 he published a book of ballads, *Das Ketzer-Brevier.*

Mehring had moved to Montparnasse in Paris in 1918. In 1922 he visited the so-called "Dada — oder Konstruktivisten-Kongress" (Dada — or Constructivist Congress) in Weimar as an active participant in the Dada movement. In 1929 Erwin Piscator directed his play *Der Kaufmann von Berlin* ("The Mer-chant from Berlin"), a drama dealing with the existing inflation, which was provoked into a theatrical scandal by the Nazis. In 1933 his play *Die höllische Komödie* ("The Comedy of Hell") was banned shortly before its first performance. Mehring was in danger of being imprisoned by the Nazis and fled to Paris on the eve of the Reichstag fire.

As the Viennese correspondent to the exiled periodical *Das Neue Tagebuch*, Mehring again had to flee in 1938, this time via Switzerland to Paris. When the war broke out he was interned in France and was permitted to emigrate to the United States from the prison camp in St. Cyprien via Martinique in 1941.

Among Mehring's most important works are the books *Müller, die Chronik einer deutschen Sippe*, which was confiscated by the German delegate in Vienna in 1934; *Die Verlorene Bibliothek* (New York, 1951); *Verrufene Malerei* (Zurich, 1958); and *Neues Ketzerbrevier* (Cologne, 1962). At present he lives in Switzerland.

Memories of an observer

My private memories of the Bauhaus in Weimar are few: the Dada meeting of 1922 with Hans Arp, Hans Richter, and Tristan Tzara, at the invitation of Theo van Doesburg; being a guest of Paul Klee, who, with Lyonel Feininger, a friend of my parents since my baby–and childhood, practiced a violin fugue composed by Feininger; being a spectator at Oskar Schlemmer's *Theatrical Dance* on the Bauhaus stage.

The personality of Walter Gropius was decisive. His plan to found a state academy lent the discredited art of Expressionism an official character. The significance of this undertaking in the Weimar Republic — its only cultural legacy — is confirmed by the measure taken against the Bauhaus by the first National Socialist Minister of the Interior, Frick, and the protest demonstrations of the citizens of Weimar against the "cultural Bolshevist mark of shame on our classical city," against "this state garbage can." The Nazi crusade against degenerate art finally drove the Bauhaus architect Gropius and his masters Kandinsky, Klee, Feininger, Itten, and Moholy-Nagy out of their last asylum in Dessau into banishment and outlawed Georg Muche. But the Bauhaus had laid the foundation for the German Expressionism recognized by art historians today.

Erich Buchholz:

Born in Bromberg in 1891. He began his career as a teacher, receiving his first and only instruction in painting from Lovis Corinth in Berlin. After the war, through the actor Karl Vogt, he worked at the theater in Bamberg as a dramaturgist and set designer. When Vogt took over as director of the Albert Theater in Dresden, Buchholz designed the sets for the premiere performance in 1920 of Strindberg's *Schwanenweiss*, for which he used only projected light as a space divider on the empty stage. While he was working in the theater, Buchholz began producing abstract drawings and paintings and in 1921 had a one-man show at Der Sturm. He was in close contact with the Dadaists, the Constructivists, and many modern architects, developing a particular friendship with Viking Eggeling. After his exhibit at Der Sturm, Buchholz concerned himself with many design problems: space-in-itself, stressed-skin construction, egg-dome construction, shipbuilding, furniture design, typography, and painting.

In the fall of 1922 at the first Russian art exhibit at the Van Diemen Gallery in Berlin, he exchanged views with El Lissitzky. Three years later he left Berlin in order to live in the country, away from the so-called "art business." In 1933 he was forbidden to exhibit and was arrested.

After the war Buchholz returned to Berlin and resumed painting and sculpture, intensifying his work in glass. His work was exhibited in several one-man shows, notably at the Rose Fried Gallery in New York (1956), the Galerie Rosen in Berlin (1957), the Haus Salve Hospes in Braunschweig, and at the Galerie am Dom in Frankfurt (1961). Various museums have acquired his early works, including the Galerie des XX. Jahrhunderts and the National Galerie in Berlin, the Museum of Modern Art, in New York, and the Carnegie Institute in Pittsburgh. His works are also contained in a number of private collections such as the Rothschild's and the Williams'. Buchholz lives in Berlin, where he still works with kinetic objects and does sculptural experiments with glass.

Bauhaus—Bauhaus—Bauhaus

It's understandable that the universal syllables "Bau-haus" could not over the span of several decades — and we are necessarily bound to speak of these things in a relative way — have acquired a fixed definition.

Not only we — the few still on hand — who took part in its birth are interested in clarification. The great mutations of those times, the great intersection, the golden twenties, they themselves illuminate the situation from several aspects. One could expand. The brewing rebellion of those times — what did it not touch? It broke over all the changes of time in the urgency of expediency (not only of sensuality), of being itself, even culminating in the blasphemous radical formulation: intellectuality is the deadly enemy of life.

What concerned us in art in those days — modulated by whether it was openly admitted or accorded only fluttering recognition — was open discussions about everything. More precisely: the elements, material of any kind, material itself at all times, and material according to its use and availability. The uncertainty of the times added other considerations. Objectively formulated: what do new materials signify and how do they correspond to their fundamental new character? New colors, new paper, possibilities developed through synthetic materials — plexiglass, pressed woods — were to be examined, tested, installed.

That despite all these momentous changes man must stand at the center was the necessary reflection of the crashing force of technology itself. In this atmosphere — then, too, after the complete collapse and the lack of any philosophy of life — these analyses and salvage attempts were the main theme.

The radicalism of a political goal that became even more urgent after the appearance of the Russians in 1922 naturally urged the tense, heightened discussions to sometimes aggressive pitch.

This the situation that was to give and did give this child his baptism: the Bauhaus. Its founding even here in Berlin basically tended toward actual consolidation (Gropius did live here from time to time). And the significance of Der Sturm at the moment of preparation (the great Bauhaus masters after all were initiated by it into the actual field of vision) may on no account be forgotten.

Considering the seriousness of the situation in complete contrast with today — which has managed grotesquely to go so far as to give even the philistines the opportunity to furnish themselves with "modern" (modish) stuff, e.g., shirts and blouses plastered with op designs — so, considering the seriousness of the situation in those days, we fully recognized even the danger points (the term "modern" was tacked onto us only later).

Since it seemed obvious to question and necessary to establish facts, all these discussions, especially concerning the Bauhaus, were most precarious; it wouldn't be denied that somewhat atavistic reflections, even in the word "Bauhaus" with its medieval connotations, could from the beginning endanger its weight and its principles. Of course, the act was an experiment and must be hailed.

Absolutely objectively, the thing developed for me personally — and I must be allowed to speak personally — thus: I did not respond to the invitation to the opening of the Bauhaus (my wife went there with Adolf Behne). My reason: if I went there I could not guarantee that there wouldn't be unpleasant discussions. It was just such fundamental discussions of all these questions, here especially concerning the Bauhaus, mixed in with questions about all sorts of doctrines (for example, Mazdaznan) that seemed to me particularly misguided. The things about which the discussions were held were far too important for us to dare burden them with a philosophy that from the beginning could have produced for us symptoms of a fatal image. Well . . . the developments proved me right in every way. The dogmatism brought in by Theo van Doesburg actually caused more confusion, proving to me its real baselessness. From the very beginning it meant to me personally the necessity of distance from the foundation by Gropius. Mies van de Rohe's invitation to me to participate at the continuation of the Bauhaus in Berlin (1932) may suffice.

Quite apart from the fact that the first Bauhaus building originated from the painter Muche — the ground plan was laid according to the conception of two dimensionality — in every respect the things that actually won the tag were already in very distinct form, available and carried out before and besides the Bauhaus. For documentation: Buchholz, Burchartz, Dexel, van Doesburg, Eggeling, Lissitzky, Peri — from 1924 on Berlewi — so far are known to us. And it is significant that the founder soon turned his back on his institute, fleeing it. The Bauhaus: a refined, dressed-up show window for unfulfilled promises, which had to content itself with pegging the market, well knowing that the records could easily slip. And it is more than a joke that in the hallway, of all things, they parade the chairs of Mies, the man who could have made a Bauhaus of the Bauhaus.

Everyone knows that the chairs were produced without the Bauhaus Idea. But the publicity — and through countless books it filters down — slaps one in the face. Incidentally, Mies van der Rohe today: "The best thing that Gropius did was to invent the name Bauhaus." Next to the legend stands the cliché — launched out of embarrassment or expediency — that trudges through time as a convenient quotation in the mechanism of an economy based on illusion.

Lou Scheper:

Born Lou Berkenkamp in 1901 in Wesel/Niederrhein. In 1920, right after her graduation, she went to the Weimar Bauhaus to work as an apprentice in the workshop for mural painting, under the guidance of Johannes Itten. She also participated in Paul Klee's course. At the same time she developed many of her own ideas on pictures, picture stories, and illustrated letters. She worked on the Haus Sommerfeld in Berlin with Hinnerk Scheper, who was responsible for the color design. He left the Bauhaus in 1922, the year Lou and he got married. In 1925 Scheper was appointed to the Bauhaus as junior master, and they moved to Dessau. There Lou Scheper participated in work for the Bauhaus theater, under the leadership of Oskar Schlemmer. At the same time she contributed paintings to the exhibition "Junge Maler am Bauhaus" (Young Painters at the Bauhaus).

From 1928 to 1931 Hinnerk Scheper took his family on a vacation from the Bauhaus to Moscow, where he served as a specialist on questions of color in architecture and town design. Later they returned to the Dessau Bauhaus. After its closing and the ensuing unrest, the Schepers moved to Berlin in 1933. During the war they worked mostly on repairing monuments and painted "for the drawer."

After the war, there was a new blossoming of the plastic and graphic arts. In 1950 the Schepers participated in the exhibition "22 Berliner Bauhäusler," as well as in group exhibits in Germany. They also published picture books for children.

After Hinnerk Scheper's death in 1957, Lou Scheper herself turned toward the problems of color and architecture and participated in various building projects, among them works at the picture gallery of the Germanic National Museum in Nuremberg, commissioned by Ludwig Grote, and at the Egyptian Museum of the Technical University in Berlin. From 1962 to 1963 Lou Scheper joined the team of Hans Scharoun, who was responsible for the color design of the new Berliner Philharmonie. Since 1967 she has been consulting collaborator on color design for the new school at Gropius City and other Gropius buildings in Berlin.

Apart from her creative activities, Mrs. Scheper is also bringing out publications on architecture, exhibitions, and repairing of monuments. Lou Scheper lives in Berlin.

Retrospective

To report on the Bauhaus in retrospect is as easy as it is difficult. Easy because the fullness of memory floods those who took part in it, experienced the development of the institute and the confusions of its various phases. Difficult because every Bauhaus member has his own point of departure and thus his own point of view in his evaluation. One might well say that each Bauhaus member has his own Bauhaus.

Each saw it from the assumptions that persuaded him to go to that particular school, so basically different from the other academies before and after the institute of design. To speak of the experiences of the Bauhaus members in the founding years: in the ambiguous manifesto that summoned them each found his own questions answered. Each expected theoretical and practical opportunities in Weimar and the realization of his own, often still vague, conceptions and wishes — opportunities that at that time were only open in that place, the Bauhaus. That is why for so many Bauhaus people the Bauhaus became home.

To reconstruct the objective situation out of subjective memory one needs documentation. But a document gives a truer picture when it is part of current experiences, not retrospective ones, when as a constructive element it lends content and form to the material gathered from one's own perceptions. Objectively verifiable facts provide the outline; presence adds colors and shading; knowledge of a place, local color. It is in just those first days, so moved by impulses and improvisations, that less is held in word and image than later, after system and method have been developed.

In general the word "community" is used to describe specifically those first Bauhaus days, those first recorded days of Bauhaus history. This community corresponded neither to the concept "commune" nor the concept "cloister," even though individual Bauhaus people preferred the ascetic's cell. The Bauhaus community was the sum of significant, independent individuals who could develop more richly in association than in isolation. At the time one did not in general write in small letters, and one talked "big" — of the postwar mood of political hope and artistic expectations, of the search for the unified work of art. Play and creative imagination and also a tendency toward mysticism, even to spiritual faith healing and to sectarianism, and in addition a delight in nature taken from the youth movement are the badge of Bauhaus members of that time, who were more artists than technicians, more craftsmen than constructers. It was only later that the call to a return to handicrafts in order to create the Cathedral of Socialism was replaced by the new formula Art and Technology — a New Unity. Though the Bauhaus had originally started to produce unique, handicrafted pieces, it later developed — in apparent contradiction — the models for industrially produced articles. Both were products of the same feeling for form, the sense of function and materials, and both were a consequence drawn from the social tasks of the times. The same road led from the individual house of the Bauhaus exhibit of 1923 to the housing settlement, from the hand-treated walls (in their original, structural character) to the Bauhaus wallpaper, from woven piece to yard goods.

The *ABC* of form was to conceive and treat space as space, line as line, surface as surface; in their elementary attributes. It was always a matter of laws: laws of color, of form, of kinetics. On the spiritual field nothing could be learned, but much was experienced — through Klee, through Feininger, through Kandinsky, or through Schlemmer.

The teaching system was as free as its masters. Methods, principles, and theories never took on the character of dogma; where there was danger of this the Bauhaus discarded them. The creative characteristics of each individual were carefully nursed; games were taken seriously. Bauhaus people without imagination were rare — they remained the exception that confirms the rule that a single law governed every creative act of a house under whose (flat) roof architects and artists were united, handicrafts and technology connected, and constructive and creative elements interrelated.

After these general observations references to the problem of color in architecture and as an area of study at the Bauhaus might follow: it's a duty of a participant. From its first beginnings until spring, 1922, the wall-painting workshop in Weimar worked with Hinnerk Scheper whose training had been in handicrafts at an academy and in an arts and crafts school. In Dessau from 1925 on he directed the workshop. In the time that he did not spend at the Bauhaus, he did fundamental work in various places and on various objects, and this was the basis of his invitation to be a Bauhaus master. The principle that he developed was the use of color in architecture as an integral element of the building, not as an added final touch.

In the early days of the workshop, as everywhere else in the house, play entered into the serious work. So in painting the canteen (in May, 1920), its walls and ceilings, down to the final little corners that could only be reached with color-soaked sponges raised high on poles, became the playground of lively ornaments of the tiniest size and gayest colors. We painted and squirted together — urged on by Peter Röhl — with delight and a guilty conscience because we were fully aware that our creations were completely nonfunctional — inappropriate to a room used for eating and relaxing. And all this while the psychology of color was beginning to be discussed and systematically examined at the Bauhaus!

Itten, the lawgiver taming our exuberance, demanded a cheerless gray-green of contemplation as background for an Oriental motto, which was to educate us while we ate. But this was the extent of his influence on mural painting at the Bauhaus. It was the end result of a view that saw a room rather as housing for people than as an architectural form, drawing inward and shutting out the outside. It was an almost cloister-like conception, which affected the colors as well.

Later, rooms were to open outward. In the interior rooms the structure of the architecture was transformed into harmoniously colorful area partitions (e.g., Scheper in the Sommerfeldhaus, 1921–1922). His redesigns for the Weimar provincial and palace museums followed — they represented a revolutionary change in the treatment of exhibition halls. For the first time the paintings and sculptures, used to gallery velvet and silk, were hung against a neutral background especially suited to them in texture and material. They contrasted with the colorful paint of the domes and ceilings, a device used to make the room seem higher or lower that had no function in itself, but merely served the objects exhibited. The function of the room became more precise and at the same time more effective. A stronger differentiation of walls, in regard to material, was begun. They were highly polished or matte, roughened or textured. By superimposing glazes of different shades the effect of diffuse color was achieved. In the Nierendorf Gallery in Berlin and the Fides Gallery in Dresden, but most strikingly in the Folkwang Museum in Essen, the principle of variable hanging surfaces in exhibition halls was to develop out of Dessau in a manner that set the example.

In 1924 the fundamental work on the university clinics in Münster began. The solution of the commission: the color design of the building complex would identify its different purposes. In general one was used to thinking of hospitals as aseptic barracks. Here there was to be comfort and cheer, achieved through the appropriate coloring of walls and ceilings, which for the patient are such important room surfaces. Light and shade were carefully considered. The ceilings in the corridors of the individual wards were characterized by stronger colors. Unlettered signs in the same shades as the ceilings led to the wards. This principle was used in the new Bauhaus building in Dessau, too. Scheper was invited to teach there in 1925. Now his ideas would become the subject of teaching and study, theoretical and practical demonstration, and practice. In the young Bauhaus masters, the Bauhaus had proved itself; they were masters of handicrafts and design. Their experiments and ideas created the models for production and industry. Think of the steel furniture, the fabrics, the advertisements, the tapestries.

For Scheper, in the meantime, the change to constructive, functional, and useful space design had finally been consummated. Color had its task to aid architecture; simultaneously it had to serve the purposes of the room. The distinction between sustaining and auxiliary elements offered the possibility of strong tension in the chiaroscuro and the opposition of textures.

Taking a leave of absence, he accepted an invitation to act as color specialist during the planning of the city of Moscow in 1928–1929. This opened a tremendous field for experiment and provided experiences valuable to both the Bauhaus and its members.

It must be mentioned that besides providing practice, the execution of large commissions gave the members of the mural workshop a means of existence. They worked economically, on a profit basis unusual in a teaching institution, but in coordination with the educational program.

Clear light and clear dark shades, pure white and pure black, and a variety of clear, clean stages of gray — this was the world of color that the evil brown and blighted red of the Third Reich broke into. Whatever had been developed before 1934 was discarded and must today be carefully reconstructed and brought back to consciousness. Whoever can remember knows how much of basic importance was developed then and now finds its uses, without even knowing, after such a long time, who developed it. There is little in the art and architecture of our times that was not pre-invented, preformulated, or anticipated, even if it seldom seemed realized and perhaps not even completely thought through. Without doubt it was a fragment, this our already-legendary Bauhaus, transfigured by the fascination of its incompletion. But it remains today still more moving than many things that were completed and stiffened in the mold. We often contradicted ourselves, but we did touch on truths and between the lines formulated understanding. And each of us gave himself to a task that transcended him.

Heinrich Konig:

Born in Leipzig in 1889 and studied political science and chemistry in Göttingen, Dresden, and Kiel. He made a long study tour through southeastern Asia in 1913–1914 and then interrupted his studies during the war to take over the direction of his father's factory. From 1917 to 1918 he was in the foreign service in Brussels. In 1920 he received his doctorate in political science. Thereafter, until 1923, he was a partner in a chemical factory of Dessau.

As a result of his many trips to Weimar, by 1919 König had become familiar with the Bauhaus. In 1921 he married Maria Elisabeth Schneewind, another follower of the Bauhaus. With Ludwig Grote, the Landeskonservator in Anhalt, König fostered the takeover of the Bauhaus in Dessau by the city government, under the leadership of the mayor, Fritz Hesse. In 1927, in Dresden, König became the general representative of the Bauhaus company, and later the representative of the State Bauhochschule in Weimar, conducted by Otto Bartning. After 1933 he gave up his creative activities and limited himself to representing technical building materials.

With Professor Will Grohmann and Stephan Hirzl, König refounded the German Werkbund in Dresden in August, 1945, remaining its business manager until the Russians forced its dissolution. In 1947 Bartning summoned him to Heidelberg to direct a new department, housing supply for Protestant relief work. This department, in conjunction with a group of modern architects, was to develop functional housing for refugees and settlers. After the currency revaluation, however, this work was given up.

From 1947 to 1964 König was honorary chairman for the German Werkbund for Württemberg-Baden. In 1949 he organized the first Werkbund exhibit in Cologne since the war, entitled "Neues Wohnen" (New Living). Because of his familiarity with the British Council of Industrial Design, König played a part in the Bundestag's adoption of the resolution that led to the foundation of the *Rat für Formgebung*. König's articles on the problems of new living and modern industrial form were published widely in leading magazines and professional journals. He died in Mannheim on October 1, 1966.

The Bauhaus—yesterday and today

To demonstrate the idea of the Bauhaus as a living connection between yesterday and today and its importance for tomorrow would certainly suit the desires of Walter Gropius, who always insisted on confronting the burgeoning myth with facts.

The facts will not only show an unending chain of ugly attacks on the Bauhaus from the outside and the Bauhaus' brave defense, but also the often great differences of opinion among the faculty and students. All of us who were friends of the Bauhaus saw this multiplicity not as a drawback but as a source of enrichment. These internal divergences did not in the long run impair the image of the Bauhaus, as can be demonstrated by the recollections of Fritz Hesse, at the time lord mayor of Dessau, who in all his otherwise accurately detailed reports did not find it necessary to mention these conflicts. All the more readable is his very lively description of the services of Hannes Meyer during his directorship from 1928 to 1930, and the objective account of the circumstances that led to his leaving.

The lord mayor, however, could not report on one important event in the history of the Bauhaus because it occurred in Weimar, before the Bauhaus' Dessau period: The first Bauhaus exhibit in 1923 and the related Bauhaus week. How the state government of Thuringia forced this exhibit and how the Bauhaus masters resisted the event is portrayed in Hans Maria Wingler's book *Das Bauhaus Weimar — Dessau — Berlin 1919–1933* (see Feininger and especially Marcks). But after the decision had been made each gave his best to make the radiant power of the Bauhaus evident in both the exhibit and the event of the Bauhaus week.

For the sake of comparison imagine the Ulm School of Design, founded in 1953, having to give an account of itself after four years — i.e., in 1957, even though the concept of good industrial design had already become familiar with a broad public. Fortunately, they were able to wait until 1963. But the Bauhaus was asked to do so after four years, and that forty years before its time. Think of what apartment and household furnishings looked like then!

Posters and folders on the exhibit and the Bauhaus week were sent to all the great travel bureaus of the five continents. But hardly any one of the rich international tourists appeared. Certainly some of the foreign students attracted friends or relatives to Weimar. The international architectural exhibit — the first one completely limited to the construction — called together architects of many countries. But the majority of those who came had struggled hard to make this trip — it was, after all, almost the height of the inflation. They were people who wanted to see and experience themselves the new events.

No doubt many were shocked, for next to the international architectural exhibit in the main building and the exhibit of fine arts in the provincial museum, the workshop exhibits were the main attractions. One could most easily perhaps become acquainted with the decorative material and furnishings, the carpets and wall hangings from the Bauhaus weaving shop with their glowing colors and stern, abstract drawings, or with the things that came out of the ceramic workshop on the Dornburg. But many could not understand even these things — much less what was on view from the carpentry, metal, and sculpture workshops. Many had to labor to the conclusion that these were primarily experiments, attempts to conquer new territory with new shapes and colors, and not finished models that could be industrially mass-produced. Many had expected simply an arts and crafts exhibit and were now having a hard time finding things that corresponded to what they had expected among the exhibits, particularly those from the metal workshops, as for example the jewelry of Naum Slutzky or tableware by Marianne Brandt, Christian Dell, K. J. Jucker, Otto Rittweger, Wolfgang Tümpel, and Wilhelm Wagenfeld. The main attraction of the whole exhibit, namely to show the variety of talents and with that the expression, was part of the demonstration of the Vorkurs, directed by Itten until 1923. This was the high point and at the same time the main stumbling block of the show. Here there *could not* be any completed work. Even the detailed nature studies were not exhibited for themselves, but as a part of the education program of free exercise in composition using different materials. And these things now belong to the carefully preserved incunabula of the Vorkurs. Many of the studies struck the malicious opponents of the Bauhaus and even the sometimes well-intentioned, though ignorant, visitors to the exhibit as the offspring of madmen or as a conscious mockery of the so-called "sane mind." None of us, probably not even Gropius and Itten nor even Moholy-Nagy and Albers, who later directed the Vorkurs, could imagine at the time that it would be this very Vorkurs that would conquer the schools of arts and crafts throughout the world.

Lastly, the model house on the Horn must be mentioned as part of the Weimar exhibit of 1923. It was designed by the painter Georg Muche, built under the direction of Adolf Meyer, and furnished in cooperation with all the Bauhaus workshops. "Cold and flat and repulsively ugly" its enemies called it. But those who longed for a fundamental change to a new life, and thus into new forms of living, were enchanted. There were things to be seen here that not long after 1923 would be serially produced — some chairs, Alma Buscher's children's toy chest, Jucker and Wagenfeld's glass table lamp, Theodor Bogler's first spherical hanging lamps and utensils. Today when we see the kitchen equipment of this experimental house designed by Marcel Breuer in 1922 (it was never mass-produced), it looks quite normal to us. But who remembers that it was the first kitchen in Germany with separated lower cupboards, suspended cupboards attached to the walls, a continuous work surface between them, and the main work space in front of the window (there was no table in the middle of the kitchen)? Twenty-five years later this kitchen arrangement returned to us as a "Swedish kitchen," and it is now the common property of the kitchen equipment industry.

Why are the memories of forty years ago revived here? Out of the hope that more well-intentioned helpers than uncomprehending opponents will be present if a single person or a group of persons should turn up with a new creative Idea, as did Walter Gropius at that time with his Bauhaus Idea. One must not only think of the Ulm School of Design, but one must remember — as was clearly stated during the fiftieth anniversary of the Swiss Werkbund in Zurich — that "our generation is the first that must come to terms with the experiences of an industrial world." Today's task is no longer simply to produce beautiful, costly things with appropriate methods and materials. But we are pressed hard to solve greater problems. Creative people have always been inconvenient; but an idea cannot always prevail against all resistance as did the Bauhaus Idea. *Videant consules!*

Helene Schmidt-Nonne:

Born in Magdeburg in 1891. From 1908 to 1912 she studied at the Kunstgewerbeschule (School of Arts and Crafts) in Magdeburg. From 1913 to 1916 she studied at the Königliche Kunstschule (Royal Art School) in Berlin. After taking her exams as a drawing teacher, she worked as a social worker for children from 1916 to 1918. Following this she continued her studies and in 1919 obtained her diploma as a practical teacher. From 1919 to 1924 Helene Nonne worked as practical teacher and drawing teacher at the Victoria-Lyseum and Frauenschule (Victoria-Lyceum and School for Girls) in Magdeburg.

Passing through Weimar during the summer of 1923, she visited the Bauhaus exhibition twice and in 1924 she decided to continue her studies at the Bauhaus. Because of her former training she was permitted to omit the preliminary course and start right away to work in the weaving workshop. In the fall of 1925 she married Bauhaus member Joost Schmidt. When Schmidt became junior master at the Bauhaus, Helene Schmidt-Nonne continued her studies at the weaving workshop and also became involved in questions of art theory as pupil of Paul Klee. She received her Bauhaus diploma in 1930. After the closing of the Bauhaus in Dessau, Joost and Helene Schmidt went to Berlin via Weimar and the Bodensee. In 1933 Schmidt was commissioned by Walter Gropius to cooperate in designing the exhibit "Nicht-Eisen-Metalle" (Nonferrous Metals) in Berlin. Later he occasionally taught at the school Kunst und Werk (Art and Work) under the direction of Hugo Häring (formerly the Reimann School). After he was denounced, he was no longer permitted to work. Helene Schmidt-Nonne did occasional work in arts and crafts during the war years, until her husband was hired by Max Taut in 1945 at the Hochschule für Bildende Künste (Highschool for Arts) in Berlin, where he took charge of basic instructions for architects. At the same time he was art director for the U.S. Exhibition Center in Berlin. Together with other Bauhaus members in Berlin Schmidt attempted to prepare a book about the Bauhaus. Due to the partitioning of Berlin into East and West Berlin, this project was dropped. Only the exhibition "22 Berliner Bauhäusler" was presented in 1950, which ex-cluded the former Bauhaus members living in East Berlin. Schmidt went with the U.S. Exhibition Center to Nuremberg in 1948, where he died on December 2.

For a short time in 1949 Helene Schmidt-Nonne worked at the editorial offices of the American Illustrated magazine *Heute* ("Today") in Munich, and then in 1950 she settled in Wangen at the Bodensee.

From there Max Bill invited her in 1953 to the Hochschule für Gestaltung (Ulm Design School) in Ulm, where Mrs. Schmidt-Nonne taught as guest professor on color theory until 1957. In 1961 she settled down in Darmstadt to prepare a publication of Joost Schmidt's work, based on her own material and the Bauhaus Archives. The book has been published in the series *Dokumente Visueller Gestaltung* ("Documents of Visual Design"), edited by Fridolin Müller in Teufen, Switzerland. She lives in Darmstadt.

The Australian art historian Basil Gilbert conducted this interview with Mrs. Schmidt-Nonne during his studies at the Bauhaus Archives in Darmstadt in 1966, in order to represent Joost Schmidt and his contribution to the Bauhaus.

Interview (by Basil Gilbert)

Q. Melbourne is quite a long way from the Bauhaus, but it was at the university there that I first heard Ludwig Hirschfeld-Mack telling the students of his experiences in Weimar. Among his colored slides was a quite unforgettable red-and-black Bauhaus poster. "This was designed by my friend Schmidtchen," he said. Instantly I had a mental picture of a tiny, friendly little man. Does that description fit your husband?

A. Well, not exactly. Joost Schmidt was certainly friendly enough, but he was far from tiny. In fact he was almost six-feet tall. But as the youngest member of his class in the Weimar Academy he received a "baby" title. Later this became a term of affection used by his student and friends.

Q. What made him decide to join the Bauhaus as a student?

A. For many years he had wanted to visit France in order to learn something of French art and to have a close look at the Gothic cathedrals, and like many of the young *Wandervogel* in Germany at that time, he loved nature and the open air and so decided to pack a rucksack and tramp to Paris. But when he finally did arrive in France it was not with cap and walking stick, but with helmet and rifle. The war had intervened. Later, when he was in an American prisoner-of-war camp in France at the end of the war, he received a letter from a friend in Weimar telling him of all the recent exciting goings-on in the new Bauhaus there. With his curiosity aroused he decided to go to Weimar to see things for himself.

Q. What were some of these "exciting goings-on"?

A. The most exciting stimulus came from the *Bauhaus Manifesto,* which Walter Gropius had published in April, 1919. On the cover was the "Cathedral of Socialism" by Lyonel Feininger, with its three shining stars, and inside was Gropius' call to all artists to unite together to build the "new building of the future . . . the crystalline symbol of a new faith." This challenging call-to-action had a great appeal to idealistic youth, and young people came to the school from all over the country. They wanted to sample the new freedom in educational methods, learn a trade in one of the Bauhaus workshops, and engage in communal activities. These activities, such as the kite festivals and the weekly dances to the Bauhaus band, added to the general air of excitement and hope following the tragedy of the war.

Q. What made Schmidt decide to join the sculpture workshop?

A. Perhaps it was his experience with the Gothic sculpture he had seen on the facades of the cathedrals when he was in France, although often his only opportunity to get a close view of these was through field glasses from a military trench in the field of battle. Of course, like many other young students, he was also fed up with the rigidity of the academy classes.

Q. Who had been his teacher at the academy?

A. He was a member of Max Thedy's class. Thedy himself later became a member of the Bauhaus staff when Walter Gropius united the academy with the former Van de Velde Arts and Crafts School, but the modern trends in painting and teaching methods were not to his liking, and so with some of the other former professors he joined the rivaling academic institution, which was re-established in the same building of the Bauhaus in the spring of 1921. This school once more introduced classes in landscape painting, perspective, anatomy, and the like, and was quite a contrast and frustration to the Bauhaus, which was attempting an educational experiment.

Q. One of Schmidt's first important works as a student at the Bauhaus was his decoration of Sommerfeld House in Berlin. Can you tell me something about this?

A. Adolf Sommerfeld was a well-established wood handler in Berlin and after the war he acquired a large quantity of teak from a ship that had recently been dismantled. Building materials were extremely scarce in those post-war days, and with this timber he commissioned Walter Gropius to build him a house in Berlin. As an apprentice in the wood-sculpture workshop, Schmidt was commissioned by Gropius to decorate the main entrance, the foyer, and the staircase leading to the first floor.

Q. Were these purely Abstract Expressionist designs?

A. No. Although they do make use of many abstract elements like the triangle and the square, they also depict scenes from those towns where Sommerfeld had wood mills or timber interests. You can see the names of some of these towns on the panels — Schneidemühl, Kolmar, Danzig, Belgrade, and so on. In the Danzig panel one can see a typical loading crane and a ship in the context of a decorative background.

Q. But this realism is not typical of Schmidt at this time?

A. No, not at all. He often said he wanted to forget Sommerfeld House, although the abstract elements in his work do show something of the general direction in which he was moving — toward abstraction based on the spatial relationships of simple geometrical elements. Schmidt was always fascinated by mathematics and geometry, and this interest of his perhaps accounts for the simple strength of many of his later poster and advertising designs at Dessau.

Q. How did your husband get interested in graphic art — seeing that he was a member of the sculpture workshop?

A. It all started with the dances that took place every Saturday night in the Ilm Schlösschen in Ober weimar. To advertise these dances the students made colorful posters for the notice board, which was situated in the vestibule of the old academy building of the Bauhaus. These were, of course, painted and drawn — many were collages — for at that time facilities were not available in the printing workshop. Probably the first printed placard that Joost made was the red-and-black lithograph for the 1923 Bauhaus Exhibition. One could see this poster all over Weimar.

Q. The script on this poster is, I believe, hand-drawn. Was this something he also learned at the Bauhaus — the art of lettering?

A. No. In those days, most of the students at the Bauhaus were extremely poor because of the inflation. Many wore suits — or should I say shirt-blouses — which had been made from uniforms left behind by the Russian prisoners-of-war. To make them less military-like the students dyed them fanciful colors. My husband's was colored dark red, others were dyed blue or dark green. But let me return to your question. The students were so poor that money had to be earned somehow. Schmidtchen earned himself a few extra marks by helping Otto Dorfner — who, apart from technically leading the bookbinding workshop in the Bauhaus, also ran his own business — to decorate such personal and celebration documents as congratulation cards, jubilee certificates, and the like. The lettering was quite fancy and had to be applied with gold leaf on to parchment. To acquire the necessary skill for this task, Schmidt borrowed some of those beautifully decorated medieval books that were in the Weimar State Library and diligently copied the hand-written script during his spare hours at home. So you see, he was really self-taught here.

Q. And what was he working on at this time in the sculpture workshop?

A. The year 1923 was a time of great activity for all the workshops of the Bauhaus — for the experimental Haus am Horn had to be constructed and furnished, and both the Bauhaus buildings had to be decorated for the coming exhibition and the activities of the Bauhaus week. Unlike the restrictions of the Sommerfeld commissioned work, this time Schmidt was given a free hand by Gropius and was able to indulge his interest in experimentation.

Q. What was the nature of the experiment?

A. The nature of the problem he set himself can perhaps be understood best in the light of an unpublished essay he wrote in 1947, recalling his work of almost a quarter of a century earlier. In the essay he wrote: "This work was the fruition of my research with primary plastic forms. I employed both positive and negative forms and sought to incorporate them compositionally into architecture . . . it was through these experiments that the expressive possibilities of the primary forms became much clearer to me. No longer for me were geometrical figures inexpressive scientific configurations. Beauty, Geometry revealed themselves to me."

Q. It is a great pity that these abstract reliefs in the vestibule of the main building were destroyed once the exhibition was over, for one cannot fully appreciate plastic forms in black-and-white reproductions. However, I recently had the good fortune to see an original work by your husband on display in a delightful exhibition of the art of the 1920s — "Less Années 25" — in the Musée des Arts Décoratifs in Paris. This work was a most beautiful semi-abstract relief of a young woman, whose contours were so subtly expressive that they reminded one of "a melody of Gluck," to use an expression of Sir Kenneth Clark. Was this return to naturalism a new trend in your husband's thought?

A. Yes, it was. It came about like this. In 1929 Joost Schmidt was placed in charge of the life-drawing class in Dessau, and so, after a lapse of fifteen years — since the time he was a student at the Weimar Academy — he was once more confronted with the living model.

Q. Would you say that this work was a successful combination of two trends in your husband's work — abstract geometric elements with the expressive qualities of the human form?

A. Whether it is successful is for the experts to judge. But this work does show his interest in using negative and positive volumes as he mentioned in his essay, combined with a naturalistic contour. It may be of interest to mention here that Schmidt had originally intended this work to be executed in wood, not out of a conventional solid block of wood but out of a block made up of a number of sheets of wood varying in type, textural structure, color, and so on. Thus the outline of the sculpture would have been reinforced by a number of secondary contours, somewhat in the manner of a relief map.

Q. To get back to more personal things, how did you and your husband react to the change-over from Weimar to Dessau?

A. I must say the change had a strong effect on both of us. Weimar in those days had a wonderful atmosphere all of its own. Not only was it the traditional home of such great spirits as Goethe and Schiller, but one could also take walks through the beautiful park or wander in the nearby woods. Since it was a small town, one felt closely related to others; there were plenty of lively discussions in the small cafes, and it was always a pleasant surprise to run into Klee or Kandinsky taking a stroll through the town. Dessau, at first, was quite different. For one thing it was a much larger town, for another it was highly industrialized. Junkers, Lufthansa, and Agfa all had factories there or in the vicinity. To make matters worse my husband and I had no place to live at first, and I had to rent a room — furnished in the worst possible taste — while Joost slept clandestinely in his studio in the Kunsthalle. This building provided provisional studios for the masters and housing for the stage workshop, until the main Bauhaus building was completed. The other workshops were accommodated at this time in some warehouses belonging to a wholesale firm, while Gropius' office, the business management — the Bauhaus was now registered as a limited liability company — and some of the classrooms found space in the old State Arts and Crafts School in the Mauerstrasse. Thus the student body was, in effect, split into three. But life was not always dull. Our social life was centered in the Kunsthalle, and one of the highlights of the activities that took place there is still vivid in my memory. It was the celebration of Walter Gropius' birthday on May 18, 1926. Gropius, as you know, was a cavalry officer during the war and so one of the students dressed himself up in a Hussar's uniform borrowed from the local state theater, one of the new young masters played the postman and read out the greeting telegrams, while the girls from the weaving workshop dressed up as — believe it or not — Salvation Army girls, handed over a number of elaborate "presents" (including cactus plants made out of lemons, cucumbers, radishes, and chocolates), and sang hearty songs of greeting accompanied by guitars!

Q. And when did you finally move into the new building?

A. The official opening took place on December 4, 1926. Compared to Weimar everything was now almost too perfect. Some of the young masters expressed a surprisingly new gentlemanly elegance in dress, and the old masters were elevated to professors. But this did not make them any less friendly. Later when Joost and I moved into the masters' housing block we were soon on good terms with our immediate neighbors — Feininger on one side, Klee and Kandinsky on the other. In our new house, Joost was soon busy preparing material for his preliminary courses and advertising class and dreaming of the perfect Bauhaus exhibition of the future. Memories of Weimar slowly faded into the past.

In fact, when I think back and recollect all the changes that have happened in my life since the beginning of the tragedy of 1933, that house in Dessau — 4 Burg Kühnauer Allee — was the last real home to me.

Gunta Stadler-Stolzl:

Born in Munich in 1897. From 1914 to 1916 she studied decorative painting in Engel's class at the Kunstgewerbeschule in Munich. She was a Red Cross nurse during the First World War.
In the autumn of 1919 Gunta Stölzl became an apprentice in the workshop for mural painting at the Weimar Bauhaus. During 1920–1921 she participated in the conversion of the hand-weaving plant into a workshop. Later she attended additional courses at the textile school and the dyers' school in Krefeld. In 1924 she installed a hand-weaving plant for Johannes Itten at the Mazdaznan-Center in Herrliberg near Zurich, but she returned to the Bauhaus dur-

ing the same year to continue her work.
In 1925, when the Bauhaus moved to Dessau, Gunta Stölzl became a teacher at the textile workshop. During this time the workshop was divided into a teaching workshop and a production workshop, and also a teaching program leading to a Bauhaus diploma was developed. Gunta Stölzl became Bauhaus master from 1927 to 1931, succeeding Georg Muche in the direction of the textile workshop. Since 1931 she has run her own workshop for textile design and a hand-weaving plant in Zurich. She also designs textiles for a variety of uses, and her work at the Bauhaus has had a great influence on the development of weaving. She lives in Zurich.

Weaving at the Bauhaus

In the weaving department of the Bauhaus at Weimar, and later at Dessau, we attempted to train young people to free artistic and technical production through handicrafts.

We did not found our workshop on a sentimental romanticism nor in protest against machine weaving. Rather, we wanted to develop the greatest variety of fabrics by the simplest means, and thus to make it possible for the students to realize their own ideas.

The study of materials — not a scientific but an aesthetic study of their effects on people — was particularly close to our hearts. We tried to capture the learners' interest by sensuous appeal, and particularly in the beginning of the course we put stress on playful, artistic experimenting rather than technical accomplishment. The characteristic effects of various yarns — wool, silk, linen — in the fabric had to be discovered by the learner himself, who was unburdened as much as possible by technical knowledge. Proper vision and proper feel could not be assumed; they had to be awakened and methodically nurtured. So we tried, especially in the beginning, to give the student as much as possible a comprehensive conception of his handiwork and to provide a certain broad freedom of motion, which is absolutely necessary for the student interested in fundamentals. After some months of experimenting, teacher and student discovered whether there really was any aptitude for textiles. Love of the material, a feeling for the many, varied characteristics of the yarns, anticipatory imagination, a sure sense of color, patience, perseverance, ingenuity, and nimbleness, both spiritual and manual, were the prerequisites for aptitude in this work.

Artistic and technical education should work together; neither the one nor the other may take precedence, for a thing is only good if all its qualities harmonize. In order to develop the artistic faculty one must have open eyes and receptive senses. Studies of materials, their equivalence, gradations, contrasts — shiny or dull, grainy or smooth, soft or rough, velvety or hairy, etc. — help to distinguish the variety of yarns. The rich scale of aesthetic values, like color, proportion, line, surface, chiaroscuro, structure, was continually treated, partly in special courses.

At Dessau the following technical studies were offered: binding, theory of materials, analyses, dyeing, and calculation (of the amount of material needed). The very well-equipped workshop at Dessau (unlike the one at Weimar) contained the most varied looms, so that the training of the students for design and program work in industry was possible. It was, after all, our goal to supply industry with persons who would blaze new spiritual and artistic trails. The proximity of people of varied ages and training, the internationalism of the students, fostered mutual learning in comradeship and created an inspiring atmosphere for us teachers.

I should like to stress especially that the coexistence of a workshop for training and a workshop producing things for profit had a very good influence on the student. He had concrete tasks set before him; from the beginning he had the correct index of efficiency and he had responsibility with respect to materials and tools. Calculation of the fabric and also calculation of a handicraft enterprise gave the student practice such as certainly few schools can offer.

Our training was divided into two contrasting fields: (1) *The unique work.* Individual fashioning, free artistic work on a self-imposed or set task — the tapestry, the wall-hanging, the "rug-in-Smyrna" technique, and (2) *Textile design.* This area demanded imagination that took its inspiration from the technical possibilities, a strong ability to imagine color and structure, and the faculty to make combined use of given possibilities in order to meet the demands of a certain program.

The connections between the various Bauhaus workshops, which made it possible to work jointly on large commissions, opened for the student a view of the whole and of his particular task — and much more.

Born in Haag, Austria in 1900. He began his professional training in Linz at the Schmidthammer Studio of Architecture and Applied Arts. In 1920 he became a voluntary apprentice to the architect Emanuel Margold at the famous Mathildenhöhe in Darmstadt. A student at the Weimar Bauhaus from 1921 to 1923, he studied mural painting under Kandinsky and also started his work on typography — so important in his later career. In 1925, after an idyllic year in Italy, touring and painting, he was appointed Master and head of the advertising and typography workshop at the Bauhaus, which had moved to Dessau. In 1928, before Gropius announced his resignation as director, Bayer decided to leave the Bauhaus for Berlin. There he strongly influenced the publication *Die neue Linie* ("The New Line"), and became art director of Dorland Studios. He was also appointed art director for the Paris edition of *Vogue* magazine and he participated in various exhibitions, among them the Werkbund Exhibition in Paris, 1930, and "Das Wunder des Lebens" (The Miracle of Life) in Berlin, 1934.

In 1938 Bayer emigrated to New York, where he was a primary participant in the "Bauhaus 1919–1928" exhibition at the Museum of Modern Art. In addition to his activities as a free-lance commercial artist, he was a consultant for John Wanamaker's Department Store and J. Walter Thompson Advertising Agency. In 1945 he became director of art and design for Dorland International.

In 1946 Walter Paepke asked him to be consultant on the development of the cultural center at Aspen, Colorado. At the same time he became a design consultant for the Container Corporation of America and, from 1956 to 1965, was director of its design department. A member of the artistic advisory committee of the American Office of Information from 1958 to 1961, he was a participating designer for various of their planning groups. In addition, he developed a complete design program for the Container Corporation, including many architectural commissions. Besides acting as adviser to the Aspen Institute for Humanistic Studies, he originated the International Design Conference of Aspen.

Bayer's paintings are represented in museums all over the United States and Europe. One of his most outstanding exhibitions was a retrospective entitled "The Way Beyond Art, 1947–1949," compiled by Alexander Dorner and shown in numerous American cities. In Germany, his entire artistic output was exhibited in 1961 in an exhibition that toured the country. Bayer is a resident of Aspen, Colorado.

A general survey of his work as designer, architect and artist is published in a documentary book 1967 in USA, England, Germany and Japan. In November 1969 Herbert Bayer received the cultural prize of the German Society for Photography in Cologne.

Homage to Gropius

he was in his office
at the van de velde bauhaus building in weimar
when i first met him,
presenting my work
to become a student at the bauhaus.

above his desk in the spacious high-ceilinged room
hung a cubist léger.
there was also a medieval architectural drawing.
gropius wore black trousers, white shirt, slim black bow tie,
and a short natural-colored leather jacket
which squeaked with each movement.
his short mustache, trim figure, and swift movements
gave him the air of a soldier
(which in fact he had been until recently).
gropius' manner of dress was in contrast
to the generally fantastic individualistic appearances
around the bauhaus.
it was a statement of his opinion
that the new artist need not oppose his society
by wearing dress that, to begin with,
would set him apart from the world he lives in,
that the first step toward common understanding
would be acceptance of such standards
as would not infringe on a free spirit.
when i recall those years
i first think of a community of highly eccentric individuals,
some of them strange or just funny, with vague notions
about their purpose for being there,
attracted mainly by the promise of the unknown,
bohemian, poor, defying weimar's bourgeoisie.
i also think of the scent of roses and lilac,
and of nightingales in goethe's moon-flooded park.
my background lay in the viennese design tradition
of art nouveau and secession.
dissatisfied with the role of the designer
as a mere beautifier,
i was drawn to the bauhaus by its first proclamation
with feininger's symbolic, romantic woodcut — a revelation.
at the time i was deeply impressed by kandinsky's book
about the spiritual in art, which i read by chance.
if even in retrospect i cannot express exactly
what brought us all together.
in gropius' mind it must have been clear,

as preceding the bauhaus he had already opened the doors
to new perspectives with his crystal-clear buildings.
and he steadfastly guided us
through yet undefined concepts
to a distinct consummation.
outside currents and inside trends contributed
to an atmosphere of explosive evolution.
most of us were stricken with romantic expressionism.
dadaism paralleled our rejection of any sanctioned order
the work of the de stijl group, attractive by its purity,
had a short-lived, formalistic influence.
constructivism added its share to the artistic turmoil,
but the world of machine production,
with its innate facts and functions,
was already coloring the future.
more evident still becomes the greatness of his vision
if we understand the utter confusion of those times.
as a student of the bauhaus i honor gropius
for he was always drawn to youth —
and youth was always attracted to him.
a prerequisite for the great educator he was,
dedication to the younger generation,
gave him strength in the face of hostility,
to deal with unending personal, artistic, internal, financial issues.
his interest in man was at the core
of his belief in the working team.
and it is here that i had the privilege
to be associated with him in later years
in collaboration on design projects.
this i learned from him:
to give and take, to live and let live.
by exchange of thought to contribute parts to the whole,
making teamwork a great and successful experience.
whether the aims were vague or clear at the bauhaus
there was a unifying air — the spirit of a group,
making each member
an active part in the explorations of the new.
friction of thought against thought

or harmony of ideas
inspired the individual.
group spirit carried feeling and thinking, living and working.
for the future
the bauhaus gave us assurance
in facing the perplexities of work;
it gave us the know-how to work,
a foundation in the crafts,
an invaluable heritage of timeless principles
as applied to the creative process.
it expressed again that we are not to impose aesthetics
on the things we use, to the structures we live in,
but that purpose and form must be seen as one —
that they seldom can stand alone,
that direction emerges when one begins to consider
concrete demands, special conditions, inherent character,
but never losing perspective
that one is after all an artist.
whereas the painter can only be guided from within,
the bauhaus existed for a short span of time,
but the potentials,
intrinsic in it principles
have only begun to be realized.
its sources of design remain forever full
of changing possibilities
the bauhaus is dead.
long live the bauhaus.
i pay homage to gropius
for his creative intuition,
for his relentless perseverance in the advancement of life,
for his strength of mind and character
in standing firm against opposition and slander,
for his inspired leadership,
for his deep concern with man and his community,
for his search for a common basis of all understanding
beyond the mastery of material and physical things,
for his belief in personality
as the ultimate decisive value.

Walter Gropius in front of
his plans for the
Törten settlement
Dessau, 1927
Photo: unknown

The main entrance of the
Bauhaus at the opening of
the new building on
December 4
Dessau, 1926
Photo: Archive of
Walter Gropius

The Bauhaus building
Dessau, 1926
Photo: Reproduction from
a picture postcard of that
period

"Bauhaus shadows," a
play put on by some
students in one of the
workshops
Dessau, 1928
Photo: Werner Zimmermann

The Bauhaus cafeteria with
Oskar Schlemmer (right)
Dessau, 1928
Photo: Archive of
Tut Schlemmer

Wassily and Nina
Kandinsky in the dining
room of his master house
Dessau, 1927
Photo: Lucia Moholy

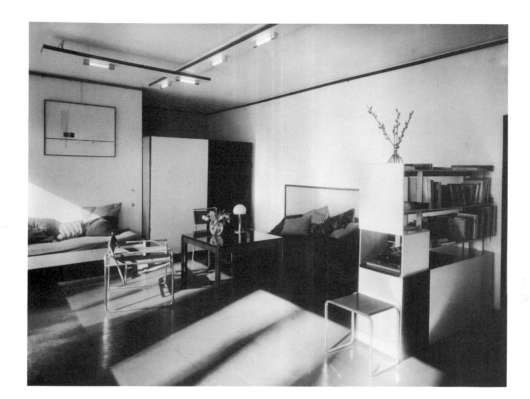

Living room in the
Moholy-Nagys' master
house
Dessau, 1927
Photo: Lucia Moholy

Lyonel Feininger with
his sons, Andreas, Lyonel,
T. Lux, Laurence
Dessau, around 1928
Photo: unknown

Fritz Hesse:

Born in Dessau in 1881. He studied law at the universities of Jena, Berlin, and Halle. After his civil service examination he established himself as a lawyer in Dessau in 1907.

Hesse made his political debut as delegate of the liberal Demokratische Vereinigung (democratic union). In 1914 he became alderman and in 1918 he was elected mayor of Dessau. At the same time he was a member of the National Assembly of Weimar. Hesse endeavored to convert Dessau from a quiet residential town to a modern industrial city. Thus he supported from the beginning the development of the Junkers-Werke and saw to it that the aircraft factory got an airport in Dessau-Alten.

At the beginning of 1925, Hesse learned of the imminent closing of the Bauhaus in Weimar through an article in the *Berliner Tageblatt*. In his memoirs he expressed his thoughts at that time: "This situation presents a great chance for the development of Dessau which will hardly come again. Dessau's cultural period was flowering under Prince Franz and went down with his death more than 100 years ago. Only in the field of the theater and the special attention to opera did the Prince's successors feel an obligation to continue the tradition. If one would offer the Bauhaus an asylum and a chance to work within the walls of Dessau, could one not also make the bells of other arts ring again?"

Hesse's considerations where confirmed by Franz von Hösslin, Dessau's general director of music, who asked the mayor about the chances of moving the Bauhaus to Dessau. Hesse asked his country curator, the young Ludwig Grote, who immediately took a very personal interest in the matter and went to Weimar upon the mayor's instructions a few days later. After Hesse's personal visit with Grote, he called a private meeting of the town council on March 25, 1925, where it was decided that the entire senate and the representatives of the relevant ministries, industries, trades, and the press would visit the Bauhaus. In Weimar Gropius introduced them to the Bauhaus Idea and the masters guided them around the workshops. On March 23, 1925, after hectic discussions by the citizens, a ballot was taken by the town council. Mayor Hesse had reached his goal with twenty-six votes against fifteen: the Bauhaus moved to Dessau. Once this decision was made, the erection of the Bauhaus building and the houses for the masters began. Their opening on December 4 and 5, 1926, was an event of international importance. The buildings are still today a sign of the Bauhaus. For a few years work on the Bauhaus went on peacefully under the wings of Fritz Hesse, who was re-elected mayor of Dessau for another twelve years in 1929.

After the well-known political catastrophy, which shut down the Bauhaus in 1932, Hesse went to Berlin as a lawyer in May, 1933, after several weeks of protective custody. After the capitulation on July 1, 1945, he was reinstated as the last freely elected mayor of Dessau by the commander of the American occupation force. After the United States troops left and the Soviet Russian occupation army entered, his position was confirmed. Fritz Hesse tried to pick up where he had left off in the twenties and invited the former Bauhaus member Hubert Hoffmann to Dessau to reopen the Bauhaus. Political trends prevented its realization, and in November, 1946, Hesse finally had to relinquish his post. Again he worked as a lawyer, again in Berlin. In 1952 he settled in Bad Pyrmont. In his memoirs *Von der Residenz zur Bauhausstadt* ("From a Residence to Bauhaus City," Hannover, 1963), Fritz Hesse described his political involvement and his endeavors for the Bauhaus in detail. He lives in Bad Neuenahr.

The Bauhaus was not an institution with a definite program, it was an idea, and Gropius himself had formulated this idea with great precision. He said: "Art and Technology — a New Unity."

When, after the end of the year 1924, the director and masters of the Staatliches Bauhaus in Weimar refused the invitation of the Thuringen state government, in February, 1925, Walter Gropius accepted my offer to move the entire institute to Dessau to continue there as a municipal institute and under more favorable conditions the work that was interrupted in Weimar. The Bauhaus had gone through an almost six-year period of development. In many ways they had been very stormy years. Its consolidation in Dessau — particularly after the erection of an extensive building with workshops and apartments for the students — bore fruits and justified the opinion of a person like Bruno Paul, who later in a letter to me called the Dessau Bauhaus "undoubtedly the most important creation in the field of art education."

What the Bauhaus actually taught — as Gropius expressed it — was equal evaluation of all kinds of creative work and their logical overlapping in our modern world order.

The teaching successes of the Bauhaus, which were also the cause for a great increase in the number of students, would not have been possible without the outstanding person who formed the faculty of the Bauhaus, and their teaching methods.

The Bauhaus student Wera Meyer-Waldeck expressed this in her reply to a questionnaire by the management of the Bauhaus directed to the students to explain where they saw the value of the Bauhaus:

"For me it is not so much what is being taught, but how it is taught, that before conveying the necessary knowledge one first produces and educates people who can think and act independently."

For me the most positive factor was the educational aspect, which is not subject to any timetable, but which signifies one of the most important parts of the work at the Bauhaus. For instance, the educational work that was required in the Vorkurs could hardly be exceeded. And if the Bauhaus had had no other courses than this, their human and artistic angle alone would had made it worthwhile to attend.

It is well known that the idea of the Bauhaus defied all animosity and efforts of suppression. After being driven out of Dessau in the autumn of 1932 and its subsequent dissolution by the National Socialists, it was spread across all frontiers by its former teachers and students. In a letter of May, 1953, Gropius wrote to me: "In retrospect one can hardly believe that in spite of mounting difficulties the Bauhaus made such an impression. When you live in Germany, you can hardly imagine how world famous the Bauhaus has become, especially in the United States and England. In both countries the curriculums of the schools of art and architecture have followed the teachings of the Bauhaus, and the official state examination for architects contains the obligatory question 'What is the Bauhaus?' Therefore, it was all worthwhile, though neither you nor I knew beforehand the great and almost insurmountable difficulties we were going to have."

Xanti Schawinsky:

Born in Basel in 1904. He first studied art and music in Zurich. From 1921 to 1923 Schawinsky worked as an unpaid assistant in an architectural office in Cologne. In 1924 he became a student at the Bauhaus in Weimar. There he contributed to the Bauhaus stage as designer, writer, and dancer and acted as Oscar Schlemmer's assistant.

In 1926–1927 Schawinsky was designer of stage scenery at the State Theater Zwickau in Saxonia. He then returned to the Bauhaus in Dessau. There he taught stage design and also became very much involved in painting. His work was exhibited with the group called Young Painters of the Bauhaus.

In 1929 Schawinsky became director of the graphic art studios of the municipal government of Magdeburg, where, under the leadership of the city planner Johannes Göderitz, a progressive program was developed, and where he was responsible for its visual design. However, already driven by political persecution by 1931, Schawinsky went to Berlin to work as a free-lance graphic artist and exhibition designer. In 1933 he emigrated to Milan, where he worked as a graphic artist in the Boggeri Studio and as a free-lance designer for companies such as Olivetti and Motta.

In 1936 Josef Albers invited Schawinsky to Black Mountain College in the United States. There, next to teaching painting, he continued his stage experiments with a group of students and he founded the "spectodrama," demonstrations of contemporary studies on the stage. In 1939 he designed the North Carolina pavilion at the Worlds Fair in New York, and he also worked together with Walter Gropius and Marcel Breuer on the Pennsylvania pavilion. Following this, Schawinsky settled in New York as painter and designer. Occasionally he lectured at New York University and City College and also held seminars at other universities in the United States. After 1950 Schawinsky again dedicated himself completely to painting. One-man shows of his latest works were held in the United States and Europe.

In 1961 he designed the complete scenery for the ballet *Stone Flower* by Prokofiev at the State Theater in Basel. During the same year he received the Copley Prize for painting.

In the exhibitions and publications arranged by the Bauhaus and dedicated to the Bauhaus, Schawinsky is represented by his works for the stage, posters, and pictures. His experiences in experimental theater have been published under the title *Play, Life, Illusion* (Spectodrama, Buenos Aires, 1954). Schawinsky lives in New York and Oggebbio (Lago Maggiore).

bauhaus metamorphosis

where am i to begin, in making a comment on the bauhaus today . . . after these many years in which that time has gained plastic depth, become much less blurred than it was then, when it was still warm and full of experiences of the stormy but also of the quietest kind, with all the nuances that may intervene — of thought, of discovery, of resignation, of madness, of reason, of doubt, of friendship and devotion, of the consciousness of human worth, of joy, and of pain, too. after all, most of what came out of it is common knowledge by this time — whether in the sphere of architecture or in that of art, environment-making or world-remaking . . . for this the times have provided sufficiently, if not a little more than sufficiently. for in this way that world of sometime action is laid softly to rest, classified, understood through and through, and highly assessed in its significance.

in the vast mosaic of bauhaus experiences, naturally, a hundred incidents occur to one, meaningful or irrelevant, which in their actual coming-to-pass were perhaps no less remarkable than a chair, a house, or a picture.

thus i happen upon the following event, not very well known,
faintly discreditable, and sad if anything, yet in which, at this distance in
time, one might find a moral.

winter, 1928. berlin. the bauhaus band is playing an engagement on the steinplatz for the poeltzig festival put on annually by the great
man's class. a certain baron x and journalist z approach the band and suggest that the members, with their joint financial backing, organize a bauhaus
band festival in berlin. where so much talent and originality are conjoined,
they say, the undertaking should lead to an event of artistic interest of a
kind that berlin has perhaps never seen before.

on the way home to dessau, encumbered with musical instruments of all sorts, on the train and afterward in the band members' studios,
the project is discussed and finally, after plenty of "to and fro," adopted
with the proviso — understandable in our wretched financial position — that
the money risk be assumed by the two gentlemen. painters all, besides our
paintings we had but scanty commissions to depend on, and there was
hardly enough for bare necessities. heinrich koch, the realist of the group,
painted the risk in glowing colors — matched only by his own eyes — while
we consumed a frugal meal of bread, onions, salt, and a bottle of wine. at
last, optimism and pessimism shook hands on it.

the band was composed of: andreas weininger, piano and fal-
setto tenor; heinrich koch, bass; jackson jacobson, percussion; clemens
röseler, second piano, trombone, banjo; fritz kuhr, second base, banjo; lux
feininger, clarinet, banjo; xanti schawinsky, soprano and alto sax, flecaton,
cello, lotus pipe; and, as occasional guest, jura fulda, banjo, solo voice.

our musical heritage derived from the countries of our birth and
origin, germany, hungary, czechoslovakia, poland, switzerland, russia, the
united states; and diverse as it was, it was unified according to the rule of
the art in a fanatically rhythmic and penetrating din. chairs, gunshots,
hand bells and giant tuning forks, sirens and pianos prepared by means of
nails, wires, and any kind of tone-modifying materials supplemented the in-
strumental outfit, which in its ensemble, from various folk sources or from
homemade compositions, was able to produce guaranteed danceable music
for hours. improvisations, however, even when they threatened to get out of
hand, seemed nailed together by the swinging sledge-hammer rhythm.

in part this group had formed, after the weimar bauhaus was broken up, in dessau, where in the first few weeks there was as yet a lack of opportunity to foregather *in corpore* for impromptu dancing and theatricals, and thus, in relaxed mood, to engage in jocose yet acute exchange of thoughts that busied minds in the isolation of their work. eventually a provincial beer establishment with a suitable dance floor and stage was discovered, where everything on two legs would throng on saturday nights, hastily transformed in garb and inwardly charged with a just-announced community topic. . . . so the thread that had been broken at the ilmschlösschen near weimar was picked up again, people at last felt reunited in the exchange of ideas, feelings, and temperaments, and it was on such occasions that the birthdays of gropius and the masters were observed with fitting uproar and gifts of the bauhäuslers' own making, distributed or, as once on lyonel feininger's feast day, sung by a mixed male sextet:

> there stands a man, a man
> as firm as any oak tree, oak tree,
> maybe he has lived through many a tempest, tempest, tempest,
> maybe by tomorrow he will be a corpse,
> like so many of his brothers before him, him, him.

sometimes when the peak seemed to have been passed in the dance, the heated revelers would prevail on andy (weininger) to sing. instantly the tumult fell into profound silence, all sat in groups on the floor in front of the podium to listen to andy's renditions, which caused many a tear to mingle with the sweat of exertion.

at such functions band and stage were neighbors, their members airing their theatrical experiments, often still in the process of creation. oskar schlemmer, say, as a musical clown; siedhoff doing a hoop, box, or stair dance; joost schmidt having a wrestling match with himself; kurt schmidt's mechanical ballet with bogler and teltscher; schawinsky's jazz and step machine; parts of the *triadic ballet* and mechanical cabaret; group works like *man at switchboard*; pantomime dances; manifestos like "square and flower — a new unity"; skits like "höhepunkt" or "olga-olga," "circus" or "rococo-cotte"; hirschfeld and schwertfeger's color-light plays; lux's masques and spirit seances; wanda von kreibig's feminine invasion of this predominantly masculine theatrical activity . . . all this was calculated to transform the dancing company into a breathless spectatorship, to the music of bach, händel, mozart, antheil, stuckenschmidt, stravinsky, hinde-mith, or the band's own improvisations. guests, too, appeared, kurt schwitters one of the most outstanding, with his sonata in primordial sounds:

> laanketerglll, pepepepepe
> oka oka oka
> lanketerglll pepepepepe
> zueka zueka zueka
> ruemph, rnph . . .

or presenting his solo, one-act play, in which he rang the changes on the complete script *ich huete-te meine schaafe-fe* until — in spite of his blue sunday suit — everybody could see not only the shepherd boy materialized on the boards, but the sheep, too. and when palucca did her provocative "loosening-up exercises," the not unperilous consequence was that the bauhäusler were ready to climb the glass facade of the bauhaus and jump off the roof, had not krajewsky screamed for caution.

lux feininger, still very young, was turning out a series of wild drawings, many of them in the most shocking colors, that were inspired by the bauhaus band. he used to make us presents of such drawings, and one day he came to see me to ask me to sponsor him for the band, as he wanted very much to join. i knew him pretty well as the stage leader and was aware that he was tone deaf. i thought this something of an obstacle, and so did the other members, though i reminded them of kurt schmidt's theory that you could sing the whole opera *carmen* without knowing one tone from another — as long as the time was right. no use, the application had to be tactfully rejected. a few months later lux revisited my studio, this time carrying an oblong case. from it he drew forth the parts of a clarinet, swiftly assembled them, stood in a corner, and flawlessly played first one bauhaus air, then another, until i was lost in astonishment and couldn't help bursting out laughing. he had been taking lessons secretly, memorized everything, and learned the positions visually so well that finally it was just the same as if he had a normal ear. we accordingly arranged an audition, and it went off perfectly. after that, when in the confusion of a night's dancing the ticklish question arose whether the next number started on *f* or *g*, we had only to call on lux, whose visual musicianship never forsook him. mostly this would happen at artists' parties outside the bauhaus, at hanover, halle, berlin, magdeburg, as a result of the somewhat too abundant flow of cognac and champagne with which the guests would regale the band.

despite intensive professional work on the part of all the band members, it was of course taken for granted that they shared the eagerness of all bauhäusler to hold festivities, according to the time-honored principle of *saure wochen, frohe feste.* occasionally these grew into major productions, to which friends were invited from far and near. whole groups would sometimes show up in a body, costumed to suit the announced theme, like our friends from burg giebichenstein in halle, or the hellerauer and others from far away, as well as from our town of dessau. there would be feverish preparations to give expression to the theme in manifold form and decorate the premises accordingly (the white festival, the metallic festival). for albers and his novices it was as easy as pie to work out their ideas in depth; and the masters also were called upon to build their altars. no limitations were imposed on originality of costuming ideas, and everybody worked as hard as though it were a matter of life and death. and then when kandinsky came out in a huge beard, klee with a turned-up snout, and gropius brilliantly executed his reckless power dive, it seemed to everyone in the flush of enjoyment that it had all been very well worthwhile.

against the everyday-life background of this slight digression, the proposition of the two berlin gentlemen baron x and journalist z may appear in a more comprehensible light. now that we had committed ourselves, the next thing to do was to move the spectacle to new quarters. heinrich stephan undertook the search for premises in berlin and found them, in a rather mysterious hotel, in the form of two large halls with elegant vestibules, dining rooms, and connecting apartments such as wardrobes, ample make-up facilities, studios, buffet and bar, far-flung kitchens and pantries, conference rooms with paintings, dressing rooms, but no stage. because of the two halls, it was decided to engage a second band, that of friedrich holländer, though they couldn't start until eleven-thirty because of a theater engagement (*threepenny opera*). so there was no fear that people would get trampled to death once the dancing really got started. most big parties had two orchestras; in fact, when the new bauhaus was opened in dessau in 1927, a second band had been engaged. so whereas the larger band quit at four o'clock in the morning, the bauhaus band played on until eight or even ten in the morning.

the theme title was "bauhaus band beard, nose and heart party." schawinsky was put in charge of decorations, herbert bayer designed the invitations, a costume advisory office was opened in berlin, an umbo obtained for a photographer's booth, a show planned — despite the lack of a stage; we would simply have to build one. time was short, the party season was drawing to a close, it was a big rush . . . the thirty-first of march was the deadline. everything was being worked on, the bauhäusler helped all they could: the girls made flower arrangements, to be sold at a bazaar; heaps of hair were turned into wigs, whiskers in every style — sundermann to chaplin — trimmed and combed, curled and waved; noses molded — according to the injustice of nature, hearts invented. the invitations were sent out in all directions. but from berlin came the news that both the baron and the journalist had vanished from the face of the globe; there was no money whatever. so it was only to be hoped that the deficit might be covered by the sale of admission tickets, ten marks each. in the meantime, everybody had to do the best he could. the theatrical show had to be dropped; we couldn't afford the freight charges. back in 1925 we had gone through something of the sort when we had tried our luck in berlin with an arsenal of figurines, decorations, and other gear, but couldn't get the chance we wanted from the agents and producers; we were much too radical. that financial fiasco had meant disbanding the weimar stage group; the work of years was moldering in warehouses . . . so take warning.

undismayed, we rode to berlin with our instruments the morning of march 31, a whole troup of bauhäusler, express fourth class. things looked bad, far too few paid admissions. the elegant construction, the lighting, the conversion of the giant chandeliers into colored sculptures, setting up the hairdresser's shop and the photographer's booth — everything went surprisingly well. expectations were high, tempered with apprehension.

afterward everybody said it was the handsomest festival ever mounted in berlin. we played as never before, the guests appeared in the most marvelous costumes, but the rooms were half empty. the restaurant concession complained that there wasn't enough eating and drinking. the waiters were making long faces; every penny in the till was gone toward the rental of the premises. our throats were dry. the crowd was not supposed to see that anything was wrong. it did not. the mood was permeated with unaccustomed formality, almost dreamlike. people moved about ceremoniously but freely, as if coached by a talented director. everybody was having a good time, as we could very well see from the bandstand, where, in spite of a show of high spirits, deep depression reigned. the holländer band had meanwhile arrived and promptly demanded its fee of fifteen hundred marks. heinrich koch was called into the studio to negotiate the situation, since stephan hadn't been getting anywhere with holländer. when i, too, was called for and came in, i heard koch's uncompromising voice, "we're not signing anything!" since our backers had disappeared, holländer was insisting on an iou. but how could we have redeemed it?

"don't sign anything," koch repeated when he saw me. i explained that we were painters and that the only assets in our private possession were our own paintings. couldn't we pay in paintings? i promised to make mine available. andy, too, was called in. he suggested auctioning off the bauhaus flowers. here at least was something instantly tangible, and holländer agreed to let his jazz band play some dance numbers.

andy announced the auction and turned in a masterful performance as auctioneer. he was, of course, a very retiring person, of delicate feelings, which went very well with the pretty flowers, but did not tend to warm up the bidding. rather he seemed to be saying, "just look at these rare blooms, imaginable only in the hereafter of a bauhaus paradise . . . who needs such enchantments in this world?"

there was more laughing than trading; still, a modest sum was gotten together and handed over, together with the percentage on drinks as a down payment to our creditor.

the party went on. no one had noticed anything.

Tut Schlemmer:

Born Tut Tutein in Mannheim in 1890. From 1910 to 1914 she studied economics at the Commercial College of Mannheim and also at the University of Heidelberg. She then became assistant at the Betriebswirtschaftliches Institut (Institute of Industry) and also cofounder of the Freie Studentenschaft (Free Student Body). During the First World War she worked for the Red Cross. In 1918 she met Oskar Schlemmer, who had just returned to his studio from the army and had just become a master pupil at the Academy of Fine Arts in Stuttgart. There, Oskar Schlemmer took up his experiments in dance again, which he had started in 1912. In 1920 he left the academy. During the same year Tut and Oskar Schlemmer were married.

At the end of 1920 Schlemmer was appointed to the Weimar Bauhaus as a teacher. First he undertook the artistic direction of the workshop for murals, later for wood and stone sculpting. In 1922 his *Triadische Ballet* had its first performance at the Landestheater Stuttgart and later, during the Bauhaus weeks of the summer of 1923, it was also performed at the German National Theater in Weimar. In 1925 Oskar and Tut moved with the Bauhaus to Dessau, where Oskar started to develop the experimental theater.

In 1929 Schlemmer was appointed a professor at the Breslau Academy, to teach a program called *Raum und Mensch* (Space and Man). When the academy was closed down due to political pressures in April, 1932, he went to Berlin and accepted a teaching job at the Vereinigte Staatsschulen für Kunst (United States Schools for Art). In March, 1933, an exhibition of his works in Stuttgart was shut down by the Nazis. During the same year he was dismissed as a teacher and moved with his family to Eichberg near Baden. There he prepared a memorial exhibition for his painter friend Otto Meyer-Amden, which was opened 1934 at the Kunsthaus Zurich. At the same time his monograph on Otto Meyer-Amden was published.

In 1937 the Schlemmers moved to Sehringen near Badenweiler, into a self-made studio house. However, he never had a chance to work there due to Germany's attitude toward modern art. In 1937, he was denounced in the exhibit "Entartete Kunst" (Degenerate Art). From 1928 until 1940 Oskar Schlemmer had to earn his living as a house painter, when Dr. Kurt Herberts invited him to join the color laboratory of his lacquer factory in Wuppertal, where Willi Baumeister, Georg Muche, Gerhard Marcks, and others were already working.

Prematurely worn-out by the discrepancies between commercial and artistic interests, which he could not handle, he died in Baden-Baden on April 13, 1943. Since 1949 Tut Schlemmer has been living in Stuttgart. Her home developed into a small Bauhaus meeting place. At that time she started the laborious task of compiling a list of former Bauhaus members and mailing it out. Thus, many Bauhaus members have found each other again. This list was taken over and completed by the Bauhaus Archives.

Upon the suggestion of Will Grohmann she gave a lecture about the Bauhaus theater at the America House in Berlin in 1949, which was compiled from Oskar Schlemmer's notes and the original slides of those days. She repeated this lecture in many cities, among them Amsterdam, Zurich, and Basel. It is due to her efforts that the Bauhaus theater has not been forgotten. She also edited *Oskar Schlemmer Letters and Diaries* (Munich, 1958). Tut Schlemmer is an honorary citizen of Sehringen near Baden. She lives in Stuttgart.

...from the living Bauhaus and its stage

Nine years we spent at the Bauhaus. It was an exciting and strenuous time, yet in spite of this, unequaled and full of imposing decisions. These years represent a period of art history, but also a historical epoch. A contest of the minds, open or secret, as possibly nowhere else, a continuous unrest that forced everyone to express a fundamental opinion of profound problems almost daily.

The highlights of memory are still in the air today. The word "Bauhaus" is magic that still holds together all of us who were there in the world today.

The Bauhaus is no legend. The new style of homes, metal, glass, pottery, lighting, carpentry, printing, posters, wallpaper, photos — today film would also be included — the stage, and the king of all workshops, architecture, all are witnesses. To have linked the ambiguity of art to the reality of handicrafts and to have reinstated the old line of descent of the arts will always be attributed to the Bauhaus, whereby architecture should be the leader, according to its orchestrally comprehensive character, which is that the building is the basis of all subsequent forms and designs.

If at this point I do not sufficiently elaborate about the excitement and drama, it is probably because the memory of the highlights of this most beautiful time — also of my life — is still before my eyes. Today the magic connected with the Bauhaus still holds all of us who were there together.

The year 1919 was the beginning in Weimar. It was wild and enthusiastic. Then, too, it was the end of a murderous war, however, the surviving and artistically oriented people of all art-loving nations emerged with new ideas and desires. The generation of 1918 sensed their duty, namely to continue the new era of artistic events that had started before the war. In Germany there was also a tremendous impetus in the theater, film, music, dance, literature, in the graphic arts, and in architecture — in the discovery of large-scale beauty the authority of the functional had its start — and all this in spite of the miseries of post-war times and inflation. Gropius' call acted like a fanfare, and enthusiasts came from all over the world.

At first people let themselves go. Boys had long hair, girls short skirts. No collars or stockings were worn, which was shocking and extravagant then (today boys have long hair again and girls wear their hair short —

every time has its fads). A Bauhaus garment was designed, the Bauhaus whistle and the Bauhaus salute were invented, and one enjoyed sitting in Goethe Park on the Ilm in the moonlight or under the large index finger of Franz Liszt (monument in the park), listening to the songs of the nightingales. One was also cold and hungry for the sake of one's ideals. In short, there was a search for new ways of life, the fire of youth, most exciting living!

One enraged the citizens, they were hurt — I believe the philistines remembered us a long time — one enjoyed this liberty tremendously and enthusiastically proclaimed new ideas. One celebrated festivals with beautiful homemade Chinese lanterns, every fall one celebrated the Festival of Kites with fantastic creations that sometimes were so beautiful, they could not even fly. They were, however, proudly carried through the city, thus reconciling some of the angry citizens and making them our friends. We celebrated our festivals on the suburban stages, and everything smelling of pathos and ethics was ridiculed. We made parodies of operas and plays and Punch — usually Felix Klee presented Bauhaus satires.

The accordion was our instrument, and we developed a Bauhaus dance — a kind of hop expressing the joy of living. Later in Dessau, with the aid of our Bauhaus band, it changed into the tap dance and jazz in dress suits. Celebrations were of the greatest importance up to the last days of the Bauhaus. I remember the White Festival and the Metallic Festival of the later days, where artistic imagination was unfolded and ignited, mostly by the imaginative Oskar Schlemmer, who usually participated. Since there was the urge to perform, a stage was available from the first day of the existence of the Bauhaus. This urge to perform — described by Schiller in his wonderful letters about the aesthetic education of man — is the power from which flows the truly creative values of man, undemanding, naive joy of creating and designing, without distinguishing between the worthy and the unworthy, sense or nonsense, good or bad.

But do not think that life at the Bauhaus was simple or uncomplicated. It was much more like being on top of a volcano, and one had to be very careful not to be torn in every direction by all that rushed in upon us. One was continuously exposed to changes: we started with almost medieval regulations on form, craftsmen, and apprentices and ultimately arrived (1933) as avant-garde in all field. Whatever happened culturally and politically was reflected in our group. There were heated discussions, but our sense of responsibility always prevailed. In retrospect I believe that I understand the secret of how the Bauhaus could develop in the face of incredible difficulties and why we stuck together till this day: we simply loved it, we were a part of it and felt responsible. And then there were special reasons: the Bauhaus did not only have excellent teachers, it also had the best pupils, they were the elite! Gropius' manifesto had attracted the right people. The less talented were automatically rejected by the Bauhaus, they could not stay longer than half a year — this was the official trial period. The teachers were also like magnets, but the Bauhaus Idea could not have been realized without its pupils. They helped to pour new wine into the old pipes.

The year 1923 was the first large Bauhaus exhibition in Weimar. It created a sensation all over the modern world. Indeed it was perhaps the real manifesto of the Bauhaus. It was a testimony to its achievements up to that time. There was an exhibit of teachers and students, there were wall constructions and sculptures. The principle of form without ornament was consistently realized. The aspirations of a collaboration with industry were demonstrated by an experimental house built by Georg Muche, and not the architect Gropius. Advertising and photomontage were also presented. The surprisingly good and today still timely and versatile *Bauhaus Book* was published. The music of Hindemith and Busoni was played in the Staatstheater; and *The Story of the Soldier* by Stravinsky, who, as well as Hindemith, was present; and the *Triadic Ballet* by Oskar Schlemmer. The Bauhaus theater, too, presented itself officially for the first time. It had then — after the experiment with Lothar Schreyer had failed — still no workshop of its own, but used any workshop it could find. It was a team of stage-struck people under the leadership of Oskar Schlemmer, who was then still an art teacher for wood and stone sculpting. The performances took place in a theater in Jena, which had been remodeled by Gropius. Later on one spoke only of the battle of Jena and Auerstedt, because this first performance was something like a flop. Before that time we only used to improvise. It was only due to our master of ceremonies, Andor Weininger, who with his wit and charm persuaded the elite audience, who had come from far and near, to wait patiently, that the people did not leave the theater under protest. The intermissions between numbers became longer and longer, one could hear excited debates from behind the curtain, hammering and cursing. Again and again Andor appeared with another excuse, and I remember that among other things he said in desperation: "It is the normal thing that the curtain goes up, but it is practically sensational that it does not go up." We returned to Weimar completely downcast, and Gropius did not even look at us.

During the further development of the Bauhaus there were times of negation, doubts whether one was on the right way, criticism dissecting and questioning everything. One grappled for a second skeptical simplicity that would compensate for this crisis. Nothing was spared the Bauhaus in this respect. Moreover, the greater became the influence of the Bauhaus on the rest of the world, the more grew the opposition in Weimar. Weimar's government was already turning politically very much to the right, and there was an end to the carefree splendor. The whole reaction against the Bauhaus resulted in press campaigns without equal, in meetings, in slanderous accusations, and, in 1924, in a declaration of disbandment for Weimar.

The City of Dessau offers a new home

If one regarded Weimar as the so-called childhood, the period of storm and stress, life for the Bauhaus started in Dessau in all seriousness. It was the year 1925–1926. The new building — at that time a great rarity in steel and glass — the many-sectioned educational establishment, and the buildings for the masters were built according to the plans of Walter Gropius. We moved in, and this was a completely different world. Since we moved from a house built in the style of the early period of Van der Velde and we were somewhat romantically inclined, many things did not seem right when we moved into glass and steel. This was the beginning of the great transformation. The workshops became model workshops and the heart of the Bauhaus. The machine was accepted. (The trade of the future was termed as the creative preliminaries for industrial production.) The workshops had only a small budget and had to support themselves. We had to get orders and industry had to be won over. We were successful: metal furniture, lighting fixtures, wallpaper, and many other branches of industry produced thousands of objects. The same far-reaching effect had the new concepts of the Bauhaus on typography, graphics, photography, photo-montage, etc. A series of Bauhaus books — already started in 1924 — were published. A quarterly magazine appeared, which informed about the events within the institute and also other artistic happenings. The beautiful pamphlets bore among others the inscription: "Young people of all lands come to the Bauhaus!" And they came from many lands. In the meantime we had become more self-assured. Laws were evolved out of awareness and chaos, and concepts like norm, prototype, synthesis showed the way that should lead to the ideas of design. From now on the Bauhaus was called the High School of Design. The tutors were promoted to professors.

One was greatly concerned to convey to the students the most complete, most comprehensive education and training. In this unique high school one tried to reach new forms of design by combining artistic and workman-like tendencies. This path was consciously followed, based on a new concept of reality to counteract the tastelessness of that time.

Naturally, these endeavors also embraced the theater, which is, after all, a product of order and planning and the scene of living form and color, and which presented the necessary opposing force against the some-times too objective tendencies of the Bauhaus — that refuge and assembly point of metaphysical interests. It was not said in vain that the theater is the flower in the button hole of the Bauhaus. Of course, this did not prevent our technical functionals, of which there were many: why the flower, the buttonhole is sufficient?

This theater was built and directed by Oskar Schlemmer in Dessau from 1925 to 1926. He put down his results and knowledge in the fundamental Bauhaus book, which is still of importance at the present time, *Mensch und Kunstfigur* ("Man and Art Figure"). Since Schlemmer was a painter, the theater was mostly concerned with form and color, space and man. The limited basis of the stage permitting, designs were tried out that were necessarily original because they had never been tried before. Our experimental theater could only be a small section — and this I want to point out — of the field of the theater and was first and foremost limited to silent action and pantomime. Speech should be added later — nonliterary conceived — as an elementary event. What was said for word and speech also held good for musical sounds. Up to that time only gong and kettle-drum were used. No stage designs were created, nor was the study of historical costumes taught, we strove only for an immediate action on the stage. It was never intended as an institute for theater art, though we also worked with the knowledge of scientific perception on the stage, but it was a question of the thing in itself. We meant to make *tabula rasa*, throw over board all the former ballast, and start again, unbiased, with the *ABC*'s, namely with the elements. Again and again one can begin with the simple and true, it just has to be newly felt and fulfilled.

The elements are space, form, color, and light: space — its planimetry, its law, and its mystery; form — any of its manifold manifestations as a plain surface or sculpture; color — as a phenomenon, its reciprocal influence, harmony, disharmony; and light — lighting, projection, transparency, and film should be essential media to demonstrate the inner laws suitable for the stage, away from naturalistic tendencies of imitation. Lighting should not produce the sun, moon, morning, evening, etc., but should appear as what it is, namely yellow, blue, red, green, violet, etc.

Mechanism was presented as an end in itself, as a self-contained machine, whereby people figured only at the switchboard. Humans were presented as an event, the privileged and authority of directness, mediators and proclaimers of speech and sound; their metamorphosis through costume and mask; their acting as a lifeless puppet, as a marionette, and thus the possible exaggeration of the figure.

This is what encompassed the realm of the theater, which should extend to stage scenery. Scenery was visualized to be of new materials, miracles of the materials of tomorrow combined with new inventions in the field of optics, mechanics, and acoustics. The stage would be no longer a peep show, but would be organized on several levels, which could be lowered or moved. Shape and color are the tools of the creative designer, space and man are the polar components around which the world of the stage revolves. Let us watch what space, shape, and color can do to influence man.

Oskar Schlemmer, who never ceased to be an optimist even as an artist, said about thirty-five years ago:

"Considering human transformation from the naked to the costumed man, to puppet and marionette, up to larger than life figures of fantasy; considering everything with its span from the comic-grotesque to the heroic-pathetic; considering, in addition, the future theater stage, created under completely new suppositions; considering the music of the spheres, the organized ether waves or the music to be produced mechanically in an unheard of intensity of sound, of which Busoni dreamed; considering that the poets — inspired by new possibilities — will arrive at completely new ideas and topics, so that they will think rather in spacious sculptural architecture than in illustrated pages; considering the progress in the field of optics and mechanics; and above all, considering that these media may serve art as an end in itself, that they do not serve to simulate the illusion of a second nature on stage, but can act directly and immediately by the elementary power of their substance, one can say that there are almost unlimited possibilities for creativity."

Ursula Schuh:

Born Ursula Diederich in Hamburg-Blankenese. She studied art history at the Hamburg, Berlin, and Heidelberg universities. While visiting the Sorbonne, she became interested in painting and studied at the Academi Calarossi in Paris. In 1931 she came to the Bauhaus in Dessau to continue her studies in painting with Kandinsky. From 1932 to 1934 she lived on a scholarship in Paris and later, up to 1937, she spent several months every year in Paris, where her painting was influenced by the artist Hans Reichel. In 1939 she married the producer Oskar Fritz Schuh.

After moving to Vienna in 1940, she started to exhibit her paintings. Her first exhibition was at the Neue Galerie in Vienna in 1942. From 1945 to 1946 Ursula Schuh was drawing in Vienna. Later she acted as picture editor and reviewer for *Welt am Montag* and *Welt am Abend*. After extensive European travels, she lived in Berlin from 1953 to 1958 and then in Cologne from 1958 to 1963. After this she settled in Hamburg. Upon the advice of Rolf Liebermann she started to design scenery and costumes for the State Opera and Deutsche Schauspielhaus in Hamburg in 1964. Among her creations are sets for Stravinsky's *Firebird*, Frisch's *Chinese Wall*, Schnitzler's *Der grüne Kakadu*, and Giraudoux's *Undine*. Outstanding among her exhibits are the one-man shows at the Galerie Gerd Rosen in Berlin in 1955 and at the Wallraff-Richartz Museum in Cologne in 1961. Ursula Schuh lives in Hamburg.

The Dessau Bauhaus was an imposing building. Reinforced concrete, glass, large white square or rectangular blocks in an open landscape, broken up by rows of reflecting windows. This was then the triumph of the lord mayor of Dessau, who was ahead of his time, a forerunner of today's city planners.

In September, 1911, I opened this door for the first time as a Kandinsky student. When I entered it was very much overheated, as is usual in academies, and I was surrounded by a hushed silence. Even the doormen talk softly there.

"Kandinsky's class, please?"

"Up these stairs, second floor left."

I am careful not to slip on the polished linoleum floor. I move up the stairs like a shadow; stairs, enormous window, stairs, first floor. Deserted corridor with closed doors. I go on: stairs, enormous window, stairs, second floor. I am all shadow and only a case under my arm containing immature, inferior work, which I feel is much too personal, completely subjective and tasteless. Searchingly I pass closed doors with often quoted imposing names, along the silent corridors to the door: painting class. Kandinsky. Thank God, *he* has not yet arrived! I find a seat. Benches and tables, like in a classroom.

He enters. Immediately everything unreal vanishes in front of these lively, fast-moving, pale blue eyes looking through sharp glasses. A glance interested in everything, which continuously seems to discover new secrets in the world around us. Suddenly questions and answers and one is right in the middle of the problems of his color system. He has brought along a great variety of rectangles, squares, disks, and triangles in various colors, which he holds in front of us to test and to build our visual perception. In one combination, for instance, yellow is in front and blue in back. If I add this black, what happens then? Etc., etc. For the painter this is a never-tiring game, magic and even torture, when one, for instance, "cannot get something to the front."

Only later did I notice Kandinsky's almost feminine, sensitive, but very controlled mouth, the graying hair, his dignified, rather preceptive appearance, the correctness of his dark suit, the snow-white shirt, the bow tie (like Braque's), brown shoes — the well-groomed elegance of a scientist in 1931. Also the certain impersonal treatment of people and objects. Altogether very attractive. He might have been a good fifty-five, perhaps sixty years old? This was the first and lasting impression one had of Kandinsky as a person.

His art, his artistic experiments suited exactly the spirit of his generation. One loved to break with old conventions, but one also loved the precision in determining and formulating new perceptions, in whatever field, in any kind of artistic manifestation. One loved abstraction, one felt "abstract." It is significant that one never aimed to paint "modern" at that time, nor did one think in terms of isms (both were left to the spectator). One was much more concerned to find the only appropriate, the unique and clear form for expressing one's own experience. Opinions about paintings might have been expressed as: "The picture is OK," "The picture is striking," "This is constructed." Or one indicated the appropriate and logical use of color and form. If it was said of a picture: "This contains nice things," it was second, third, or fifth rate, but had exactly outlined and determined valuable parts.

To "arrange" a picture was despised. If a picture was arranged it meant: A square was capably filled by more or less agreeable shapes, but lacking genuine experience. It was not composed, i.e., inner experience and formal knowledge did not form a unity.

The greatness of Kandinsky's artistic character consisted of his relentlessness, his consistency, his love of truth in art. This was the great example for the development of standards for the younger generation, even if later on they should go toward completely different paths, or rather were forced to, since the more consistent they were, the more they went their own way.

Kandinsky perceived the visible world as not the vital point. Of significance to him were the imminent qualities of the manifestations of his environment and his own inner perceptions. These he wanted to expose. This accounts for the titles of his pictures "Light," "To Each Other," "Suspended," etc. Or, when he was drunk with the pleasure of exploring free use of color and form, the thus-created picture was called "Improvisation" and not "Composition," because composition meant for him a conceived, precisely measured picture. In art one was very strict with oneself and with others.

In fine art, too, the parallel with music was felt very strongly: the seemingly free forms and colors were yet developed according to certain laws. Again and again this was expressed in the titles of pictures such as "Fugue," "Variation," "Crescendo," or "Allegro." It is significant that Kandinsky very much admired the dancer Palucca, because her dancing was, so to speak, pure dance, entirely developed out of the possibilities of body rhythms, without literary or pictorial deviation from the given themes.

I did not stay long at the Bauhaus, but returned to Paris, since the artistic atmosphere was strongly undermined by cultural, political conflicts. There I also met Kandinsky personally for the last time. This took place in his home at Neuilly, a modern, western suburb of Paris, after his emigration in 1933. Fortunately I was still in Paris to see both great exhibitions of Klee and Kandinsky, which in a sense confirmed their international and general importance.

Will Grohmann:

Born in Bautzen in 1887. He visited, when still a highschool student in 1904, the great International Art Exhibition in Dresden and became very interested in art; at first, however, his interest lay more in painting than in aesthetics. He then studied Oriental languages, archaeology, the history of art, and German philology at the universities of Dresden and Leipzig. He took his doctors degree at the Leipzig University in 1913. During and after the First World War he taught.

After 1923 he collaborated on the magazine *Der Cicerone* and also worked at the publishing offices of the Thieme-Becker *Künstlerlexikon* in Leipzig. At that time he also started his close association with modern artists and became an important defender of their aims. By 1924 he had already published a monograph on Wassily Kandinsky, followed by many books and numerous essays on the topic of modern art. After its opening he became a frequent visitor to the Bauhaus, in particular to the studios of the painters Wassily Kandinsky and Paul Klee. In 1923 he visited Ernst Ludwig Kirchner in Frauenkirch near Davos and in 1925 he published a book on Kirchner's drawings, in 1926 a book on his complete works. He wrote important monographs about Paul Klee in 1929, in 1930 again on Wassily Kandinsky, in 1931 on Willi Baumeister, and in 1933 a book about the collection of Ida Bienert.

In 1933 he was dismissed from his job for political reasons. Thereafter he involved himself in questions of archaeology, among them the art of migrant peoples. He made it his job during these difficult times to prepare an annotated edition of the writings of the Asian explorer Josef Strzygowski, who described around 1900 the influence of the Orient on Western culture. Unfortunately this manuscript was destroyed by fire at the end of the war.

In Dresden after the war, he made strong efforts to revive cultural life as head of the Department for Popular Education. In 1948 he was appointed to the Hochschule für Bildende Kunst in Berlin as professor of art history and at the same time he acted as chief art critic on the *Neue Zeitung* in Berlin. In 1955 he returned to his real interest, modern art, and published a number of large monographs, which appeared in various languages. Outstanding among them are *Paul Klee* (1954); *Karl Schmidt-Rottluff* (1956); *Wassily Kandinsky and Ernst Ludwig Kirchner* (1958); *Henry Moore* (1959); *Willi Baumeister* (1963); *Oskar Schlemmer, Drawings* (1965); *Hans Hartung, Aquarells* (1966); and again, *Paul Klee*. In 1959 Grohmann received the Viareggio Italian Prize for Literature and in 1962 he was elected honorary president of the Association Internationale des Critiques d'Art and honorary member of the Museum of Modern Art in New York. In 1967, on his eightieth birthday, the Deutsche Gesellschaft für Bildende Kunst (Kunstverein Berlin) established a Will Grohmann Prize in appreciation of his efforts of many years in the cause of beginning artists, and the Akademie der Künste in Berlin made him an honorary member. During the same year he recorded his personal associations with the artists of his time in a book titled *Lieber Freund — Künstler Schreiben an Will Grohmann* ("Dear Friend — Artists Write Will Grohmann"). This book reflects the strong impact of his work on modern art. Grohmann died in Berlin on May 5, 1968.

The Bauhaus and modern art

It is quite unusual that we should still be talking about an art school that existed for thirteen years, and during this time was shattered and reconstructed. There are academies in Germany having a life span of more than a hundred years that were still of no interest, and there are private schools, some of which at least will be remembered, for instance the one of Azbes in Munich, counting among its students Kandinsky and Jawlensky. Only in 1900 did Kandinsky come to the academy to study with Franz Stuck

simultaneously with Klee, and both men met again after the war at the Bauhaus in Weimar. Klee started his activities in January, 1920, Kandinsky, in
June, 1922. And Lyonel Feininger, who had joined their exhibit at the famous
Herbstsalon of Der Sturm in 1913, had already been at the Bauhaus since
1919. The other masters came from different realms of the artistic world.

The Bauhaus was more less an idea originated by Gropius.
He was bold enough to find collaborators of whom he expected as much as
he did of himself, first of all, their own thoughts and opinions. Very often it
was hard going during the first years. There were hot arguments between
teachers and students, but Gropius tolerated truths and contradictions. As
a human being, he was a gentleman, as director, a good organizer and educator, and he was an *esprit fort.* Proof of his importance came when after
ten years he resigned from the very taxing appointment to work again as an
independent architect. He could not be replaced, not even by Mies van de
Rohe, the genius among the master architects. To be the director of such an
institute meant not shying away from the pettiness and dealings with the
authorities, the politicians, and industry, but at the same time one had to
remain flexible and always prepared to replace good with better, to start
anew again and again.

The Bauhaus was a target for attacks as long as it existed.
Though the best people were on its side, these were in the minority. The
idea of the Bauhaus was in the air. Immediately after the war when the
Arbeitsrat für Kunst was founded, its aims were closely related to those of
the Bauhaus: reform of the art schools, education based on craftsmanship,
synthesis of the arts, resistance to boundless individualism, etc. And the
Arbeitsrat comprised almost all leading figures: Erick Heckel, Karl Schmidt-
Rottluff, Lyonel Feininger, Gerhard Marcks, Hans Poelzig, Wilhelm Valen-
tiner, Paul Cassirer, and, naturally, also Gropius. But Gropius had his
Program in Progress already set. He knew what he wanted, only he did not
yet know just whom he should appoint for the Bauhaus.

Gropius had just returned from the war and believed that nothing was impossible. The years after 1918 were the most exciting and daring
ones of the twentieth century in Germany, the most hopeful years. Everybody wanted to better the world, everybody was a philosopher or poet or

had utopian schemes. At first it was clear what Gropius wanted, the trouble started only when the people, swept aside by the revolution, recovered and gained the upper hand again.

Gropius' idea was to concentrate all artistic forces on architecture; he aimed at an education based on craftsmanship so that every apprentice would be useful and fit into the whole set-up. There were no professors and students, but masters and apprentices, not free and applied art, but creators supplementing each other to serve a common cause. According to Gropius, art cannot be taught, only manual skills and knowledge. Genius is not part of the school curriculum, but free creation does grow out of mechanical education. Should the artist who was an apprentice of the Bauhaus be unable to live by his art, he could always fall back on his original craft.

There were the preliminary studies (exercises in plastic art and materials), studies in the workshop (stone, wood, metal, textiles, glass, color) combined with plastic art (nature studies, construction, space, color), and finally, the study of building construction, terminated by the masters degree. The students were instructed in two ways, in a practical way by the master of crafts and in the formal way by the artist. In Weimar there were no painting or sculpturing classes, there were "form-masters." Kandinsky, for instance, taught mural painting; Klee, glass painting; Moholy-Nagy, metalwork; Marcks, ceramics; Muche, textiles; Feininger, printing; Schlemmer, sculpture, which was later applied to stage and theater. Only in Dessau did Kandinsky and Klee give painting lessons, and only in Dessau was tuition placed in one hand, since former students could now function as form-masters and craftsmen. They had been prepared for both. In Dessau the workshops became more and more like laboratories where sample models (prototypes) were developed. The students of architecture had to study the house as a problem of a mass need, with methods of construction and prefabrication of building elements. Science and techniques were accepted, but the question of design took first place.

The aim was a synthesis, the collaboration of everybody, and even during apprenticeship, everyone had to subordinate himself without losing his own personality. Even the nongenius finds his place in the orchestra. The Bauhaus revived the medieval *Bauhuette.* Most students went into practical work after completion of their studies, carried on the ideas stimulated by their teachers, and found their task in the field of environmental design. Comparatively few became painters or sculptors, like Fritz Winter. The Bauhaus was not an art school; Hochschule für Gestaltung (School of Design) was then the correct name, but Bauhaus was better.

The success of its teaching was seen in 1930 in the "Exposition de la Société des Artistes Décorateurs" in Paris. The Werkbund commissioned Gropius to design the Section Allemande, and for the first time an international public saw models and objects that were beautiful and functional at the same time. The much-criticized functionalism proved to be neither dry nor without feeling for building or commodities, it was no more than a necessary regulator of the imagination, a technical and economical partner.

It seems miraculous that for a period of ten years (only in 1928 did the team begin to break apart) so many unusual talents worked together, lived peacefully with each other, personally and professionally. Whoever had an insight into the operation of the institute, or participated in performances and celebrations of the Bauhaus, will never forget the spirit of friendship, or the *élan* distinguishing the work. Even minor talents grew above themselves in this atmosphere. The masters were demanding and so became the students. Failures were discarded without mercy, successes were praised unreservedly. There was no petty jealousy, only healthy competition.

And they regarded the festivities as just as important as their work. They always had a motto like "metal" or "black-white." It was a matter of honor to create everything themselves, even the music. The jazz band of the Bauhäusler was famous all over Germany and even abroad. The students could thereby earn money for their studies, just as they received a share from the profits of their designs and patterns that were accepted by the industry. Part of the budget of the Bauhaus in Dessau was met this way, and the industry liked to work with its teachers and students. The Bauhaus wallpaper brought more money each year.

On leafing through the Bauhaus books today — thirteen have been published — one wonders how many famous objects were created within such a short period. The Bauhaus lamp, metal furniture, ashtrays, etc. All these articles are still in use because they were not just fashionable. The word "fashion" did not exist at the Bauhaus, it had a bad sound. A precise work, sensibly designed, automatically has the actual style of the time. Personality came second — still one could guess the designer of some objects, often more than one — but with each work the joint collaboration was more noticeable than the individual.

When in 1926 the young masters in Dessau were in charge of the workshops, it was run as Gropius intended it from the beginning. Josef Albers and Moholy-Nagy were responsible for the Vorkurs. The students made experiments with a variety of materials and learned to use them in construction. Before nobody suspected, for instance, how much could be done with paper; even today many of Max Bill's projects for sculptures are made of paper. One preferred to work with one's hands, using a bare minimum of tools. The method was inductive and stimulated inventions. Space was not explained, but rather discovered on biological grounds of experiencing space. Already during the Vorkurs the students were able to find out their strong and weak points, whether their talents were more technical or more intuitive and artistic. In Dessau Albers became one of the leading art educators. There Kandinsky and Klee had their painting classes and in addition lectures on art education, parts of which were published by them. Klee included them in his *Paedagogischen Skizzenbuch* (1925), Kandinsky in *Punkt und Linie zu Flaeche* (1926). These works demonstrate that at the Bauhaus something like a theory of harmony — comparable to music — was developed.

The Bauhaus magazine (1926 to 1931), published by the institute, contained important information compiled by teachers and students as well as outsiders. The Bauhaus put great importance on contact with the outside world — scientists of all disciplines and all nationalities — in order to keep the students up to date and also in order not to neglect their orientation on the level of life next to their "orientation on the creative level" — in Klee's words. For this reason a Circle of Friends of the Bauhaus was founded, whose function was also to fill out the budget through members' contributions.

Gropius, responsible for the *Baulehre*, had his turn as an architect only in Dessau. He was commissioned by the city and its mayor Fritz

Hesse, who had invited the institute to his city after its dissolution in Weimar, to design the new building for the Bauhaus, which is one of the most beautiful buildings of the twentieth century, and also seven master houses in the Burgkuehnauer Allee for the teachers. Most of these houses were furnished on Bauhaus lines. They were model houses with wonderful studios, and many of the teachers had for the first time an opportunity to have studios worthy of their work.

Living together increased the feeling of belonging together, which had hardly suffered during the confusion of the years of construction and political fights. Also at that time Gropius built a workers' colony of 316 houses in Dessau-Törten, according to the latest methods and with prefabricated elements. One should have thought that Germany was proud of his achievements, but they were completely obliterated when the nonintellectual movement of National Socialism flooded the country. What has remained is the memory of an undertaking that was unique in its time, of teachers who were great artists as well as educators, of a community in which everyone, even each student, had his place surpassing his own abilities, and of an atmosphere where art, science, and technology, intuition and the spirit of research were on good terms and inspired each other.

Josef Albers:

Born in Bottrop (Ruhr District) in 1888. He studied at the Teachers College in Bueren from 1905 to 1908 and there received a teacher's certificate. Following this, Albers became a teacher in his home town. From 1913 to 1915 he continued his studies at the Königliche Kunstschule (Royal Art School) in Berlin. By 1908 he had already come in contact with new trends in art through the Folkwang Museum in Hagen, and there he met the patron of the arts Karl-Ernst Osthaus and painter Christian Rohlfs. He paid frequent visits to the Berlin museums and avant-garde galleries, in particular to Paul Cassirrer and Herwarth Walden (Der Sturm). In 1913 he painted his first abstract pictures.

After graduating as an art educator, he continued his studies at the School of Arts and Crafts in Essen from 1916 to 1919, and for a short time at the Munich Academy in the class of Franz von Stuck. This was the preparation Josef Albers had had in 1920 — at thirty-two — when he entered the preliminary course at Weimar as an apprentice.

In 1922, after passing his test as a journeyman, Albers took over the installation of the glass workshop. At the same time he made his first glass pictures, among them the ones for the Sommerfeld House in Berlin. By 1923

Walter Gropius had entrusted him with the teaching of the preliminary course for materials and design at the Bauhaus.

When the Bauhaus moved to Dessau, Albers became Bauhaus master. He was put in charge of the preliminary course for entering students. He also continued his experiments in the glass workshop and worked in the fields of typography, letter design, and furniture development. After Marcel Breuer left the Bauhaus in 1928, Albers also took charge of the furniture workshop and became assistant director of the Bauhaus. In 1932, after the closing of the Bauhaus in Dessau, he went with Ludwig Mies van der Rohe and the rest of the students to the private Bauhaus in Berlin, remaining until its final closing in April, 1933.

During the same year Josef and Anni Albers were invited to the newly opened Black Mountain College in North Carolina, where Albers became professor of art. From 1936 to 1940 he also taught at the Graduate School of Design at Harvard University in Cambridge. In 1949 he resigned from Black Mountain College and in 1950 he was appointed to Yale University in New Haven as head of the Department of Design. Albers also directed a great number of guest seminars, mainly at North and South American colleges and universities. In 1953 and 1955 he acted as guest lecturer at the Hochschule für Gestaltung (Ulm Design School) in Ulm.

Josef Albers taught for ten years at the Bauhaus, longer than any other teacher. This Bauhaus experience and his activities in the United States (sixteen years at Black Mountain College and ten years at Yale University) have made him an influential interpreter of the Bauhaus Idea. Since the twenties his paintings have been exhibited in international one-man shows and group exhibitions in many important museums. In appreciation of his philosophy of art and its influence on today's art his work was shown in special rooms at "The Responsive Eye," Museum of Modern Art, 1965, at the "Documenta IV," Kassel, 1968, and at the first Biennale of Constructivist Art, Nuremberg, 1969. Among his many awards is the title of Doctor of Fine Arts from the University of Hartford (1957), Yale University (1962), and California College of Arts and Crafts (1964).

His experiences in the study of color at Yale University have been collected in his important book *Interaction of Color* (New Haven, 1963). In Germany Eugen Gomringer has published a detailed monograph about Albers' work as painter and philosopher in 1968. Albers lives in New Haven.

Thirteen years at the Bauhaus

I spent three years as student and ten years as teacher at the Bauhaus (this means longer than anyone else). In 1919, when the Bauhaus was founded, I was in Munich, and at the beginning of 1920 I studied with Franz von Stuck at the Munich Academy, as did Kandinsky and Klee before me. Although I grew particularly fond of Munich, I was soon very strongly drawn to Weimar because of the tempting possibilities of studying under an unusual name — the name was Bauhaus. Obviously this name meant something else than "academy." Also the names "institute" or even "Hochschule" were not alarming. And instead of workshop, which it actually was, it was most modestly called "house," and significantly not "house for art and industry," nor some other combination of both, but "Bauhaus," therefore a house for building, and again modestly and discreetly, for building and design. Even today I am convinced that the invention of this name, the invention of the word "Bauhaus," was a particularly happy and important action of Gropius. This happened at a time when art was written with a capital *A*, after a much too retrospective nineteenth century, when one talked too frequently of the golden age of the Renaissance, so that there was hardly any time left for one's own work. In spite of the independent, unconventional name of Bauhaus we did not even in Weimar remain without some indications and warnings of the past. But the more we studied the old memories, the more certain we became that analyzing and dissecting was no goal. It was even more significant that the so called masters there did not look back toward even older masters, but intentionally opposed what had already been done and said, in order to dedicate themselves more intensively to their own development. We therefore preferred to watch new and living masters who were determined not to follow others, and Gropius was the man who bravely introduced us to such masters.

The greatest success of the Bauhaus was to win over and interest industry. We realized this aim only to a small degree. Time was too short and possibly not yet ready for it. Instead, we gained something else, something much more effective: a new visual education. We had a disorganized but very far-reaching influence on general education. This was an unexpected success. I do not believe that during the ten years of my life at the Bauhaus I heard the word "education" mentioned. We talked a lot about design, production, and industry, but hardly about education. We simply tried to teach anew. In America today the mistake is made of talking of a Bauhaus method. We have heard that it is of no use to talk about the Bauhaus style because no style was sought. A Bauhaus teaching method was never intended, because each master developed his own method of teaching, independent of the others and especially independent of any agreed principles and aims of teaching.

And this also explains the pedagogic success of the Bauhaus. As every success in learning and teaching depends on the personality of the teacher, so it was in teaching of design, i.e., of Shaping and Construction at the Bauhaus.

At first the Bauhaus meant opposition for me. Naturally, the strongest opposition came from young people, and this was supported by the work and attitude of the masters, who also did not follow others nor repeat others. The result was that the students influenced the development of the Bauhaus. It is typical that the very first course at the Bauhaus, the preliminary course, had to succumb to the opposition of the students. Subsequent courses could not and would not act as a continuation of the preliminary course, if only because later lecturers could not and would not be heirs to a way of teaching that had been rejected.

T. Lux Feininger:

Born in Berlin in 1910. In 1919 he moved with his parents to Weimar, where his father, Lyonel Feininger, was one of the first teachers to be appointed to the Bauhaus. In 1926 he started his studies at the Bauhaus in Dessau. From 1927 to 1929 he worked as collaborator at Oskar Schlemmer's experimental theater. He remained an active member of the Bauhaus theater even after Schlemmer left the institute in 1929. Since 1928 Feininger was also a member of the Bauhaus jazz band. Among his special teachers were Josef Albers, Laszlo Moholy-Nagy, Oskar Schlemmer, Paul Klee, and Wassily Kandinsky.

Apart from his studies at the Bauhaus he developed a particular interest in photography and from 1927 to 1931 he worked as a well-known photographic reporter for prominent periodicals and illustrated newspapers at the Agency Dephot in Berlin. After 1929 he devoted himself to painting. Up to 1947 he exhibited his work in America and Europe under the name of Theodore Lux, later under his full name.

After the closing of the Bauhaus in Dessau, Feininger settled in Paris. In 1935 he returned to Germany, where he had a large exhibition of his paintings in Berlin and Hamburg. At the end of 1936 Feininger went to New York. From 1942 to 1945 he served in the army. Afterward he again settled down in New York as a painter and from 1950 to 1952 he held a position teaching design at Sarah Lawrence College. In 1953 Feininger was appointed as lecturer at the Fogg Museum, Harvard University, Cambridge. From there he was appointed an instructor in painting at the Boston Museum School in 1962, where he is still working today.

Among his main interests are his activities as a writer of art reviews. Next to his writing on modern art, his father's (Lyonel Feininger) life and work demands most of his attention. Works by Lux Feininger are to be found at the Museum of Modern Art, New York, the Busch-Reisinger Museum, Harvard, where a retrospective exhibition was held in 1962, and in many American and European private collections. Feininger lives in Cambridge.

The Bauhaus: evolution of an idea

I grew up with and at the Bauhaus. I was nine years old when my father was invited to join the founding staff in 1919, which necessitated our family's removal from Berlin to Weimar. In my memory, the moving was attended by cheery circumstances. In the first spring since the cessation of hostilities a great upsurge of hope was evident everywhere. I liked the town and surroundings of Weimar, and best of all was the Bauhaus atmosphere itself. A boy does not trouble his head about the origin and history of things, and I accepted the interesting people and their works, and the attention they paid to me and my works, as something which might have been there always, but which was certainly very agreeable and delightfully different from the musty disciplines of the Gymnasium. The Bauhaus population was fond of gaiety and given to playing and the celebrating of feasts; a paper lantern serenade under our windows on my father's birthday remains an unforgettable experience.

In the following years, as was inevitable, other preoccupations intruded upon the Arcadian felicity of the beginning, and when, seven years later, I became a student at the Bauhaus myself (the youngest ever admitted), I could probably have dimly remembered the childish participation but was engrossed in so new and different a situation that it seemed like a new world altogether.

Forty years have gone by since that time; and the more I ponder now what has always seemed so familiar, the more material for wonder I find opening to me. These findings are of a dual, intertwining nature. I am impressed with the effect and forming power the school has had on my own development, but especially with the uniqueness, the scope, the bold novelty of inception, of a community into which I had wandered, when young, as unquestionably as I might have strolled casually into some ancient church; something that "had always been there." I discover that it had not always been there and that soon it was not to be there any more at all. I must attempt to separate the strands of personal recollection and gradual enlightenment as to the social meaning of what is known as "The Bauhaus," an organization born out of the collaboration of many minds. At the beginning of it all, with his strong spirit of devotion, stands the vision and the genius of Walter Gropius.

Never was the truth of the prophet being derided at home more applicable than in his case. His prophecy begins, as is proper, with a word. The name of his creation was to be: "The Bauhaus, *Hochschule für Gestaltung.*" The word "Gestaltung" embodies the philosophy he envisaged.

If the term "Bauhaus" was a new adaptation of the medieval concept of the "Bauhütte," the headquarters of the cathedral builders, the term "Gestaltung" is old, meaningful and so nearly untranslatable that it has found its way into English usage. Beyond the significance of shaping, forming, thinking through, it has the flavor underlining the totality of such fashioning, whether of an artifact or of an idea. It forbids the nebulous and the diffuse. In its fullest philosophical meaning it expresses the Platonic *eidolon*, the *Urbild*, the pre-existing form. The feeling for the close neighborhood of pure thought and concrete substance is essentially German. In the sense and nonsense of the poetry of Christian Morgenstern, I should not dare to decide which is uppermost. A quatrain of his, antedating the founding of the Bauhaus, speaks of the dilemma of *nous* and *physis*, and although I wish to state that no conscious parallel can be proven, it remains a curiously felicitous anticipation:

> Wenn ich sitze möcht' ich nicht
> sitzen wie mein Sitzfleisch möchte,
> sondern wie mein Sitzgeist sich,
> sässe er, den Sitz sich flöchte.

While still in army service, Gropius had been invited to plan for a reorganization and possible fusion of two schools in Weimar, the Academy of Fine Arts and the Arts and Crafts School, both under the auspices of the Grand Duke of Saxe-Weimar. Given full powers and funds to start with, Gropius was able to issue his first invitations to three artists in 1919: Johannes Itten, Lyonel Feininger and Gerhard Marcks. Paul Klee and Oskar Schlemmer accepted calls in 1921, Kandinsky in 1922, and Moholy-Nagy in 1923. Of the seven artists, six were painters, one a sculptor; only one of them, Johannes Itten, had definite ideas about art education and had taught previously. These men were to be "Masters of Form," each presiding jointly with technical "Master of Craft" over one of the workshops: Carpentry (furniture), Metal, Weaving, Ceramics, Color Design (wall painting), Stone-cutting, Printing and Bookbinding, Glass. The Stage class assumed importance only gradually. In the program of studies drawn up at the opening of school and reported by Gropius under the title Idee und Aubau des Staatlichen Bauhauses ("Idea and Structure of the Bauhaus"), a well-designed curriculum was stipulated, in which the mainstay of instruction was to be built around the apprentice-journeyman-master relationship of the German Artisans' Guilds. A theory of design was to evolve out of a return to the crafts, both practice and theory to be informed by the common spirit of architecture. This was the scaffolding around which life and instruction at the Bauhaus was to unfold.

If, in our time, the term "revolutionary" is perhaps a little too readily applied to the latest detergent or an extra fin clapped onto the latest car model, it does rightly belong to the Bauhaus idea; not, as has often been thought, because chairs, pots, lamps, etc. designed at the Bauhaus looked very different from other lamps, pots, and chairs, but because of the pedagogical thought. Where in pre-revolutionary Germany (or elsewhere) had there been a school in which the masters carefully inquired of the students what, and how, they ought to be taught? One cannot repeat often enough that, if a design following a particular bent developed later, there had been, at the outset, no preconceived idea of what it should look like. Even the industrial angle, the designing of new types of goods for mass production, so characteristic of later, was not "taught" at first. If it was in the back of Gropius' mind, it was not in the students'. This change came, as the form masters thought, prematurely and because of undue outside pressure from the legislature, which wanted to be able to show "results" to their constituents. The really revolutionary concept is to be found in the method of teaching rather than in the anticipated results. Gropius' steadfast ideal was the "collective work of art — Architecture" (der Bau), and means to realize this had to be found. The way as he saw it, was the grouping of a staff of strongly formed individuals into a nucleus of "influence." "Form," once achieved in one field, for example in painting, must be applicable to other fields. The painter or sculptor, without giving up his art, must bring his formal findings to bear on the student's problems of design; he must teach not painting, but "form." Not a little to ask. Yet it came about. But it could never have happened, had not the students of the early years been what they were, "goal-directed" as we would say today, through privation, suffering, indignation at the failure of a system; hungry for a spiritual rebirth. They came to the Bauhaus ready for the experiment. An authoritarian epoch had come abruptly to a close with the flight of the Kaiser. Out of political, economic, moral chaos, the intellectual avant-garde, only yesterday a derided minority, was called upon to help to regenerate society. The incomparable shock action of the Bauhaus idea came from the unity of purpose of a group of people fortifying themselves against a wilderness. There was nothing of the ivory tower in this isolation. It was the necessary defense of the pioneer in his stockade: he meant to establish himself in the land. Everybody was poor — the inflation saw to that; but the early Bauhaus community represented the religious attitude of the poor in spirit. If the standard of living was low (things came to such a pass that tuition fees had to be waived altogether), the sights were set high. The "Bauhäusler" of 1920 was a lean-jawed, wide-eyed apparition, in extraordinary garments, running to bare legs and sandals, long locks on male heads and bobbed hair on women, causing unending scandal to the citizens. But beneath the eccentric appearance there was devotion to an idea, a burning desire for spiritual things, a willingness to pass through the most harassing errors on the quest — a horde of seekers from a page of Dostoevsky. Enthusiasm alternated with profound dejection. They were indefatigable arguers; obstructionist and full of complaints one day, the next they would set to work in a concerted effort without rest, if the cause required it. Distrustful of leadership and touchy even about "influence," they could show self-discipline and loyalty toward their director and masters when threatened from the outside.

Lyonel Feininger reported some of his early impressions of prospective students as follows:

May 1919. The students I have seen up to now look very self-confident. Almost all have been in the army, it is a new type, a new generation. They are not as timid and harmless as the old professors here imagine.

(The "old professors" were the pre-war faculty of the academy, who withdrew from the Bauhaus shortly afterward.)

May 1919. How often I am struck these days with the fact that these young people are not babies . . . that they accept nothing without a quite merciless scrutiny. . . . Expressionism for them is the symbol of their generation and of their belongings.

June 1919. These consultations with students are amongst the affairs uppermost in my mind. I often ponder on the way of establishing a working relationship with students. I think I have it now: leading and help- ing them along, talking freely to them and exchanging thoughts and ideas. I feel strong and rich, I am convinced that I can contribute to their develop- ment without forcing them into something foreign to their nature. The trust they place in me is very wonderful.

The form masters were free to accept pupils for their own instruction, but the official plan did not incorporate painting classes as such. Lyonel Fein- inger was in charge of the printing workshop.

Gropius' attitude towards the beaux arts is expressed in the document referred to above (Idee und Aufbau): "The fundamental peda- gogic mistake of the Academy arose from its preoccupation with the idea of individual genius, and its discounting the value of commendable achieve- ment on a less exalted level." This is beautifully clear, both in its rejection of a former approach, and in its adoption of the new attitude of the Bauhaus. Like many other ideological statements, it is not free from paradox. The noble, republican distrust of the academic hierarchy of yesterday came from a man whose very soul was that of the gentleman, aristocratic *malgré lui*. And, in order to build up a school in which achievement was to be valued on a "less exalted level" he invited famous painters who might well attempt to found a new academy under his nose. This danger was averted, not without frequent clashes and even an occasional crash: sessions of the Meister-Rat (council of masters) were apt to be fiery affairs.

To return to Lyonel Feininger for a moment: the quotations speak of the inner searches of an artist about to face a very new situation. While this was also true for the other appointees, with the exception of Itten, who needed no coaxing, they were by temperament more inclined to enter into the spirit of collaborating on a common curriculum than my father, who adhered to the idea of the "artist in residence" and relied upon influence rather than classroom teaching. He thus chose to stay with the Bauhaus after the transfer to Dessau, as an unsalaried and non-teaching member of the community. The trend of teaching, however, grew steadily in the opposite direction, toward classes and lectures. But in considering these differences of approach I seem to see the best illustration of the visionary power of Gropius' plan, which was based on his expectations of results coming from the total personality of his collaborators rather than from their opinions. In this light it is interesting to note that the most "trained" and experienced educator on the staff, Itten, was the least able to submit to the collective plan and left the Bauhaus early.

The period from 1922 to 1924 was crucial for the Bauhaus. The big Bauhaus exhibition of 1923 was decided upon in 1922. This had been the result of outside pressure, to which Gropius added the weight of his own persuasion against the inclination both of masters and students, who felt that this demand for public demonstration was premature and apt to endanger the educational growth. Gropius was able to convince the staff that without this concession the days of the school were numbered. The exhibition, today a landmark in the history of modern art, showed conclusively the validity of the aims of the institution. Although it marks the beginning of the end of the Weimar period, it established without doubt that the Bauhaus was of interest not only to the nation, but to Europe. The effect of the demonstration was overwhelmingly favorable everywhere except among the local reactionaries. The invitation of the city of Dessau for the Bauhaus to move there was a direct result.

Not surprisingly we find that during this period of intense effort the ideological picture began to clarify. The era of pure experimentation had come to an end. Profitable production, to be achieved only through collaboration with industry, was declared to be essential henceforth. This turn was distinctly unpalatable to a portion of the Bauhaus population, although the majority of masters and students accepted it, partly as inevitable and partly as wholly desirable. The ways are beginning to part: if henceforth the workshops were to concentrate on type design for industrial production, and an architecture class requiring mathematics, physics, and appropriate courses in statics, graphics, etc. was to replace the private "Baubüro," on the other hand the "artists" obtained more recognition of their aims. Regular courses were instituted by Klee and Kandinsky; these became obligatory for all students in Dessau. Beyond this, free painting under the tutelage of these two masters was made available. If in this way gains were registered for both wings of opinion at the school, it is only just to point out that the very forming of these wings constituted a weakening of the initial structure, in which unity was sought through exploration of the interrelatedness of all the disciplines, when all problems of design were formal, and where the eventual creation of a chair for instance (in the Morgensternian sense alluded to earlier) could be the result of processes not differing in their nature from the creation of a painting or a piece of sculpture.

With this loss of the pristine joy and innocence of discovery the Bauhaus entered its mature age. A great deal of substance had been acquired. Although the move to Dessau in 1925 saw various departures in other directions, five students rose to master rank, all destined to make significant contributions: Josef Albers, Herbert Bayer, Marcel Breuer, Hinnerk Scheper, Joost Schmidt. Of the original three masters, only Feininger went on to Dessau, as resident artist; the teaching staff was thus completely renewed. The workshops also underwent changes. Stone cutting, ceramics, glass workshops were discontinued; the former block-printing and book-binding shop evolved into a typographical print shop with elements of advertising art taught jointly with the craft, first under Herbert Bayer and later under Joost Schmidt. The stage, a somewhat poorly defined undertaking in the beginning, was to become a regular workshop furnished with an experimental theater and put under the guidance of Oskar Schlemmer.

The invitation to Dessau, and the erection of the magnificent complex of buildings for Bauhaus use were due to the forward-looking and liberal city council under the progressive leadership of the mayor, Fritz Hesse. The Bauhaus, after seeing its fulfillment in Dessau in a seven-year period — under the direction of Gropius (1925–1928), Hannes Meyer (1928–1930) and Mies van der Rohe (1930–1932) — succumbed together with other institutions to the Nazi régime. Toward the end it had been under attack from left- as well as right-wing extremists.

The outlook in December 1926, when the building was formally inaugurated, was certainly bright. The school had a right to feel that it had proven itself. The population of the State of Anhalt was industrial and liberal, instead of agricultural and backward. The halls and ghosts of the Grand-Ducal academy had been left behind. The harassing era of inflation had ended two years earlier, and stabilization of the German currency had brought a period of optimism and bright business outlook.

From this period on I am able to speak of "teaching at the Bauhaus" from personal experience. All masters conformed to the idea in appealing to self-discipline on the part of the students, and in refraining from imposing tasks and assignments. Ideas were emitted, and if a student chose to work with the idea, well and good; if not, no more was said about it. There were no "grades," no tests nor examinations. Performance in the workshops was reviewed periodically by the form and technical masters, and warnings were issued to doubtful cases; continual failure to produce might result in exclusion from the school. No doubt it was possible to attend a good many classes without learning anything. But this was, at the Bauhaus as well as at a more traditional school, the loss of the student, and, no degrees being given, it is certain that the Bauhaus graduated fewer incompetents than any other institution I can think of. This is largely due to the high motivation of the great majority of applicants for admission. Only in the last few years was there a decline in the standards for acceptance. Participation in party politics was first permitted under the directorship of Hannes Meyer and its corroding effect hastened the process of dissolution begun when Gropius relinquished his post.

The most characteristic of all Bauhaus courses was the Vorkurs of Josef Albers. The idea of a probationary experimental semester, at the end of which admission to a workshop and the school proper could be granted or refused, was carried over from the Weimar years, when it had existed under Itten and Georg Muche. The concept of the course itself, however, was so drastically changed by Albers that nothing but the name remained. The emphasis was on possibilities of construction in a variety of materials, principally wood, paper, metal. The properties of the materials were to be experienced through dividing and combining them, with a minimum of tools and with as little waste as possible. In fastening pieces together, the resources of each respective material were to be exploited to the full; for example, metal can be bent, but wood cannot without a considerable apparatus; metal needs to be cut, but paper can be torn, etc. Expendable materials of ordinary daily life were favored; I remember a most impressive structure composed of nothing but used safety razor blades (which are slotted and punched by the manufacturer) and burnt-up wooden matches. The most marvelous aspect of this kind of work is that it was not "taught" in any strict sense of the word at all. Very much in the spirit we have seen in Schlemmer's discourse, ideas were broached in a general way, some kind of hidden talent of invention was appealed to, and the resulting response was astonishing. But one felt a tremendous conviction emanating from Albers, a great joy in what he was doing, also a certain humility with which even quite wretched works were discussed with the purpose of inducing deeper insight in the student. One of my first impressions of the Vorkurs is Albers introducing a stapler, not so common then as now, and demonstrating its various possibilities with great inward satisfaction, including a statement of the American origin of the machine. I also remember his leading us through a cardboard box factory, a depressing place to me (I confess), and pointing out manufacturing particulars, both good and bad (i.e. capable of improvement), with the kind of religious concentration one would expect from a lecturer in the Louvre. The criteria for evaluation of the works were structural invention and static and tensile strength. Aesthetic values were not sought, and were condemned as a point of departure. The absence of any "purpose" in these exercises strengthened the "functional" feeling: another paradox! The function was, to be as much wood, metal, paper, as possible, to be paper to the top of one's bent, so to speak. These things are nowadays almost common property, but they weren't thirty-three years ago. Moreover, they were not done to be an end in themselves, but in order to find out what workshop would be best suited to the student's abilities.

I am evoking early memories of my own encounter with an artist whose post-Bauhaus work is probably better known in this country than that of any other Bauhaus master — through his teaching at Black Mountain College and, since 1950, at Yale, as well as through his exhibitions. I have heard Albers called anti-intellectual, but I think that his preoccupation with what he calls "ordinary sense" conceals a deeper meaning. He does not so much glorify the "lowbrow" as reproach the highbrow with his one-sidedness. He wants to put his students in touch with unknown parts of themselves; his aim is really psychological even though his doctrine is, or affects to be, quite matter-of-fact and practical. To the patient persuasion of his early teaching method he has added in later years the feature of shocking his audience into recognition of the pre-existence of formal relations. He sees no reason to give up control over the artifact; he distinguishes between "the work of art" and "the ability to paint." He has said of himself: "I believe that thought is as useful in art as anywhere else, and that a clear head does not bar access to feeling (*aux sentiments purs*)."

One may say that the function of Albers' teaching was to seek to create the highest degree of "useful uselessness": something which was a true symbol (and therefore valid), an instrument of understanding, something needful to painter as well as to educator, architect and designer. And in conjunction with the necessary reverence for precision in geometrical exploration, I would underscore the important factor of the *play* with simple geometrical form. Its meaning can become portentously symbolic if it makes us re-examine such forbidding philosophies as nineteenth century utilitarianism, which sought to outlaw play (cf. Dickens' *Hard Times*). In our own time the need for play has been discovered to have an almost, or perhaps quite, deadly earnestness about it, by no means confined to the young, although perhaps best understood when playing with them. One is here confronted with an archetype. Play is in its nature symbolic, and the symbol is generative of consciousness. Direction is not excluded: we direct children but the mature learn easily how to direct their own play; and if they are talented (this sort of experience presupposes some talent if it is to extend into adult dimensions) they learn to recognize the signs of proximity to the hidden treasure of comprehension (that is, an addition to consciousness). When the sign is beheld, work replaces play. The treasure must not only be raised, but spent wisely. One without the other remains infantile. Paul Klee in his highly specialized language is saying the same thing, and his art draws its vitality from the same, the only, source: man's fugitive chemistry rooted in the cosmos, the immortal soul in the born and dying body with its senses.

At the termination of the probationary semester, the work done by each student was exhibited, a choice of a workshop was made, and the council of form masters under the chairmanship of Gropius passed on the merit of the performance and of the selection of the future field of studies. I squeaked through with a warning from the masters to pay more attention to the program of studies, and was admitted to the stage workshop.

My choice was the outcome of seeing with breathless excitement, admiration, and wonder an evening's performance of the stage class in the Bauhaus theater. At an early age I had occupied myself intensely with the making of masks in various materials, I hardly could say why, yet sensing dimly that in this form of creation a meaning lay hidden for me. On the Bauhaus stage, these intuitions seemed to acquire body and life. I had beheld the "Dance of Gestures" and the "Dance of Forms," executed by dancers in metallic masks and costumed in padded, sculptural suits. The stage, with jet-black backdrop and wings, contained magically spotlighted, geometrical furniture: a cube, a white sphere, steps; the actors paced, strode, slunk, trotted, dashed, stopped short, turned slowly and majestically; arms with colored gloves were extended in a beckoning gesture; the copper and gold and silver heads (the masks were full round, covering the entire head, and, apart from the color of the metal foil they were covered with, were identical in shape and design) were laid together, flew apart; the silence was broken by a whirring sound, ending in a small thump; a crescendo of buzzing noises culminated in a crash followed by portentous and dismayed silence. Another phase of the dance had all the formal and contained violence of a chorus of cats, down to the meowling and bass growls, which were marvelously accentuated by the resonant mask-heads. Pace and gesture, figure and prop, color and sound, all had the quality of elementary form, demonstrating anew the problem of the theater of Schlemmer's concept: man in space. What we had seen had the significance of expounding the stage elements (Die Bühnenelemente), a project developed more fully in the work of the following years. The stage elements were assembled, re-grouped, amplified, and gradually grew into something like a "play," we never found out whether comedy or tragedy, because its career was stopped by changes befalling the stage class. The interesting feature about it was that, with a set of formal elements agreed upon and, on this common basis, added to fairly freely by members of the class, "play" with meaningful form was expected eventually to yield meaning, sense or message; that gestures and sounds would become speech and plot. Who knows? This was, essentially, a dancers' theater and as such, sufficient unto itself as Oskar Schlemmer's genius had created it; but it was also a "class," a locale of learning, and this rather magnificent undertaking was Schlemmer's tool of instruction.

Periodically sketches and productions were performed to a Bauhaus or public audience. The composition of the troupe is difficult to characterize in few words; the Bauhaus stage did not train pupils in ballet or choreography, but it attracted persons who had ideas and interest in this field and gave them an opportunity to lend their talents to the work. Some of the best dancers were volunteers working their way through the school in some other workshop (Walter Kaminsky, Lou Scheper, Werner

Siedhoff). For a full-scale performance, Schlemmer could muster an impressive number of participants (in the late twenties the Bauhaus stage gave performances by invitation in several major theaters throughout the country), while the work of the numerically small stage class proper consisted in the design, making and taking care of masks, costumes, equipment, and, in the form of a council with Schlemmer presiding, the planning, guiding, coordinating of further choreographic developments, sketches and inventions.

Schlemmer's teaching methods were stamped by great self-denial. To me, as an enthusiastic and very young admirer, it often seemed incomprehensible that a man with so much to give should yield so meekly to a not always enlightened majority. I wanted him to assert himself. It took many years to realize that this way was closed to him, and that the secret lay in his personal psychology — that in this respect he could not choose. Conviction was smouldering within, one felt, but could not be voiced. I vividly remember his exclamation in times of mental stress: "Janein!" — and only action, demonstration, a physical manifestation could bring relief. Then indeed it was a treat to watch the precision, aplomb, the power and the delicacy of action. His language, too, although unable to assume command, was an expressive tool. His was the most personal vocabulary I have ever known. His invention of metaphors was inexhaustible; he loved unaccustomed juxtapositions, paradoxical alliterations, baroque hyperbole. The satirical wit of his writings is quite untranslatable.

Of the other masters with whom I was acquainted, I can report but little that would contribute to the picture of teaching at the Bauhaus I am trying to give. If, of Paul Klee and of Wassily Kandinsky, I retain indeed an immense respect and warm personal affection for their personalities, and of Moholy-Nagy a memory of infectious enthusiasm and delight in experimentation, I miss, on the other hand, that element of response in me which seems to me so characteristic for the intellectual climate of the Bauhaus, that degree of interaction of teacher and pupil. In a contribution to a Festschrift for Schlemmer's seventieth birthday* I said that I learned from Schlemmer not so much stagecraft as teaching, and this I would extend to

* Privately published in September, 1958, by Frau Tut Schlemmer in Stuttgart.

my contact with Albers. I must have been one of the worst students ever to pass through his course, as far as the immediate outcome of the contact is concerned. But I find that he has made a lasting imprint upon my awareness through his insistence on basic elements of design. He and Schlemmer induced independent action on the part of the student through an appeal to inherent and collective faculties: the urge to play. And Schlemmer's dancer, in his costume and mask, in his relations to architectural space, remains an experience as fertile formally as Albers' prime geometrical shapes. Through their personal intercourse with the symbol, both men have expanded the frontiers of consciousness — the ultimate purpose of all teaching.

When, nineteen years ago, I was to become a teacher myself, I had in common with the early Bauhaus members the fact that I had been a soldier in a war. All else was diametrically opposed: I was *not* famished, there had been *no* revolution, the war I had "fought" in was won, not lost. And where the Bauhaus student of 1919 embraced freedom for the first time in his life, the students at my first college were so steeped in all kinds of freedom that they did not know what to do with it. The one word that caught my attention during the first interviews was the stated need for discipline. And in essence I find that it is still so now, the need for order in a chaos not social but spiritual. In the art of our time we are in the midst of a fantastic revolution. Art, as the last resort of the manifestation of "useless" values, in the fact of an all-devouring and hideous materialism *not* alleviated by "65% of the population participating in some form of church activity," has become impenetrably mysterious, inward, romantic, menacing — perhaps psychotic. The last attempts to extract objective meaning from its embodiments are hopelessly obscured by the fact that it has become a highly marketable commodity.

Since I teach painting, not philosophy, the truth which I believe capable of saving us is embodied in geometrical form. In my method of instruction I proceed from the surface to the depths; beginning with the raw material of painting — color, pigments — we progress toward perceptions of the relations of color and shapes in nature. Trying, at this impressionistic stage of development, to arrange color-shapes in a pictorial sense (still-life) we discover the function of light, at first as a modeling agent of optical shapes. If light (and shade) can express the surface aspects of ob-

186 jects, color becomes superfluous. If, on the other hand, color is wanted in painting because of its pure, that is to say emotive and spiritual, qualities, which by themselves have nothing to do with terms of light and shade, the concept of the picture must necessarily penetrate beyond surface aspects of objects. Already the inner being of the student is engaged at this phase, and he eagerly asks for new shapes to give to the awakening inventiveness. Here freedom ought to step in and just here it is where it becomes so weighty a burden: "Do we have to do what we want to do?" How hard it is to abandon the question for the meaning of things! How brutally hard, to digest that Mephistophelian truth:

> Wie würde dich die Einsicht kränken
> wer kann was Dummes, wer was Kluges denken,
> das nicht die Vorwelt schon gedacht?

If I had encountered, and suffered from, this atrocious stage of growth myself, I recognized a little afterward that what had happened to me was fairly typical of our time. It was then that the significance of my Bauhaus studies revealed itself to me: constructible precision of form necessarily led back to the ultimate ground from which all imagination springs (let us call it "geometrical" for lack of a better word); so long as we remember that "measuring the earth" was, in the infancy of mankind, a differently venturesome proceeding from what it would be today. Geometrical relations then became for me the carriers of new color ideas — for a while. This experience of renovation I try to make accessible to students. It is not necessary to underline constantly the symbolic meaning of such relations. The symbol is effective despite our initial (and perhaps perpetual) lack of consciousness. All that is necessary is to have experienced it oneself. I conclude with another, and last, discovery of parallel formulation: in a poem by Josef Albers, I found the lines:

> Thus art is not an object
> but experience.

Ludwig Mies van der Rohe
with students of his
architectural seminar
Dessau, 1931
Photo: Pius Pahl

Advertising workshop at
the Bauhaus
Dessau, around 1928
Photo: unknown

Weaving plant at the
Bauhaus
Dessau, around 1927
Photo: Archive of Gunta
Stadler-Stölzl

The Bauhaus jazz band
Dessau, 1928
Photo: T. Lux Feininger

"jonny-schawinsky
spielt auf"
Xanti Schawinsky with
saxophone
Photo: T. Lux Feininger

Werner Jackson and
T. Lux Feininger (right)
on the roof of the
Feininger/Moholy-Nagy
master house
Dessau, around 1927
Photo: unknown

Bauhaus students "ready
to dance"
Dessau, 1928
Photo: unknown

Alfred Arndt on his
Bauhaus student
identification card
Dessau, 1926
Photo: Archive of
Alfred Arndt

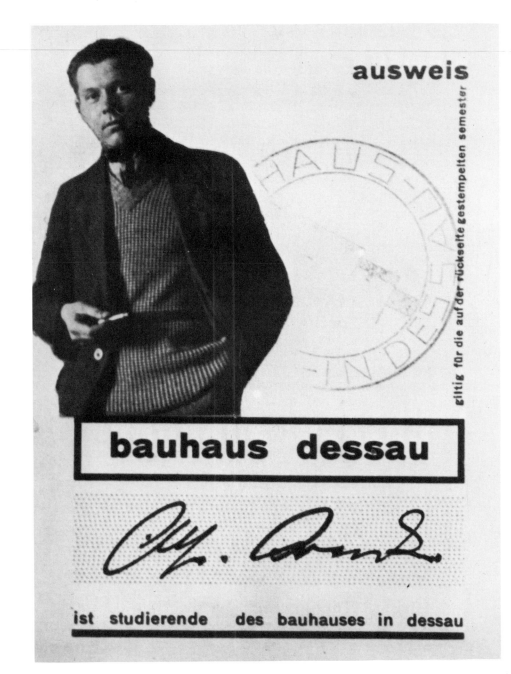

ausweis

gültig für die auf der rückseite gestempelten semester

bauhaus dessau

ist studierende des bauhauses in dessau

Hannes Beckmann:

Born in Stuttgart in 1909. He studied at the Bauhaus in Dessau starting in 1928. At the end of his studies in 1932 Beckmann received a Bauhaus diploma for his work in stage design. Among his teachers at the Bauhaus were Josef Albers, Paul Klee, and Wassily Kandinsky. After his studies Beckmann was offered a position as set designer for the Landestheater in Dessau. However, the political climate of hostility toward the members of the Bauhaus at that time prevented his acceptance of the offer. In Vienna Hannes Beckmann studied photography at the Grafischen Lehr- und Versuchsanstalt and in 1934 he established himself in Prague as a press and theatrical photographer. Since his wife was Jewish, he was frequently interrogated by the Gestapo and was finally sent to Janovice concentration camp, from which he was liberated at the end of the war. In 1947 he was granted Czechoslovakian citizenship and a year later emigrated to the United States.

In New York for the next few years, he was the head of the photography department of the Solomon R. Guggenheim Museum of Art. Since 1953 Beckmann has been professor of two-dimensional design and color theory at Cooper Union School of Art and Architecture in New York. In 1961–1962 he was guest lecturer at Yale University. His paintings hang in several museums and important private collections in the United States, and he has taken part in many group shows, among them "The Responsive Eye" at the Museum of Modern Art in 1965. He lives in New York.

Formative years

It is, of course, difficult after thirty-eight years to remember events that took place when I was young and not fully aware of the importance of them. But looking back I know that the work done by the Bauhaus impressed me as a new creative force on the cultural scene. I was then nineteen years old and studying at the Kunstschule in Hamburg under Professor X.

On the first day I was placed in an enormously large studio in front of a cactus plant, which I had to draw for many hours, everyday for several weeks, and all these weeks I was alone in the studio. Two other students of Professor X, who called themselves master students, worked in another studio. Twice during the day, Professor X entered the room to take a look at my drawings, glancing over the rim of his spectacles and shaking his head disapprovingly before leaving the room, without saying a word. I was very unhappy then.

One day I met my former art teacher from high school. I told him about my Kafka-like experience. He said in his Berlin dialect: "Man, you are nuts to waste your time there. If I were young today I would go and study at the Bauhaus. There they have some quite different ideas from your Herr Professor X."

So, one day after having traveled all night from Hamburg to Dessau, I was standing in front of the then ultra-modern Bauhaus building. Its architecture represented to me the beginning of a new era.

There was, as I found out, a spirit of confidence — of optimism and excitement at this school that I had missed so much at the Hamburg Kunstschule, and so I became an enthusiastic and devoted Bauhäusler.

One of the most important and decisive experiences for me was the Vorkurs conducted by Josef Albers. Every student had to go through this preliminary course to prove his abilities, before he was finally accepted.

I remember vividly the first day of the Vorkurs, Josef Albers entered the room, carrying with him a bunch of newspapers, which were distributed among the students. He then addressed us, saying something like this: "Ladies and gentlemen, we are poor, not rich. We can't afford to waste materials or time. We have to make the most out of the least. All art starts with a material, and therefore we have first to investigate what our material can do. So, at the beginning we will experiment without aiming at making a product. At the moment we prefer cleverness to beauty. Economy of form depends on the material we are working with. Notice that often you will have more by doing less. Our studies should lead to constructive think-ing. All right? I want you now to take the newspapers you got and try to make something out of them that is more than you have now. I want you to respect the material and use it in a way that makes sense — preserve its inherent characteristics. If you can do without tools like knives and scis-sors, and without glue, the better. Good luck." And with these words he left the room, leaving us quite flabbergasted. He returned hours later and asked us to put the result of our efforts on the floor.

There were masks, boats, castles, airplanes, animals, and all kinds of cute little figurines. He referred to all this as kindergarten products, which could often have been made better in other materials. He pointed then at a study of extreme simplicity, made by a young Hungarian architect. He simply had taken the newspaper and folded it lengthwise so that it was standing up like a folding screen. Josef Albers explained to us how well the material was understood and utilized — how the folding process was natural to paper, because it resulted in making a pliable material stiff, so stiff that it could stand up on its smallest part: the border of the paper. He further pointed out to us that a newspaper lying on the table would have only one page visually active, where as the rest would be hidden. Now that the paper was standing up, both sides had become visually active. The paper had lost its tired look — its lazy appearance. After a while we caught on to his way of seeing and thinking. Fascinating studies in all kinds of materials, like paper, corrugated cardboard, kitchen matches, wire, metal, were produced.

We were provided with brass plates approximately nine by twelve inches (twenty-four by thirty centimeters) in size, and metal scissors. The assignment was to use the material in such a way that its inherent quality was preserved. I simply cut along the diagonals of the rectangular brass plate, stopping just before the center of the plate. Then I twisted the two triangular forms at the top and bottom ninety degrees. The four resulting wings were connected by the half-inch center point where the four diagonal cuts met. Such point connection is, of course, only possible in metal. Any further twisting would have broken off the wings. Josef Albers in his criticism pointed out that the process used to make this study was of the greatest simplicity: four equilength cuts and two twists. He suggested one further improvement. Up until now the metal study was standing on four points. By twisting very gently the two side wings at the bottom, the center pieces would be raised and the whole metal study would now rest on only three points, taking on a more dynamic appearance resembling a bird in flight. "Why stand on four legs when three will do?" Albers remarked.

Through the Vorkurs a whole new world of seeing and thinking opened up to us. Most students had come to the Bauhaus with set ideas about art and design. They were usually romantic cliché ideas. But we soon learned that habitual thinking was in the way of creative thinking. The Vorkurs was a kind of group therapy. Seeing the solutions made by other students, we learned quickly to recognize the most elegant solution to a given problem. We also learned to exercise self-criticism, which was considered more important than criticism. No doubt this type of "brainwashing" that we were exposed to in the Vorkurs resulted in clearer thinking.

I was fortunate to meet Josef Albers again after the war, in the United States, where he was already known as a great teacher and fine painter. He conducted at the time a course in New York City called Laboratory in Design. I had signed up for this course. He introduced me to the class, saying jokingly: "This man studied with me twenty-one years ago, and now he comes back to listen to my nonsense all over again." But it was just his NO-nonsense approach that made me come back.

One of the most original contributions to art education that Josef Albers made in the United States was his color course. Similar courses are now conducted at universities and art schools all over the country by several of his former students, including myself. The basic principle of this course is to learn about color by direct perception. Rather than getting involved in the intricacies of pigment performance, it is preferable to choose colors from a set of over two-hundred colored papers. (In the United States such papers are available under the name Color-Aid paper.) Paper, as such, suggests the use of clean-cut forms to produce simple two-dimensional designs, which permit color changes, transparency effects, optical mixtures, vibrations, and other basic color phenomena to show. The constant necessity to compare the sheets of colored papers until one finds the right color develops sensitivity and color memory.

In 1963 Yale University published a big volume by Josef Albers, under the title *Interaction of Color.* It contains eighty-one silk-screen-printed, large folders of fascinating color studies, many done by his students.

Looking back at the Bauhaus years, I cannot help asking in which direction the Bauhaus would have developed, assuming that the irrationalism of nationalism had not brutally interrupted its development.

During the *Sturm und Drang Jahre des Bauhaus* in Weimar, its founder Walter Gropius proclaimed: "Architects, sculptors, painters, we must all turn to crafts." But when the Bauhaus moved from Weimar to Dessau, technological functionalism, rather than a revival of the crafts, was stressed, often at the expense of psychological function.

Painting and other artistic activities were in danger of becoming isolated, and the Bauhaus seemed to develop into a school of architecture and industrial design only. It was at this time that the student council requested that lectures about Gestalt psychology should be given. The request was granted, and von Dürkheim came from Leipzig to give a series of lectures on this subject. Up until this time design problems were more or less solved on the feeling level. It looked as if the artist asked the scientists for reassurance that they were on the right track. The Gestalt psychologists had after all for years investigated how we perceive and interpret form and color in the mind. They explained the reason why some configurations make for good reading — for a good Gestalt, where the whole makes more than the sum of its parts — whereas other configurations will make for bad reading, for a bad Gestalt, where parts remain apart.

It may be that the interest of the Bauhaus, a school in Gestalt psychology itself, Hochschule für Gestaltung, points to the direction that future art schools will take. Realizing that art, as such, can not be taught, the emphasis may be on visual education, partly based on Gestalt psychological insight, with an aim to achieve what Josef Albers calls: "A meaningful approach to the production of form."

Sigfried Giedion:

SEE BIOGRAPHY, PAGE 76

About the practical output of the Bauhaus

The achievements of the Bauhaus are twofold: the creation of new prototypes and the creation of a new teaching method. In pedagogy one utilizes scholastically already-known facts, in order to introduce students to their professions. It was different at the Bauhaus. In its high-tension atmosphere types were created that did not exist before.

As is well known, the Bauhaus intended to bridge the gap between artistic form and industrial production. There possibly Walter Gropius' early impressions, which he received as manager of the studio of Peter Behrens in Berlin, have contributed. The industrialist Ernst Rathenau enabled Behrens to influence industrial design in a large company for the first time. The Bauhaus aimed at educating the rising generation in the practical field, producing a generation capable of designing prototypes of pure form for industrial mass production. It cannot be described here how the student was educated to participate in the long refining process from the design to the industrial model.

In Dessau from 1925 to 1928 the experimental laboratories of Weimar or, as Paul Klee termed them: "the association with visual media," paid off.

A completely new generation came to the foreground, grown up in the atmosphere of the Bauhaus, including such masters as Josef Albers (Vorkurs), Herbert Bayer (typography), Marcel Breuer (carpentry), and many more. This is quite an achievement for an educational institution lasting only a few years.

Newly designed mass products sprung from seemingly secluded studios. Typical of this is the invention of the steel tube chair by Marcel Breuer in 1925. In the beginning the industry was not exactly enthused. When Gropius requested a few yards of steel tubing from the Mannesmann Werke for experimental purposes, he was told that there was no material available for such childish amusements. Later, however, industry changed their attitude considerably.

In the field of architecture only one example shall be mentioned. A new type of apartment house grew completely out of the atmosphere of the Bauhaus: the skyscraper made of glass panels, the skyscraper of eight to twelve stories, which is found everywhere today. This type of skyscraper was designed by Marcel Breuer for the first time in a contest for inexpensive apartments held by the Bauwelt in 1924, disproving the idea of concentrated mass due to its platelike shape. Walter Gropius fought in vain an intensive but hopeless battle for the realization of this type of dwelling up to 1933. The first glass-panel house in Rotterdam was built by van Tijen in 1934.

Georg Muche:

Born in Querfurt in 1895 and spent his childhood and youth at the Rhön. In 1913 he went to Munich to study painting at the art school of Azbé. During the same year he saw Kandinsky's work at the Galerie Goltz, which confirmed everything he had ever dreamed of in his own artistic fantasies. One year later Muche moved to Berlin and began his collaboration with Herwarth Walden at the gallery Der Sturm. He had his first exhibition together with Max Ernst, Paul Klee, and Alexander Archipenko. Around 1916–1917 he taught at the art school Der Sturm, then he joined the army, remaining until the end of the First World War.

In 1920 Walter Gropius invited him to the Bauhaus in Weimar to teach and direct the weaving workshop and to participate in the educational structure of the Bauhaus program. In 1923, he became director of preparations for the Bauhaus Exhibition in Weimar and he designed and decorated the first experimental house of the Bauhaus, the Einfamilienhaus am Horn (The One Family House at the Horn), together with all the Bauhaus workshops, and its interior decoration. In 1924 he made an educational journey to the United States, in connection with projects for high-rise buildings. In 1925 he moved to Dessau with the Bauhaus. There he erected a prefabricated dwelling made of steel.

During 1927 Georg Muche left the Bauhaus and taught at the Itten School in Berlin. In 1931 he was appointed to the progressive Kunstakademie (Academy of Art) in Breslau as professor. In 1933 he was dismissed from government employment. Again in Berlin, Muche occupied himself with the technique of fresco and at the same time he taught art at a school directed by Hugo Häring.

Muche had two pictures in the Nazi exhibit "Entartete Kunst" at the *Haus der Kunst* in Munich in 1937. Other works that were the property of the museum were confiscated. In 1939 he founded a master class for textile arts at the School of Textile Engineering in Krefeld, where he utilized and completed his experiences from the Bauhaus weaving workshop. In 1942 Georg Muche worked together with Oskar Schlemmer and Willi Baumeister at the Institut für Malstoffkunde (Institute for the Science of Painting Materials) in Wuppertal, which was established *for the assistance* of artists by the industrialist Dr. Kurt Herberts.

After the war Georg Muche started to paint and exhibit again, particularly large mural paintings in fresco. He was represented in all Bauhaus exhibitions as well as all Bauhaus publications. Georg Muche collected his own essays in a book: *Blickpunkt, Sturm — Dada — Bauhaus — Gegenwart* ("Focal Point, Storm — Dada — Bauhaus — Present," Munich, 1961 and Tubingen, 1965). In 1963 he was guest of honor at the Villa Massimo in Rome. During recent years he has conducted experiments with electronic techniques in graphics. He lives in Lindau at the Bodensee.

Bauhaus epitaph

The decisive origins of the Bauhaus lay in the decade preceding its founding. In March, 1912, the Werkbund had already published something like a Bauhaus program in one of its yearbooks. "The aim of the Werkbund is the penetration of work by the collaboration of art, industry, and trade through education." In the foreword the cooperation of industry and artists in the field of mass production is already mentioned. Then comes the remarkable restriction of the later Bauhaus program, which owed its great promotional effect to the circumstance that it was romantic and that Gropius put at the center of his plan the artist's return to handicrafts. In the Werkbund yearbook, however, it is specified: "One expects salvation by the medieval artisan. The Werkbund should honor the romantics, but bravely face presence and future."

The Bauhaus was a revolutionary institution. It was also investigated in the "Arbeitsrat für Kunst" (Work Council of Art) when it was planned in Berlin. This Arbeitsrat für Kunst was a variation of the councils for workers and soldiers. In this Work Council of Art, where Walter Gropius was presiding, the problems of the school were sometimes investigated in an ideologically too subtle and unreal way. But Gropius remained faithful to the Werkbund program. By 1918 he had had the good fortune to receive instructions from the Grossherzog von Sachsen-Weimar-Eisenach to combine the school of arts and crafts and the academy, and it was even more fortunate that the revolutionary government regarded him as an exponent of the spiritual renovation and left him in charge. The Bauhaus could only gain a firm footing as a public institution because the authority of the state was unstable. At that time there were new men in the government who knew little of Klee, Feininger, and Kandinsky, nor of Gropius, but strived for a complete renovation. They therefore had no objection when Gropius surrounded himself with many "obscure" people. Obviously in our country this was a favorable situation for the beginning of such a daring undertaking as the Bauhaus.

History seems to me somewhat frightening, and I therefore want to try to write an epitaph for the Bauhaus as one who had been there, because an epitaph has to express accurately and precisely what happened. At the beginning of this epitaph it would have to be written: "Inexperience permits youth to fulfill what old age believe to be impossible." — *Tristan Bernard*. Then there would be — divided into groups — the names of Kandinsky; Feininger, Klee; these were the old and wise ones at the Bauhaus. Behind their names would be their ages at the time when Gropius called them to the Bauhaus: Kandinsky, fifty-six, Feininger, forty-eight, Klee, forty-two years. Next a small group: Gropius, thirty-six and Marcks, thirty years old. In the postscript would be explained why they formed the nucleus. The third group: Schreyer, Schlemmer, Itten, Moholy-Nagy, Muche; at the time of their appointments they were thirty-five, thirty-three, thirty-one, twenty-eight, and twenty-five years respectively. This meeting of generations is of great significance. Finally there would be a group of Bauhaus masters: Albers, Bayer, Breuer, Scheper, Stölzl, and Arndt. Among them, solitary and alone: Mies van der Rohe. Below all this would be the sentence:

"Only the middle and the end enlighten the darkness of the beginning."
— *Goethe*.

What came out of the meeting of generations, the old one — Kandinsky, Feininger, Klee, and the young one — Schreyer, Schlemmer, Itten, Moholy-Nagy, and Muche; and what distinguished them?

We had the advantage of our youth, we abandoned ourselves to a common cause, thus forgetting our own aims. They had the advantage of their age, they never lost sight of their aims. They operated quietly, we were prepared to work like slaves without participating in the harvest and profit. Theirs was the glory. They were the originators of a new world of imagination. We, each of us, were born too late. They were the explorers of a new continent in the ocean of the intellectual stream at the beginning of the century. We were building paths through the jungle of their discoveries and we designed the plans. They had conquered their adversaries. We needed courage to make brave decisions for new adventures. Only one thing we had in common. Their creative work and our creative work each had its origin in painting. Painting formed the base of our understanding and teaching when we — one after the other — met the architect Walter Gropius in Weimar, who was the founder of the Bauhaus, and Gerhard Marcks, the sculptor, who best represented Gropius' ideas on teaching of crafts. Both belonged to the Werkbund.

To their creators, creative actions that, seen from a distance, seem miraculous, were always most self-evident. We understood Gropius' ideas and transformed them, and we were transformed by Gropius. The Bauhaus was born out of the solution of contradictions and tensions. First Johannes Itten strewed new seeds into the furrows that had been dug by Gropius. These ripened a thousandfold and are still in bloom today, reaching far into the field of pedagogics. Johannes Itten's teaching of creativity went beyond the aims of Gropius. These would have been weakened if neither of them had given in. Itten yielded and left before the great Bauhaus Exhibition in 1923. But Gropius, too, had to make a sacrifice. He could not build the house that he, the founder and architect, wanted to build as a symbol of his Idea and the center of the exhibition. He could not build it because he was unable to convince the young members of the Bauhaus of the sober plans and examples in his architectural office. Their ears were deaf.

I should relate the events that occurred when it was a matter of bend or break, because they were the decisive ones. Everything at the Bauhaus was either for or against Gropius. He had the ability to lead to a common goal forces strained to breaking point. But it is not enough to praise his successes, he did more, he overcame or united oppositions by his intelligence and the courage of his heart.

It is the opinion of Ludwig Mies van der Rohe that the reason for the great influence of the Bauhaus all over the world lay in the fact that the Bauhaus was an idea. Was this the real reason? I cannot believe this because much too often ideas remain without any effect. If, however, it was an idea, then it must have been one nobody else had. Something mysteriously obscure? This, too, I do not want to believe. What was it then? What made the Bauhaus so effective? It was the gathering of a few people of distinct individualities who acknowledged the same cause and yet did not comprise a team, but produced a chord that was eventually heard all over the world. The independent guidance of several leaders changed often and very fast at the Bauhaus. Everybody was at one time the most important person and another time the most superfluous one.

Born in Halle on the Saale in 1893. He took his degree at the Halle University under Professor Karl Frankl. In 1924 Grote was nominated as permanent curator and director of the Dessau Municipal Gallery. There he worked extensively with Mayor Fritz Hesse to have the Bauhaus moved from Weimar to Dessau, and he remained in close and friendly contact with the Bauhaus people. Because of his interest in the Bauhaus and also his connection with modern art, he was dismissed from his government post in 1933.

He then settled in Berlin as free-lance writer, and later in Munich. From 1949 to 1951 he was in charge of the exhibitions at the Haus der Kunst (House of Art) in Munich. These included works by Der blaue Reiter; Max Beckmann; Oskar Kokoscha; and in 1950, as a first survey after the war, the painters at the Bauhaus. In 1951 he was appointed general director of the Germanic National Museum at Nuremberg. Since 1963, he has been working professionally once again and is participating in the preparation of the exhibition "50 Years of the Bauhaus," which originated at Stuttgart in 1968. At present Grote is living in Gauting near Munich.

The Bauhaus and functionalism

It has become fashionable to assign the term functionalism to the new architectural movement which began in the early twenties, and to look upon the Bauhaus as the orthodox representation of form derived from function only. For several years new tendencies in architecture have become noticeable and have stood up against the functionalism of the fathers' and grandfathers' generation by proclaiming humanization and individualization in the creation of form.

The German *Werkbund,* from which sprang the New Architecture, is also trying to keep its perspective and to find new objectives. Here, too, functionalism is the stumbling block. Hans Schwippert, the present chairman, arranged for three lectures in Baden Baden in 1964. A philosopher, a zoologist, and a politician expounded their views on the topic "Form — Its Meaning and Precepts." The personalities of the speakers — Warnach, Portmann, and Arndt — and their lectures were very impressive and afforded deep insights. What they said about the relationship between function and form, however, did not fall in with the theory of the New Architecture.

All three spoke of functionalism as an absolute and isolated concept, disregarding Gropius' or Mies' theoretical interpretation of functionalism and the way it was realized in their works. Arndt, after having rejected Mies' well-known Thomistic quotation, became openly aggressive: "Along with Hans Schwippert, I hope, therefore, that the dream of the equation of function and form has come to an end. I don't even consider this dream beautiful, but rather a nightmare, for neither the individual nor the community can be determined in merely functional terms."

This criticism was indeed directed against a dream, against an idea that was never championed by the creators of the New Architecture. Gropius has often and unmistakably clearly denied that function and form are equal.

In August of 1923 the Bauhaus and its achievements up to that time were presented to an international audience at the exhibition to which Gropius had given the title "Art and Technology — a New Unity." That is to say that form must be the synthesis of art and technology. The new credo of the Bauhaus documented its spiritual and artistic autonomy vis-à-vis 'De Stijl' and is based (as Gropius explained in volume 1 of the Bauhaus books: 'Internationale Architektur') on the realization that artistic creation must originate in life itself; and that through the revolution of the artistic mind tremendous insights into the new process of creating were gained, and through the technical revolution the tools to create. All efforts were directed toward influencing both intellectual groups. Gropius denied even then that the Bauhaus represented an apotheosis of rationalism. He tried, in fact, to determine the mutual bases and limits for both the creative and the technical areas. Every object is determined by its nature. In order to create it so as to function correctly, its nature must be explored, because the purpose must be served perfectly; this means that the object must function practically, must be durable, cheap and "beautiful." Standardization of daily vital processes is not aimed at new enslavement and mechanization of the individual; it is meant, instead, to free life from unnecessary burdens, so that it may become less hemmed in and more rewarding.

"I have always emphasized that aspect of life also which considers satisfying emotional and spiritual needs equally as important as satisfying material needs; and which sees a new concept of space as something more than mere structural economy and functional perfection. . . . The slogan 'If it's functional it's beautiful' is only half true. . . . Only perfect harmony of both the technical function and the proportions of form can produce beauty. Good architecture must reflect the life of its epoch, and that demands intimate knowledge of the biological, sociological, technical, and artistic problems. . . . It is our noblest goal to educate man so that he can see life in its totality instead of loosing himself too early in the channels of specialization." In order to place the Bauhaus amid the stream of life, Gropius gave the institute an open form that kept it from rigidity and mannerism. As soon as a new area of creativity presented itself, it was taken up and its possibilities were ascertained. When the Leica freed photography, it became a subject of instruction — as did advertising when its great importance in modern life became evident. No task was taken up in isolation but always within the framework of new order and the making of the entire human environment. Each successful creation of form made a contribution toward overcoming the state of chaos at that time. Fulfillment of purpose meant for the Bauhaus nothing other than serving mankind — humanism in the best sense of the word.

During his short-lived reign Gropius' successor, Hannes Meyer, together with his propagandist Ernst Kállai, advocated, theoretically, the narrow view that form should be determined by function only. Meyer called himself a scientific Marxist and attempted to understand human needs by means of Socialism, tables, and calculations and to eliminate the irrational influence of art. But form in his architecture and designs is obviously guided by the sense of abstraction, also. It was his formalism that forced him to leave Soviet Russia. Integration of modern art and technology has produced the New Architecture in which function is not an end in itself but rather the means to the realization of new esthetics. Therefore, the concept of functionalism does not at all do justice to the phenomenon. It would be far more appropriate to speak of abstract architecture. The unity of modern architecture and modern art is evident due to the representation of the style of its time which possesses the same capacity of assimilation as other historic styles. It is inherent in the organic nature of a good style that it does not stop developing. It is a mark of the vital strength of our style that it enters now, after 40 years, a new phase — not mutation, but growth from the same root. Obviously, I do not speak against the new in my exposition.

Born in Winterthur, Switzerland in 1908. From 1924 to 1927 he studied at the School of Arts and Crafts in Zurich and from 1927 to 1929 at the Bauhaus in Dessau. In 1930 Bill established himself as an architect and for some time he did graphic design for industry. From 1930 to 1963 he was a member of the Swiss Werkbund and for many years he was active in their executive committees. As painter and sculptor he became a member of the Abstraction-Création group in Paris in 1932. As an architect he has been a member of CIAM since 1938 and the Bund Schweizer Architekten since 1959. In 1936 and again in 1951 he designed the Swiss pavilion at the Milan Triennale, both times receiving first prize for his design. Bill has published and lectured on the Theoretical and Practical Foundations for an Environment in Harmony with a Technological Civilization. In 1944 he organized the first exhibit of "Concrete Art" for the Kunsthalle in Basel. In 1948 he founded the Institute for Progressive Culture and lectured at the Technical University in Darmstadt. In 1949 he received the Kandinsky Prize and initiated exhibits of "Good Form" at the Swiss Sample Fair in Basel and at the Werkbund exhibit in Cologne.

In 1950 Bill became the cofounder of the Hochschule für Gestaltung (Ulm Design School), which became known for its revival of the Bauhaus Idea in Germany. From 1951 to 1956 he was rector of the college and director of the Departments of Architecture and Product Design. During this time he designed the college faculty building and the student dormitories. In 1951 he was awarded first prize for sculpture at the Sao Paulo Biennal International Art Exhibit.

In 1957, after some internal disagreements at the college, Bill left and returned to Zurich. He designed the exhibit "The Unknown Present" for the Globus Department Stores in Zurich, St. Gallen, Basel, Chur, and Aarau and in 1960 he organized the exhibit "Concrete Art — 50 Years of Development" in Zurich. He became chief architect of the section on "Creation and Education" for the Swiss National Exhibition in Lausanne (Expo '64). In 1961 he was appointed by the Swiss government to its federal art commission and in the same year was elected to the Zurich City Council. In 1964 he was named honorary member of the American Institute of Architects and in 1965 honorary member of Oeuvre, the Swiss Union of Arts, Crafts, and Industry. Since 1967 he has been professor of environmental design at the State College for Arts, Hamburg. In 1967 he was elected to the Swiss parliament by the Canton of Zurich and in 1968 he was named member of the Swiss Society of Painters, Sculptors and Architects. His works have been exhibited widely in one-man and group shows and are represented in many public and private collections. He lives in Zumikon near Zurich.

The Bauhaus must go on

my intensive preoccupation with the principle of the bauhaus idea as well as the bauhaus method of education (and also with the person who had a decisive influence at the bauhaus) proves that i still regard them as valid today.

of course, again and again i am forced to admit that the bauhaus prepared the ground for many possibilities without being in a position to make full use of them at that time. it is my conviction that the then unused possibilities are by far still not utilized today, and, what is worse, when further pursued, are completely misunderstood.

my hopes at the time of the founding of the ulm school of design unfortunately also did not come true there. nor do i see today a real continuing development of the bauhaus ideas as a whole in any other place. they are much rather portions taken out and incorrectly interpreted, making a faithful rendering of further development impossible.

inspite of all these wrong developments i am still firmly convinced that the basic principle of the bauhaus carried over today, adapted to present developments, is the only real chance to escape the insecurities of design in our world and to counteract the flourishing commercial-design drive by genuine and responsible design.

at the time when i was at the ulm school of design, my program contained this possibility.

Emil Rasch:

Born in Bramsche near Osnabrück in 1904. From 1922 to 1927 he studied law and political science. Through his sister, Maria Rasch, who studied at the Bauhaus in Weimar, he was introduced to the Bauhaus Idea. In 1928, after he had started to work at his father's wallpaper factory in Bramsche, he suggested to Hannes Meyer that the Bauhaus design wallpaper for him. This wallpaper, marketed under the name "Bauhaus Tapeten," was the first product to bear the trademark of the movement. This business venture led to a collaboration with the Bauhaus that lasted until its closing in Berlin. Bauhaus wallpaper is still manufactured today by Rasch Bros.

After the war Rasch devoted himself to public life. From 1947 to 1950 he was a member of the Lower Saxony Landtag. He was also chairman of the Verein Deutsche Tapetenfabrikanten. Concerned over the relations between industry and culture, he served with the Verein Industrieform (Society for Industrial Design) in Essen and the Rat für Formgebung (Design Council), Darmstadt.
Rasch has continued to foster the idea of the Bauhaus. He supported the exhibit "Bauhaus — Idee, Form, Zweck, Zeit" at the Göppinger Gallery in Frankfurt in 1964. This book is based on the catalogue of that exhibit. Rasch lives in Bramsche near Osnabrück.

Working with the Bauhaus

I encountered the Bauhaus in all three places: in Weimar, in Dessau, and in Berlin. My first associations in Weimar, at the time of the inflation, were merely of a private nature. My sister Maria studied painting at the Bauhaus.

Unlike youth after the Second World War, young people at that time were greatly attracted by revolutionary ideas, and therefore the Bauhaus made a great impression on me. I was, however, disturbed by the many catchwords, which lost their value like inflation money and did not mean too much, and which the students changed daily. I was also under the impression that one enjoyed theories, but that there was lacking a sense of reality. I did not come in contact with members of the faculty, therefore I could only judge by impressions received in associating with students. It may be significant of their attitude that my sister asked me quite seriously at that time never to mention at the Bauhaus that she was the daughter of a manufacturer, even worse, a manufacturer of wallpaper.

It was therefore no surprise to me when in the course of my second encounter with the Bauhaus in Dessau, 1928, arranged by Hinnerk Scheper, I found Hannes Meyer, its director at that time, to be reserved when I suggested developing Bauhaus wallpaper. Hannes Meyer, whose principle aim was a collaboration between the Bauhaus and industry to enlarge the economical basis of the school in order to open up for the students new possibilities of practical education, finally accepted my suggestion, and our further collaboration was a very harmonious one. Once when I complimented him on the correct and punctual execution of our program and for his sound, business-like attitude, he told me: "You need not be surprised about this, I come from a Basel family of merchants."

My collaboration with Mies van der Rohe was no less pleasant, though in talking to him one never quite lost the feeling of dealing with an outstanding personality who was only slightly interested in business matters. My Berlin encounters were unfortunately under the shadow of a political situation that threatened termination of the Bauhaus.

Only after the war was I able to make up for not having met Gropius in Weimar. He therefore lives in my memory not as the founder of the Bauhaus, but rather as the symbolic advocate of the spiritual and moral powers who had been driven out of the country by a deluded Germany. Today we know that he and the idea of the Bauhaus have become property of the world.

Gustav Hassenpflug:

Born in Düsseldorf in 1907. From 1927 to 1930 he studied painting and interior design and industrial design at the Bauhaus in Dessau. Later he studied architecture. From 1929 to 1931 he worked with Marcel Breuer in Dessau and Berlin. From 1931 to 1934 Hassenpflug worked as a city planner and architect in Moscow. Thereafter he established himself as a free-lance architect and designer in Berlin. After the war Professor Sauerbruch commissioned him to rebuild the war-ravaged hospitals of Berlin.

In 1946 Hassenpflug became professor of city planning and land development at the College of Architecture in Weimar. From 1950 to 1956 he directed the Landeskunst School in Hamburg, which became a college during this time. From 1951 to 1956 he was the chairman of the Werkbundes Nordwestdeutschland. He took part in the Interbau Exhibit in Berlin in 1957, designing a highrise apartment house in the Hansa Viertel. Some of his most important buildings are: the aquarium and biological institute on Heligoland, the Rechtsuniversität and the Weddestrasse School in Hamburg, and the Institute of the Technical College, Munich. Hassenpflug has published several books in his fields of study. Since 1956 Hassenpflug has been professor of building design at the Technical College in Munich. He is a member of the Academy for Town and Country Planning and the Academy of Fine Arts in Hamburg.

A look at the Bauhaus today

The Bauhaus style was not limited by time, but rather represented a new intellectual and artistic attitude. Obviously today contemporary environmental design and its teaching cannot be the same as at the time of the Bauhaus. This aspect of the Bauhaus is no longer valid because the possibilities of design and its requirements have changed in four decades. But another aspect is still topical today — the intellectual and artistic approach imprinted by the Bauhaus. The history of the Bauhaus is the history of an artistic development from Art Nouveau up to the modern building trend, in all its shimmering phases and with many changes and deviations. This breakthrough of new possibilities could only be attained by a new artistic attitude, by the rejection of the intellectual society of that time and its rigid program, by education of new, versatile artistic people. This was when new painting, new pedagogics, a new architecture, and a new design of industrial products originated. The Bauhaus played an important part in this development. This was amazing, considering that the Bauhaus was a small school with never more than 120 students — usually less — three times forced to close, and existing for only fourteen years. Certainly this was the right time for artistic changes, certainly the rare meeting of incredibly strong teaching personalities was particularly favorable, but the idea of the Bauhaus was the decisive factor.

Today, if we should try to build up a school with similar basic principles, we would probably encounter the same difficulties as the Bauhaus did then. Of course, these difficulties would at least in part be of a different nature than they were at the time of the Bauhaus. While then education had to be loosened up and dissolved, today it would be necessary to find new basic concepts, new summing-up, instead of the loosening-up of existing ones. In place of an increasing lack of ideas, a new and firm basis would have to be found. By the way, similar dangers are threatening now as at the time of the Bauhaus. Arts and crafts are celebrating a resurrection in a bad sense, not only through synthetic products but in materialistic attitude, showing in some cases obvious signs of fatigue in intellectual and cultural fields. Our miraculous economical wealth favors artistic tumors and apparent prosperity. These would be sufficient reasons for carrying over to our time the freshness and liveliness, the intellectual and artistic attitudes from the history of the Bauhaus.

Howard Dearstyne:

Born in Albany in 1903. He studied at Columbia University in New York City from 1921 to 1925, earning a Bachelor of Arts degree. Thereafter he turned to architecture. Learning of the Bauhaus on a European trip, he went to Dessau where he studied under Mies van der Rohe from 1928 to 1932. (Dearstyne is the only American to have received a Bauhaus diploma.) At the Bauhaus he established lasting friendships with Kandinsky, in whose classes he gave lectures on painting, Mies van der Rohe, and Ludwig Hilberseimer. After the closing of the Bauhaus in Berlin in 1933, Dearstyne studied privately for a year with Mies van der Rohe.

Returning to the United States, he worked for leading architectural firms, notably Wallace K. Harrison in New York. In 1941, on the recommendation of Mies van der Rohe, he was appointed instructor in architecture at Black Mountain College in North Carolina. Other teaching appointments followed, among them ten years at the College of William and Mary in Williamsburg, Virginia. In 1957 he was invited by Mies van der Rohe to the Illinois Institute of Technology in Chicago, where he is now associate professor of architecture.

In addition to teaching, Dearstyne specializes in color photography. His photographs were first shown at the Second Armory Exhibition in New York City in 1945 and in the following year at the Museum of Modern Art. Dearstyne has collaborated on two books in the fields of art and architecture and translated Bauhaus books by Kandinsky and Malevich. At present he is completing a book entitled "Inside the Bauhaus," which will be a critical survey of its leading figures and their accomplishments. Dearstyne lives in Chicago.

Mies van der Rohe's teaching at the Bauhaus in Dessau

When Hannes Meyer was fired (*fristlos entlassen*) from the directorship of the Bauhaus in Dessau in the summer of 1930, a storm of protest arose from the students, provoked in part, at least, by a handful of very vocal Communists, who were ostensibly studying at the school. I had been at the Bauhaus for something less than two years, having entered it in the fall of 1928. I had always liked Hannes Meyer because of his hearty, outgoing manner and because he went out of his way to be friendly to me, an American and a *rara avis* at the Bauhaus. But I was interested in architecture as an art, whereas Hannes (as everybody called him) steadfastly proclaimed his opposition to art in general, and to art in architecture in particular, insisting that the latter was wholly utilitarian in nature. I believe that, in the matter of Hannes' rigorous rejection of aesthetics, his bark was worse than his bite, for he was caught red-handed more than once in the act of weighing the proportions of a building, surely an unseemly exercise for an out-and-out functionalist. In any case, I had begun to entertain some vague ideas of quitting the Bauhaus and continuing my studies in Peter Behrens' Meisterschule (architecture school) at the academy in Vienna.

Then came Hannes Meyer's dismissal and the appointment of Mies van der Rohe as new director of the Bauhaus. When Mies arrived in Dessau, I really didn't know him from Adam (I mean the Scottish architect, of course). I remembered having seen, in a linoleum trade magazine, a photo of a room designed by him for the glass industry in the Werkbund Exposition held in Stuttgart in 1927, and this had impressed me because of its great simplicity. I had never heard of the Weissenhofsiedlung, the Barcelona pavilion, and the rest of Mies' executed works and projects. But certain of the students who were acquainted with them claimed that they were formalistic and that Mies built mansions for the wealthy when he should have provided dwellings for the poor. They demanded that he exhibit his work to enable them to judge whether or not he was qualified to be director of their beloved school. They also held turbulent mass meetings in the Bauhaus canteen, at which they expressed their indignation at the firing of Hannes and the hiring of Mies. In the course of one of these they dared Mies to descend from his sanctuary on the "bridge" spanning the street between the Bauhaus and the trades school to defend himself. The new director, incensed at this lese majesty, ordered the canteen cleared and, when the students refused to leave, called in the Dessau gendarmes to disperse them. I have always looked upon this drastic action of Mies' as an error in judgment. Hannes Meyer or Walter Gropius, in a similar situation, would have confronted the students, reasoned with them, and probably pacified them. Mies was not cut out to be an administrator, but he proved to be a great teacher.

The insubordination at the Bauhaus finally caused Mayor Hesse and the council of masters to close the institution for some weeks. During the lull a number of the ringleaders of the revolt were expelled, and when the school reopened things had quieted down. Mies deemed it advisable nevertheless, as a precautionary measure, to interview each and every student individually, in his private office. When my turn came I was at a loss for something to say to the director, for he himself failed to open the conversation. So I ventured to raise a question that was close to my heart, asking, "Is it no longer right to seek beauty in architecture?" He quickly assured me that it was right. The very fact that I asked the question shows how completely ignorant I was at the time of Mies' nature and aims. I was to find, indeed, that the attainment of beauty in architecture had been his own lifelong goal and that he would soon launch his students in quest of it.

By the time Mies arrived in Dessau, I had completed the studies that were prerequisite to entry into the architecture department, so I became one of his students. This was the first architecture class that Mies taught at the Bauhaus and, in fact, the first teaching he had done anywhere. There were only a half-dozen people in the group, and certain of these, Eduard Ludwig, Hermann Blomeier, and Willi Heyerhoff, became my particular friends. Mies started us off with a simple problem, the design of a single-bedroom "court house," a house, that is, facing a walled garden. The plans we did for this house were all pretty much alike, varying only in details. Mr. Wingler has published Ludwig's version in his book on the Bauhaus, and Philip Johnson based the design of his house in Cambridge, Massachusetts on solutions of this project made at the school.

Mies was so concerned with uprooting our misconceptions and setting us on the right track that he sometimes, unintentionally, injured the sensitivities of his students. Those inseparable friends Blomeier and Heyerhoff, for example, had been prize students at Paul Klopfer's architecture school in Holzminden. On one occasion, early in the term, they showed Mies prints of building plans made by them there, confident that he would praise them. I was standing by and winced when Mies rode roughshod over them, marking them up with a black pencil to indicate how they should have been done. Hermann and Willi were so hurt by Mies' ruthlessness that they remained away from class for a month, nursing their wounds. But we all had to get used to having our fondest schemes rejected. Time after time when I had made sketch plans that seemed good to me, Mies would examine them and say, laconically, *"Versuchen Sie es wieder"* (try it again), and I had the good sense not to argue. Little by little we began to understand.

Mies himself was doing houses for the most part in those days and he kept us planning houses, one after another. He used to remark that if one could design a house well, he could design anything. I have become so firmly convinced of the truth of this that I repeat it to my students today to impress upon their minds the importance of mastering the simpler problems.

After making many sketches (Mies said that one should make at least a hundred) I finally came up with a house plan that he liked. The house was a one-story court house, with an elongated living-dining room and a single bedroom that communicated with this. Two external sides of the house were continuous with the walls of the court, while the living room and bedroom had floor-to-ceiling glass facing the garden. A porch roof, supported by free-standing columns, connected the house with the court wall opposite. I shall not forget the trouble we had smoothing out the rough spots. At one point we were about to abandon the scheme because we could find no place in the kitchen for the garbage pail! The entrance also posed a difficult problem. In my original plan the connection of the foyer with the living room was too abrupt. After sketching over my layout for hours, Mies finally hit upon a solution that provided an indirect transition from the foyer to the living room and, at the same time, an indirect route from the kitchen to the dining area. This kind of circuitous passage from one space to another is a continuing characteristic of Mies' work.

I kept my folks in the United States informed about my studies at the Bauhaus, and, fortunately, my mother saved every scrap of mail I sent her. In a letter written December 20, 1931, I spoke as follows of the work with Mies:

"I'm using the few days until Christmas to put the finishing touches on the house design I've been working on since I arrived [from a trip to the United States]. The house is a small one with living room, one bedroom and the necessary utility rooms such as bath, kitchen, etc. The house is of the same character as the two I had with me in America. Mies van der Rohe continues to hold us to the small problems. But that he is right in doing this is indicated by the fact that it takes weeks or months to do a small house of this nature in a decent way. The very simplicity of these houses is their chief difficulty. It's much easier to do a complicated affair than something clear and simple.

"We're learning a tremendous lot from Mies van der Rohe. If he doesn't make good architects of us he'll at least teach us to judge what good architecture is. One of the uncomfortable (perhaps) sides of associating with an architect of the first rank is that he ruins your taste for about all but one-half of one percent of all the architecture that's being done the world over. Mies van der Rohe not only comes down hard on the American architects (for which he has, without the shadow of a doubt, the most perfect justification), but holds that one doesn't need the fingers of one hand to count the German architects who are doing good work. He sets a very high standard, which is a fact that should only cause us to rejoice. It's much easier to work under less critical men and content yourself with middle-rate work. That's what I was doing at Columbia and what most of the students in America (and here) are doing. But I thank my stars that I landed where I did!"

Mies had taken one of the master houses and he spent three days each week in Dessau. He and Ludwig Hilberseimer, who taught city planning at the Bauhaus, had worked out an arrangement whereby they commuted between Berlin and Dessau alternately, so that one of them was in the capital while the other was at the Bauhaus. We saw much of Mies during his weekly sojourns in Dessau, and I often think how privileged we were to have this close association with him. Our students in the Department of Architecture of the Illinois Institute of Technology, who revere him as their great master, are lucky today if they lay eyes on him once during their entire five-year course.

When the final semester arrived, our class was reduced to four people. I know that Eduard Ludwig and Edgar Hecht were two of these and I am fairly certain that Hubert Döllner was the fourth man who, with me, completed the quartet. We moved to a private ground-floor studio, which was kept locked and to which we each had a key. Here we worked on our *Diplomarbeiten* (diploma problems). I chose to do a bathing pavilion for the Kühnau Lake on the outskirts of Dessau, and Mies walked out with me to see the site. In this last semester we had enviable opportunities to talk with Mies; isolated from the rest of the school in our private room, we had him to ourselves for hours at a time. I wrote to my folks at home about this on June 12, 1932:

"We saw a lot of Mies van der Rohe last week. He came on three different days to our atelier. Wednesday he spent over three hours with us and ordered coffee for us from the canteen. Thursday he came for about an hour. Friday he came twice and spent about 5 hours with us all told. We had coffee again. We (our semester, 4 people) have gotten well acquainted with him and he seems to enjoy talking with us more than with the lower semesters. We discuss everything, architecture, art, philosophy, politics, etc. These discussions don't, therefore, always have a direct bearing upon our work but are tremendously interesting and valuable because Mies van der Rohe is a man of profundity and richness of experience. It would be worth my while being here just for these discussions if I did no designing whatever. My hope is that the Bauhaus doesn't break up and that I can return [from a planned trip to America]."

All four of us, as I recall, received our Bauhaus diplomas in July, 1932, although Hecht almost failed to make it, chiefly because he put such atrocious-looking trees in a rendering of his project. We got in just under the wire, for political coercion, which for years had hung over our heads like a Damocles sword, was finally brought to bear upon the Bauhaus. The Nazis, who had persistently sworn to close the school and, for that matter, to raze the building, at last gained control of the Dessau legislature. Fully intending to do away with the hated Bauhaus, they nevertheless saw fit to give their contemplated action the appearance of legality by arranging a trial bearing the semblance of justice. They required the director to make an exhibition of Bauhaus work and appointed as judge Paul Schultze-Naumburg, an ultra-conservative architect who despised the Bauhaus and who, in turn, was despised by it. So Mies assembled the best of the student work for the fruitless exhibit. We were all intent upon putting our best foot forward so I asked Hinnerk Scheper, our color teacher at the Bauhaus, to make a rendering of my bathing pavilion for the exhibition. He cheerfully complied, and I am still happy today to possess this memento of that talented and modest man.

Before the inevitable blow fell, I left for a vacation in the United States. When I returned to Dessau in October, 1932, the Bauhaus was closed, and Mies and most of the instructors and students had departed for Berlin, where Mies established a new Bauhaus on a private basis. I gave up my apartment in Dessau and followed them.

Bauhaus people building
''their own'' private
Bauhaus at
Berlin-Steglitz
Berlin, 1932
Photo: Pius Pahl

220

Ludwig Hilberseimer,
Lilli Reich and students
consulting together on their
future after the final
closing of the Bauhaus on
April 11
Berlin, 1933
Photo: Pius Pahl

The Bauhaus building as it
looked after the war
Dessau, 1959
Photo: Eckhard Neumann

View of the restoration of
Feininger's master house
Dessau, 1959
Photo: Eckhard Neumann

Entrance to the master
house once occupied by
Lyonel Feininger
Dessau, 1959
Photo: Eckhard Neumann

224

A group of restored houses
of the Törten settlement,
originally designed by
Walter Gropius
Dessau, 1959
Photo: Eckhard Neumann

The Bauhaus today
Dessau, 1967
Photo: Reproduction from
a current picture postcard

226

Main Entrance of the
Bauhaus with the
incorrectly reconstructed
glass panel and a banner
of the Communist youth
movement
Dessau, 1965
Photo: Klaus F. Schmidt

Pius E. Pahl:

Born in Ludwigshafen in 1909. He began his training in carpentry, then turned to interior design, which he studied at the Staatstechnikum in Karlsruhe. From 1930 to 1933 at Bauhaus in Dessau and Berlin, he studied architecture with Ludwig Hilberseimer and Mies van der Rohe. From 1934 to 1942 he worked as an architect in various firms in Zurich and Germany. After the war he opened an architectural office in Ludwigshafen and taught at the Staatbauschule in Mainz. In 1952 Pahl went to South Africa and established a new architectural office in Stellenbosch. He taught part-time at the School of Architecture at the University of Cape Town and made several study trips through Europe, North and South Africa, and the United States. Pahl lives in Stellenbosch.

Experiences of an architectural student

A touring exhibition of the Bauhaus at the art gallery of Mannheim (1929) was the occasion of my first comprehensive view of its work. I was greatly impressed by the exhibition. Up to that time my education as an interior decorator had demanded that I use period furniture or design modern interiors inspired by the Italian Renaissance, etc. At the Staatstechnikum, where I had subsequently studied architecture, a sound technical education could be obtained, but no architecture was taught. The modern designs of various schools of art had, in part, impressed me very favorably; at the Bauhaus Exhibition, however, I felt for the first time that the exhibits and designs represented more than merely novel forms. As a result of this exhibition I decided forthwith to enroll for the winter semester, 1930.

There was no comparison between the atmosphere at the Bauhaus and that of any of the other schools I had attended. The Bauhäusler regarded themselves as part of the Bauhaus, just as monks might regard themselves as part of their monastery. The novice was confronted with many new opinions, and much that had until then been accepted lost its validity in a very short while. The recognition of the connections in industrial developments, the shifting of production, the necessary changes in the sociological structure, the intellectual assimilation of these factors, the threat to individuality in an industrial state, and other problems all were of great concern to us Bauhäusler.

The work at the Bauhaus and its intellectual foundations has been methodically reported by qualified authors. These lines, which are largely limited to the "Mies era," are intended especially as a description of the atmosphere of that period. The following are some experiences:

Experience 1. The teaching method is quite informal. Because of my previous education I may join the third semester immediately. During the fourth semester I also try to read town planning with Hilberseimer. I enter the room in which the lectures are given and sit down a little away from the others. They come in one by one and find places on tables, benches, stools, and window benches. They debate. I am waiting for Hilbs, but in vain. After some time one of the older students, perched on a radiator, is addressed as Hilbs. What a surprise for a former student of the Höheres Staatliches Technikum!

Experience 2. Often there is no end to the discussions, but even in their sometimes negative form they are quite stimulating. An invitation to about ten students to the house of the Bauhaus teacher Engelmann. Hours of discussion about industrialization, new forms of society, cultural effects of mechanization, etc. Opinions clash. I love granite and marble, a few of the others reject their use in new building. They should only serve as aggregate for the production of artificial stone panels, which are supposed to be more attractive than natural stone.

A Bauhäusler goes and lies down on the sofa (on the first visit to his teacher's apartment). What manners!

Experience 3. A competition among students for mass-produced furniture. In the description that had to be annexed to the designs I had written: The designs are developed out of the purpose, material, construction, available means of production, and aesthetics. They are indulgent about the novice's aesthetics, nevertheless I am thoroughly aroused.

Experience 4.   No papers are written or exams taken during the semester. At the end of the semester each Bauhäusler puts his work in a portfolio on a table. Behind the table two or three drawings are pinned to the wall, together with a photo of the exhibiting student.

General protest against a prefabricated Alpine hut I designed. For various reasons I had constructed the hut out of a triangle, of which one side provided the floor and the other two the roof. Crossbeams added in the center formed the floor of the sleeping quarters situated in the upper spandrel. That was probably the first pitched-roof design at the Bauhaus.

Experience 5.   Mies takes us for the fourth semester. The studio hours are always very interesting. Mies walks from table to table and helps in his clear and calm way.

First Design: The furnishing of a long and narrow room, with old furniture that we measured up somewhere. One student arrives at the studio with millimeter paper DIN A 4, on which he has drawn the plan to a scale of 1 to 100, using the millimeter divisions. Another has bought cheaply from a printer the crumbled remainder of a roll of newsprint and shows the room from all directions in large consecutive freehand perspectives. Mies is very pleased when the student spreads the ten-meter-long "ribbon" on the floor. What individualists!

Second Design: A small one-story house. When Mies comes to the table of our colleague Selman Selmanagic, he muses for a while and then says: "Selman, we shall have to start all over again." Selman is very surprised and starts explaining very eagerly how well the ground plan functions. He draws the circulation, seating arrangement, etc. (This was shortly after the era of Hannes Meyer, and the overrating of function had not yet been overcome.) "Come now, Selman, if you meet twin sisters who are equally healthy, intelligent, and wealthy, and both can bear children, but one is ugly, the other beautiful, which one would you marry?" General laughter!

Experience 6.   The Bauhaus family consisted partly of pronounced individualists. Small wonder that during the controversial years of the thirties, opinions clashed very strongly, especially immediately after lectures and demonstrations by scientists and artists. It was after the lecture of a Swiss architect to a large audience that an argument started. The functionalists substantially supported the speaker, while a large section of the students protested, but not too successfully, until Howard Dearstyne described the commendable clothes of the speaker, including the impressive red tie, and asked the opponents for an explanation of the function of the tie.

When discussing such experiences, one could not expect the various groups to reach an agreement. Political and ideological circumstances varied too much. Nevertheless, without its readiness to express an opinion the Bauhaus would not have been the Bauhaus. However, the political fights that were brought into the Bauhaus and organized mainly from the outside were destructive. One could divide the students in two parts, a smaller, yet very active group with Communist tendencies, and the larger remainder, with strong social-fundamental ideas, without adhering to any particular party. I never experienced radical-right aspirations at the Bauhaus.

On several occasions there were serious arguments between the radical group, which was very effective due to its united action, and the other students, for instance when electing students' representatives, when expelling communistic students. Occasionally even strikes were organized by the left. The last internal arguments developed when a committee of the German National Socialist Party (NSDAP) of the Dessau town council, under the direction of Professor Schulze Naumburg, was supposed to visit the end of term exhibit in autumn, 1932, to determine if the works exhibited would justify further financial assistance by the city of Dessau. We all knew that the decision of the party committee could only be a negative one. Nevertheless the teachers and most of the students knew that the exhibition had to be held in any case, as usual. The left wing announced that they would not exhibit and managed to persuade some of the undecided members of the Bauhaus to go on strike also, whereupon the exhibition was concentrated to a few rooms and was a complete success. In spite of this, the committee, who went through the whole exhibition in a few minutes, gave the expected negative judgment, and the National Socialist Council, together with the middle-class parties, voted against the grant of the needed funds, and thus the era Dessau was brought to an end.

When I came to Berlin for the winter term, building work had started on the deserted old factory that was to house the new Bauhaus. We all helped, demolished walls, and built new ones. The financial status of the Bauhaus was hopeless, tuition could only be maintained through great personal sacrifices of the Bauhaus masters. Nobody knew if the political scales would tip to the extreme right or left. Nevertheless during these six months work went well again and without internal disturbances. There was a successful Bauhaus festival visited by many friends. Also the end of term exhibition was a success, considering the fact that the Bauhaus could only be revived in Berlin on a smaller scale.

The end came on April 11, 1933, during the first days of the summer term. Early in the morning police arrived with trucks and closed the Bauhaus. Bauhaus members without proper identification (and who had these?) were loaded on the trucks and taken away. Later in the morning Hilberseimer, Mrs. Reich, and a few older Bauhaus members met, very much downcast, outside the Bauhaus to consider what could be saved. A few days later a small group met in Mies' apartment. We decided to send a petition to the culturally responsible offices. Above all, a transfer of the Bauhaus to another country was discussed, and where to. Mies himself was very much against an emigration; he hoped, as all of us did, for a better understanding of cultural questions in the NSDAP, after the party came to power. And surely, this hope had some justification, though a small one, because shortly afterward it became known that the head of the Chamber of Arts and Culture announced in public that he expected Mies to someday build a palace of culture for Hitler. Years later, Baldur von Schirach, the Reich's youth leader, declared publicly that the buildings of the younger generation should be erected of steel, concrete, and glass as a symbol of our time.

In the autumn of 1933, when I met Mies by chance at an exhibition in Milan, our last hopes had vanished for a sensible cultural development in Germany.

Alfred Hoppe:

Born in Lennep/Rhineland in 1891. He studied German philology at the universities of Tübingen, Bonn, Freiburg, and Zurich. In 1921 he discontinued his studies to become an editor in Berlin. Later he acted as a free-lance advertising consultant. In 1925 Hoppe became promotion manager for the Junkers-Werke in Dessau, a position which fostered his lasting relationship with the Bauhaus. Under his leadership the Junkers-Werke commissioned the Bauhaus in 1928 to design their information booth at the Gas and Water Exhibition in Berlin. In 1938 Hoppe moved to Stuttgart to work with the Robert Bosch AG, for whom he ordered an exhibition stand for the Leipzig Fair, to be designed by Gustav Hassenpflug and Herbert Bayer.

After 1939 Hoppe turned to other endeavors and in 1945 he became chief of the Dessau Chamber of Industry and Commerce. In 1949 he became promotion manager of Robert Bosch AG in Stuttgart once again, retiring in 1956. Hoppe died on November 28, 1966 in Munich.

An example

On the occasion of the large exhibition "Gas and Water" at the Berlin radio tower in 1928, I persuaded my management that the extensive exhibition stand of our firm should be planned and executed in detail by the Bauhaus, according to a building concept worked out by me from a promotional, selling, and technical point of view. This exhibition stand brought recognition to the Bauhaus style in this field and was, in its way, epoch-making.

No description can convey the effect on the visitor, and the successful results for the sale of our products at home and abroad. I just want to relate one fact, which probably comes under the heading of their exhibition "Idea — Form — Purpose — Time": The gas water heaters were installed, ready for use, in some of the stands designed in the Bauhaus style showing bathrooms, kitchens, or utility rooms. They had corrugated or forged copper covers. When Professor Junkers saw the appliances in these environments, he said: "Something has to be done for these appliances. They don't fit in here!" He immediately recognized that their design, in a technical sense, was old fashioned. First, the copper disappeared, and the covers were enameled; later, the design of the actual appliance was changed. This task was not given to a designer, as is sometimes done today, but to the technical construction department of the firm.

Perhaps a few other details are of interest. The stands were 50 meters long, but only 4 meters wide. At the entrance the visitor's interest was attracted by pictures, with and without motion, which were to induce him to enter the stand and walk through its considerable length. This was usually achieved.

The entrance demonstrated the importance of hot water for hygiene and home. In one passage, between chrome-framed colored glass, small gas appliances for industrial purposes were hung in a way that would be modern and effective even today. Leading from this passage, at a right angle, were the already-mentioned exhibition boxes. Then came consultation rooms, which could also be entered from the outside. Following these was a room where the fundamentals of the Junkers' research work were demonstrated: technical and material research, technical development, finishing. The presentation in detail of this research work was designed and visualized and produced excellently by the workshops of the Bauhaus. This work was done by all the workshops of the Bauhaus.

The carpenter's shop designed and manufactured new chairs. The weaving mill wove their covers. The metal workshop executed the metal work, including the kinetic mechanisms. The advertising department developed and produced the graphic designs for the exhibition stands as well as the folders. The preparation and execution of the stands was done in a cooperative and friendly atmosphere, which today is called teamwork.

The carrying-out of the plans, which were written down, was entirely in the hands of the workshops, therefore in the hands of the students themselves. Johan Niegeman, who is living in Holland today, was responsible for architecture and construction of the stands, and Xanti Schawinsky, today in New York, did the graphic designs. Joost Schmidt, who was then in charge of the advertising department, was responsible for the entire project.

Editor's note. *The following Bauhaus members contributed to the design of the exhibition stand "The Bath" for Junkers & Company in*

Dessau at the exhibition "Gas and Water" in Berlin in 1928: all-over design, Xanti Schawinsky; technical building direction, Johan Niegeman; design of the special stall for the Gas-heating Stove, Joost Schmidt (director of the Bauhaus Advertising Department); as well as students of various departments. Participating photographers were Sasha Stone (not at the Bauhaus) and Walter Peterhans.

Richard Koppe:

Born in St. Paul, Minnesota, in 1916. From 1933 to 1937 he studied painting at the St. Paul School of Art. Through Cameron Booth he became acquainted with the latest trends in art in Europe, among them the ideas of Gleizes, Hoffman, Kandinsky, Klee, and the Bauhaus. Inspired by these theoretical discussions about new art he went to the newly founded New Bauhaus in Chicago from 1937 to 1938, where Laszlo Moholy-Nagy, Gyorgy Kepes, Alexander Archipenko, and Hin Bredendick were teaching.

In 1939, Koppe joined the Federal Art Project as one of the few abstract painters. Later he became group leader in production illustration for the Air Force. In 1944–1945 he started his academic career as an instructor at the University of Texas in Fort Worth.

When returning to Chicago in 1946, he was appointed as a member of Moholy-Nagy's staff at the Art Institute of Chicago, where he taught the preliminary course. In 1949 Koppe was appointed head of the Visual Design Department by Serge Chermayeff, who was then the director. From 1961 to 1963, he was head of the Fine Arts Department. In 1963 he went to the University of Illinois in Chicago, where he became professor of art in 1965, and taught at the College of Architecture.

Since 1936 Koppe's paintings and sculptures have been shown in many one-man and group exhibitions in the United States and Europe. In 1961 the Institute of Design of the Illinois Institute of Technology organized a huge retrospective of his work. He received a number of awards and his paintings are in the collections of important American museums such as the Whitney Museum and the St. Paul Art Center, and private collections. In 1965 Syracuse University established a Richard Koppe Collection and Archives, containing his paintings, drawings, and documents. Koppe is living in Chicago.

The New Bauhaus, Chicago

Over twenty-seven years ago the New Bauhaus, American School of Design (later the Institute of Design), under the direction of Laszlo Moholy-Nagy, opened its doors to students in the Marshall Field mansion in Chicago, under the auspices of the Association of Arts and Industries.

This was in the fall of 1937, and these same doors were to close toward the end of the following summer, 1938.

I was in the first group to join the school in a class of thirty-five students. In Walter Gropius' words, quoted from an address given in Chicago in 1950, "A genuine tool of cultural growth, the Institute [of Design] took root after a stormy beginning." The New Bauhaus was certainly that "stormy beginning." The financial collapse of the school, resulting in a settlement of the director's contract and the dismissal of the faculty, student unrest over curriculum and ideological matters, and later the end of the Association of Arts and Industries were a part of that storm. Far more serious was the termination of an educational process started for sixty students. We were also to hear that the word "Bauhaus" was not to be used in a name for any future school. To ignore or minimize these events would do a great disservice to any serious historical appraisal of this most important movement. It is a tribute to Moholy's particular kind of genius and perseverance that he was able to later establish roots for a continuum under his School of Design, finally renamed "Institute of Design."

The Association of Arts and Industries had experienced a previous attempt to establish an industrial art school within the Art Institute of Chicago and raised 360,000 dollars for that purpose. In Chicago, private fund raising for such a cause must have been a Herculean effort, in the midst of a financial depression in the United States. The association separated from the art institute and decided to establish its own independent school. After a long search and on the recommendation of Gropius, Moholy-Nagy was chosen as the director. Funds had been spent on remodeling the Marshall Field mansion, and the association was reputed to have 110,000 dollars on hand when Moholy signed his contract. Yet additional contributions would have to be raised if it was to remain solvent. Later the Association of Arts and Industries was reported to have invested heavily in bonds, and these along with stocks sharply declined in the little stock market crash of that time. Apparently there was no hope for recovery. I have no intention of reiterating many of the events of the time, because they were ably set forth by Sibyl Moholy-Nagy in her biography on Moholy.

How then could anything constructive come out of this apparent turmoil? Fortunately the storm was outside of the classrooms and had little effect, if any, on the educational process itself. Moholy's book *New Vision,* published in 1938, and the magazine *More Business* (Nov., 1938) document in part and attest to both the quality and quantity of the student work of that year. The effect of Bauhaus teaching, in spite of its detractors, was eventually to invade schools of art, architecture, design, and art education, in one form or another, in almost every institute of higher learning in the United States.

Certainly the Bauhaus in Germany had influenced thinking in the United States prior to this time, but it was mostly indirect and open to individual interpretation. The almost parallel efforts of Gropius and Breuer in the Department of Architecture at Harvard; Albers and Schawinsky at Black Mountain College; later, Albers at Yale; as well as Mies van der Rohe, Hilberseimer, and Peterhans in the Department of Architecture at Illinois Institute of Technology were examples of direct contact, but considerably more limited.

Moholy, however, attempted the prodigious task of transferring the Bauhaus as an educational idea in its entirety to the United States and establishing a new school at the same time. To this end he surrounded himself with some of the most able and brilliant men both here and abroad. This dream was not to be fully realized for sometime to come. Gropius was professor of architecture at Harvard and acted as adviser in all school matters. The staff included: Hin Bredendieck (a student at the German Bauhaus), head of the basic design workshop; Gyorgy Kepes, also from Europe, drawing and light studio; Alexander Archipenko, the famous pioneer in modern sculpture who had been in the United States since 1923, modeling; Henry Holmes Smith, photography; David Dushkin, music and building musical instruments. The sciences were taught by: Carl Eckart, physics and mathematics; Ralph W. Gerard, biology and physiology; and Charles W. Morris, semantics and intellectual integration, all professors at the University of Chicago belonging to the Unity of Science movement. Lectures were scheduled by James Johnson Sweeney, Franz Alexander, Howard Vincent O'brien, Alexander Doerner, Louis L. Thurston, to name a few.

The prospects for a noteworthy education were unlimited, and there was much enthusiasm. The student body was composed of people who were attracted from all over the United States to Moholy-Nagy and the

Bauhaus Idea. This group, especially in the first semester, bears close scrutiny. They came from all walks of life, and the majority had a long training in higher education in universities and art schools. They were not only well informed and highly trained, even in the most advanced thinking of the time, but extremely lucid and varied as to geographical and educational background. Most had read as much material as possible on the Bauhaus and related movements — Moholy's *New Vision,* Kandinsky's *Point, Line, and Plane* and *Art of Spiritual Harmony* — and were familiar with the Bauhaus books. Many of us were attracted by the prospects of working in new materials, methods, and theories and establishing direct contact with the people who were active in these movements in Europe. Above all else, I think we were interested in an educational idea. Some students entered the New Bauhaus in the spirit of graduate students, and it became a catalyst to our previous education, while for others it was only a beginning.

In my particular case, for example, I had already felt the effects of contemporary European thought, influence, and education in four years at the St. Paul School of Art in Minnesota, one of the most advanced schools at that time. Cameron Booth, the director, had studied with Andre L'hote in Paris and Hans Hoffman in Munich, and Leroy Turner, of the faculty, had studied with Edmund Kinzinger and was a member of the Abstraction Creation Group in Paris. Many of my fellow students had similar backgrounds.

It would be difficult if not impossible to separate the school from Moholy as a person. He was extremely active and worked closely with the other members of the staff in every area. He lectured on general orientation concerning the entire contemporary art world and held regular sessions for this. He showed his large collection of Bauhaus material in slides as well as in huge photographic enlargements. I can remember on one occasion he and the entire student body were down on their hands and knees looking through the forest of table legs to illustrate a point he had made about space. He showed numerous films, including his own *Black, White, and Grey,* along with the mobile sculpture he had built for it. He had done several films in England and had produced the special effects for the H.G. Wells film *Things to Come.* He often spoke of working in a large film studio and seemed so amazed that one could ask for almost anything and it would be built and that others would do it for you. In classes we were introduced to the photogram, photomontage, hand sculpture, the tactile chart, space modulators (we called them "space cakes"), light modulators, the paper problem, machine investigation, and photography, all highly inventive in nature. Along with this were color theory, drawing, lettering, drafting, etc., but far different than most conventional art schools. The work went smoothly in all of the classes. Everyone worked extremely hard, and there was considerable enthusiastic response to all of this stimulation. In many respects, I have never seen so many and so varied results produced by any class within the scope of this curriculum. Perhaps a higher value was placed on inventive creativeness than on aesthetic consideration, though they were part and parcel of the same order. This evidently had been a very large factor at the Bauhaus in Germany as well and was to help in establishing the principle of function and form as one. Too often form and surface were merely applied as an aesthetic afterthought.

Students were often invited to Moholy's apartment on Astor Street, which was painted entirely in white. Here he had a foyer gallery for his Constructivist paintings and light modulators. He had also been working in plastics and other synthetic materials. I can remember well the baked-enamel painting, the design for which had been dictated over the telephone. We also saw Marcel Breuer's furniture and Marcel Duchamp's roto-reliefs and listened to Kurt Schwitter's poetry recited by the artist on a recording. There were many people from all over the world who visited the school regularly and were entertained at Moholy's home.

Moholy was one of the most dynamic personalities I have ever met. He had the energy of a dozen men. He was active in photography, film, typography, advertising design, stage design, exhibition, display, painting, and sculpture (constructions). He was a brilliant lecturer and writer. This very diversity allowed and perhaps demanded integration as an educational principle. His most singular and greatest contribution was as educator. What was most interesting about Moholy was that he represented, in essence, the Constructivist and Dadist attitude. Certainly his photomontage studies and his script for *Once a Chicken Always a Chicken* attested to the Dada influence, and one of his close friends in Germany had been Kurt Schwitters. Moholy had a tremendous interest in light. Where the Impressionists had a scientific interest in light, principally out of doors and in atmospheric effects, Moholy's interests were in scientific, artificial, and abstract light. Some of his Constructivist paintings in oil and water color had the feeling of paths of intersecting light and planes in space, and their resultant mixture or transparency.

This, then, was Moholy's "Brave New World," and the circulation among the students of Aldous Huxley's book of the same name lent an almost satirical atmosphere to the New Bauhaus. His ability to stimulate businessmen, scientists, technicians, publishers, and educators was legendary. All were attracted to his ideas. What, then, caused ideological differences of an educational nature among the students? One might easily infer that ideological differences indicate a form of resistance to a new educational idea. Far larger difficulties were, apparently, a true misunderstanding and, possibly, an over-evaluation of the whole Bauhaus Idea by the students before attending the school. These, against a climate of actual educational practice, apparently led to many conflicts. I think that Moholy and some of the others also misjudged the American student, who seldom has held great men in adoration, especially educators and artists, as reputations mean little until proven at first hand. The Bauhaus curriculum framework, too, seemed out of place in American society. The particular apprentice system leading to some professions, widely accepted in Germany then, was practically nonexistent in the United States. Students had a high school education before entering college, few had thorough hand- or machine-tool training and certainly no high level of craft. This tended to negate the prospects of the specialized shops of wood, metal, plastic, etc. If you were an industrial designer in this country, for example, you were expected to have a knowledge of many materials and processes, unfortunately not always at first hand. Also, to take a curriculum as denoted in the Bauhaus plan for four years and then to become an architect in two additional years seemed unthinkable under the American system of higher education. Moholy seemed almost fixed and unyielding in some of these matters. Undoubtedly he felt that these relationships could not be altered without changing the entire concept of the Bauhaus. In later years he gradually changed his ideas in many areas without disturbing his basic beliefs.

Another area of deep and unresolved conflict for many students was the Bauhaus Idea in relation to the painter and sculptor. It was simply indicated at the New Bauhaus that these were private matters to be pursued outside of the school environment, except for orientation discussion purposes. As students, this dimmed our views on the association of Kandinsky, Klee, Feininger, and Schlemmer with the Bauhaus in Germany and also on the numerous illustrations and references Moholy had used in his book *The New Vision,* which seemed to link the Bauhaus with so many of the modern movements in art. This conflict is largely unresolved in many schools even today.

The foundation course at the New Bauhaus demonstrated the principles of a new education in its purest form, largely devoid of apparent practical application except to education. The basic design workshop classes were involved in pure explorations into tactile surface and form sensations that soon convinced the eye and mind as well. The machine investigations were geared to pure creative, inventive use of power tools and materials devoid of a priori technical or aesthetic considerations, as were the intricate paper folds based on the use of sheet material without waste or artificial joining, yet changing dimensional and structural characteristics. Glass and wire were brought together into structures by ingenious fabrication where repetitive units dominated freer sculptural concepts. Spatial considerations, both two- and three-dimensional articulation, were investigated in capsulated form through mirroring, intricate linear elements, surface aspects, juxtaposition, movement, and spatial tensions that were the forerunners, in many respects, of the optical art we know today. This and the light workshop in connection with photography opened new vistas not normally encountered by art students and led to many fresh approaches by means of the photogram, enlargement without film, light projection, and through light modulators fabricated especially to catch and alter light. In photography, the pinhole camera, still photography and cinematography, "the worm's-eye view" and "bird's-eye view," solarization, double exposure, camera movement, reticulation, and color separation were explored. Two-dimensional color work in many media consisted of an investigation of color systems (Goethe, Munsell, and Oswald), mixture, transparency, and scientific principles along with simple drawing and photomontage. Clay and plaster took on new forms in the modeling workshop.

Though experimentation was encouraged, it either had evidence of a direction or a result or it became a means of altering conventional approaches through creative invention. Many of the problems were as ingenious in their concepts as the results they were expected to achieve. Though the initial intention of the Bauhaus may have been to reintegrate the artist and society and to embrace new technological developments, I believe that as an educational principle, it has far reaching implications largely untapped even today.

Certainly Moholy inaugurated a greater alignment with science, philosophy, psychology, and sociology and much of this was largely implemented by the three professors from the University of Chicago. Semantics and intellectual integration became the bridge between science and the other activities of the curriculum. Both Moholy and Bredendieck, because of their experiences in Germany, spoke against any outside political involvements where the school was concerned. Politics and political discussions within the educational framework of the school were virtually taboo. In its final distillation, one could apply the various stimuli of the foundation course along with scientific attitudes and principles to practical industrial or commercial uses, to painting or sculpture, or to education itself.

At this point the Bauhaus Idea was brought within the framework of higher education and away from narrow technological specialization, the trade school, commercial art school, and fine arts academy. With its basic principles and broader base, the foundation course has far-reaching implications that extend beyond the arts, with possibilities for education in numerous other fields. Thus we can see the idea of a basic principle being applied widely within rather diversified areas of related arts and design, or beyond. These principles form the link with numerous specializations. How widely and effectively this can function is open to speculation, since one must also apply this vertically to specializations as well. Without this, the Bauhaus Idea would only become another tool of liberal education and perhaps dissolve its true function, that is, to aid in integrating advance areas of specialized education.

One is eventually impressed that each person teaching within such an educational idea gives up some part of his own specialized field for the good of the whole. Some have mistakenly called this team-teaching. It is basically to teach the principles of one's own field and realize its relatedness to a host of other fields of equal importance. The danger, of course, is to be so enamored of certain principles and not to realize that even those principles are subject to change. Many of these ideas were apparent at the New Bauhaus and are the essential essence of that year's experience.

Moholy, I believe, attempted to move the Bauhaus Idea beyond the old technology of mass-production methodology into the realm of being a true adjunct to scientific and sociological developments in general, but especially through education. After the close of the New Bauhaus in 1938, I was not to again have close contact with Moholy until I joined the staff of the Institute of Design in 1946, after the Second World War and just prior to his death.

Hubert Hoffmann:

Born in Berlin in 1904 of an old established family of architects. From 1926 to 1930 he studied at the Dessau Bauhaus, first in the carpentry department and later in the building department. He then became principal assistant at the Technical University, Berlin, and taught city planning and communications. His first work outside the academic world was in the office of Fred Forbat in Berlin. After that he started to work on his own as architect, city planner, and designer; and, together with his wife, Irene Hoffmann, in advertising graphics. In 1932 Hoffmann became a member of CIAM and contributed to the "Charta of Athens."
Right after the war, in 1945, he was invited to Dessau by Mayor Fritz Hesse to reinstate the Bauhaus, but was prevented from doing so because of the political situation in East Germany. In the autumn of 1946 he tried as chairman of the "Planungsgemeinschaft Bauhaus" to arrange an international Bauhaus exhibition. Mayor Hesse's flight and the attitude of the Soviet government frustrated all further plans for the Bauhaus at Dessau. Back in Berlin, Hoffmann organized the exhibition "22 Bauhaus People," thus reuniting scattered members of the Bauhaus.
In Berlin he was one of the initiators of the international building exhibition "Interbau" in 1957 at the Hansa-Viertel, where he built a residential block (together with Wassily Luckhardt) and established "Die Stadt von Morgen" (The City of Tomorrow) exhibit. Since 1950 he has been acting as the delegate of Berlin to the CIAM and since 1958 as secretary of the architectural society *Der Ring*. In 1959 Hoffmann became professor of city planning and design at the Institute of Technology in Graz, and at the same time he became director of the Institute for Town and Country Planning. In 1965 he was invited to the Auburn University in Alabama as a guest lecturer. On his sixtieth birthday his lifework was exhibited in a one-man show at the Forum Stadtpark in Granz. In addition to his various activities in city building, architecture, and teaching, Hoffmann has written polemics advocating the redesign of our surroundings according to the changed conditions of our time. Among his books are *Neue deutsche Architektur* ("New German Architecture," Stuttgart, 1956), *Wohnen oder Hausen* ("Residing or Dwelling," Graz, 1964), and *Urbaner Flachbau* ("Urban Low Level Building," Stuttgart, 1966). Hoffmann is now living in Graz.

The revival of the Bauhaus after 1945

lord mayor hesse called me to dessau in 1945, to bring the bauhaus back to life. this plan seemed adventurous in view of the destruction of the city, which equaled a burned-out crater. its center was completely destroyed and on the outskirts there were also few buildings without war damage. dessau's life blood — the large industrial plant — had been dismantled by the russians (and after its reconstruction had been dismantled a second time, when five thousand engineers, laborers, and overseers were deported). there was famine and disease, and the population lived mostly in cellars and barracks. the bauhaus was burned down and the homes of the masters partly destroyed by bombs.

hesse had the quality of combining latent optimism with sober realistic understanding. he always saw the whole picture and left me the freedom of experimenting, even when he was not of the same opinion. at first i took over the city-planning office, later also the planning office of the district government, became a member of the city parliament and chairman of the federation for democratic renewal of germany. all this to realize the bauhaus idea "to reunite art and life," proceeding from a concrete position of power, to set an example in dessau. i did not want the new bauhaus to experience the fate of the old bauhaus, which (with exceptions) created a few pieces of furniture, houses, and appliances for snobs. much more did i endeavor to make the new bauhaus a center for the design of our surroundings, an institution that should document a new era in space and objects surrounding us and that had started with country planning by way of rebuilding city and landscape and gone on to such needs as furniture, appliances, and textiles in large quantities. with the aid of the economical direction of the zone this seemed to me a possible goal, due to the enormous need for apartments, furniture, and appliances at that time. this was an extraordinary chance because it is a known fact that the user accepts good-quality products without criticism as well as products of less value, if nothing else is offered him.

in berlin, in a circle that met every week in my apartment and that included scharoun, taut, luckhardt, rossow, rainer, hassenpflug, and the later berliner kollektiv, we discussed again and again the possibilities that would open up after the end of the third reich. we were so enthusiastic and optimistic about our profusion of ideas and particularly about being able to start again, that we hardly suspected or anticipated any obstacles — later on we still thought they were exceptions.

one of my first measures was to make a theater of the only auditorium that had been saved. helpers arrived: georg a. neidenberger from weimar, who decorated interiors, designed industrial buildings, and gave a new face to the graphic arts of the city; hinnerk and lou scheper, who helped with the color schemes of municipal buildings; fieger and pfeil, who worked for the municipal building office; and stamm and hess, who took over the planning of the villages.

soon a dozen former and a few new bauhaus members assembled in dessau to participate in the revival of the bauhaus — among them the present senator for the educational system in berlin, karl-heinz evers, and his wife mechtild. with the aid of the curator of the country, schubert, the bauhaus buildings were declared historical property, not to be destroyed, and i had them provisionally rebuilt so they could be used. five schools benefited from this by using the buildings in shifts. then we were able to secure equipment for the teaching workships of the planned bauhaus. i had hand looms built according to the instructions of a former weaving master.

rausch started in his workshop with the design of dishes for mass production, stolp prepared an institute for picture statistics, while ursinn installed a carpenters' shop at the orangerie of the luisium, and radack and marx installed studios for advertising graphics and photography in the master buildings.

since the bauhaus buildings could not be cleared for the time being, lord mayor hesse put at our disposal two castles. the luisium was completed and later became the theater workshops, which should contain the representational arts and a guest house. castle kühnau was particularly suited for the departments of horticulture and the greenery, urban and country planning, while the bauhaus buildings were prepared later for the housing of the building-planning workshop and all other workshops.

the temporary theater opened with *iphigenie*. then followed concerts with works by mahler, schönberg, hindemith, shostakovich and prokofiev. every week there were public discussions about culture, city planning, and political questions. we organized exhibitions and contests to interest the population of dessau in our undertaking. scharoun and mächter, mertens, mattern and funke, bruno paul, kurt lahs, and others came to dessau to discuss the question of revival and continuation of the bauhaus. i contacted will grohmann in dresden, henselmann in weimar, and hopp in halle, who all wanted to introduce certain basic principles of the bauhaus education in their schools.

in the meantime we managed to draw up a general building plan for rebuilding the city, against strong political opposition. the rebuilding of apartments started according to plan and the degree of the damage, at first with easily repaired projects. sixty-two village plans were put up by my planning department in the course of the governmental agrarian reform. together with the official curator of the country, doctor schubert, i was able to prevent the demolition of valuable castles and the destruction of parks by declaring them suitable for old-age homes or for cultural or party purposes. a list was prepared of the teaching staff appointed for the new bauhaus, in consultation with hesse, scheper, schmied, the cultural adviser in halle, and the members of the bauhaus. after our experiences before 1933, we tried to achieve an aggregate of very varied personalities, a scale of the most diverse directions and temperaments, who promised an atmosphere of fruitful tensions. according to the former structure of the institute we provided for its division in three parts, the preliminary studies, the workshop tuition and the planning departments. an innovation was the horticultural workshop and the greenery planning as well as a building workshop. the two landscape departments were not just regarded as a loose appendix to the bauhaus, but rather there so that each student of the preliminary course could study biological processes in nature in the greenhouse. an extension of the workshop to include plastics was planned, whereby a collaboration with the local industries in bitterfeld seemed possible.

the scientific doctrines should receive their own department head, further, one considered a commercial director, who should act as liaison between bauhaus and industry, to draw up the necessary contracts and to see to the completion of the production of samples.

the work for building as well as city and country planning could be settled on an official level, also the projected inclusion of the housing authorities. i succeeded in putting through a budget of almost three hundred thousand german marks, of which one-third was intended to be carried by the city and two-thirds by the country. the city was also prepared to undertake the final furnishing of the added castles for the bauhaus buildings, including a one time expense for the bauhaus show. with the bauhaus show a prelude was planned, which should introduce the opening of the institute. as a first part of the projected exhibition the already furnished workshops were planned, combined with a survey of the change in education, especially in the field of design, and the deviation of the bauhaus tuition from other colleges (academies, industrial schools, technical colleges, and universities). the second part was intended to present a survey of the effects of the bauhaus, in particular, the emigration of its members all over the world and its influence on other schools in various countries.

for the third part it was planned to show products and results from the bauhaus workshops and studios: furniture, appliances, buildings, and city planning; and the possibilities of extending this production and utilizing it for the rebuilding of the destroyed cities and households. a large number of former bauhaus members from many countries had agreed to participate. gropius and hesse undertook the protectorate of the bauhaus show. then came the elections. the socialist unity party won with a majority of 0.5 percent. hesse refused to continue running the municipal government by subordinating himself to the political directives of the socialist unity party and a new lord mayor appeared: adolfs, seven years the announcer for the *freiheitssender moskau* (free broadcasting station moscow). purges started. secret police agents appeared. the hatred of the philistines against the bauhaus was resurrected, the natives' aversion toward the foreigners was used politically. we misunderstood each other immediately and thoroughly. "i hear this word 'bauhaus' for the first time," said adolfs, "but one thing i can tell you right away, your elite is out of the question! we want mass education! two thousand apprentices can be taught here! and if you talk of an attraction at the bauhaus show, i agree — a merry-go-round should be on the grounds!" i was confounded by this suggestion and thought that the bauhaus originator did not mean this exactly. when i timidly tried to explain to him the idea of the bauhaus, he declared me a complete reactionary.

alderman doctor klumpp from quedlinburg, a bauhaus member owning the largest feininger collection in germany, declared immediately that quedlinburg would be in a position to house the complete planned institution, in case its realization was impossible in dessau. a positive decision was reached at the quedlinburg town council. then followed negotiations and journeys between dessau and the still well-preserved harz city. buildings were available on the domfelsen. in the meantime adolfs was reprimanded by the government in halle and his own party. then came his revenge.

at first my food ration card was withdrawn, then arrest and evacuation by the russians threatened due to some informer (supposedly i had made a secret out of my activities in the baltic provinces during the war). i disappeared for fourteen days to watch what was going to happen. hesse could no longer help me, and i was advised to flee to west germany.

when, after three months, i reappeared in dessau illegally, the social realism had begun to conquer the field, a manifestation of a clique enslaved by the party. i went to berlin, talked to becher, strauss, and abusch. they were sorry for me personally — "no doubt the bauhaus may be a valuable institution . . . but politics come first!" one was affected by stalin's conception of fine and representational art, which came surprisingly close to that of the third reich. we had come out of the frying pan into the fire. hesse and most of our dessau friends came to berlin a year later. will grohmann, hassenpflug, doctor hanna and ott hoffmann, lindig, arndt, lahs; the leading graphic artists left the east zone in the course of the next two years. long ago adolfs was replaced. his successor — a former salesgirl in a department store — endeavored even more to retain the party line. city planning was disposed of, and blocks of flats, dreadful monsters in pseudo-classical style, were aimlessly piled up in the center of the city. during the first third of its realization, our village planning was abruptly interrupted in favor of a direct industrial concentration of forces.

at first we thought all this was a mistake — a terrible nightmare — until slowly we came to realize that this exaggerated idealism during the national socialist era, these infinite sacrifices toward wrong ideals, resulted in a reaction of the most blatant materialistic idealogy in the east as well as in the west. when our efforts in the east proved to no avail, we started our endeavors in the west: hassenpflug in hamburg, mattern in kassel, the berlin bauhaus members at the hochschule für bildende künste; max bill and inge scholl in ulm. all of them tried to convert the traditional schools into institutes according to the principles of the bauhaus, to rebuild such an institute. each of them had to make numerous compromises or were only partly successful. it would be a mistake to draw the conclusion that the bauhaus idea is out dated, this can only be attributed to superficial observations. it seems to me that the framework set up by the masters will be valid for a long time. around 1950 i once more showed in the exhibition "22 bauhaus members in berlin", works by most of its collaborators and friends. this was the first demonstration after 1945, when architecture, town planning, furniture, appliances, and textiles were shown in connection with graphic art for advertising, sculpture, and painting.

Teo Otto:

Born in Remscheid in 1904. After a technical education he went to work, continuing his studies at the Kunstakademie in Kassel from 1923 to 1926. After spending some time in Paris studying, he became assistant at the Bauhochschule Weimar for a short while in 1926.

At twenty-one he had already designed his first stage scenery for the state theater in Kassel. He joined the Kroll Opera in Berlin as scenic designer in 1927. In 1931 he was put in charge of the scenery at the Prussian State Theater and at the same time he became collaborator at the Staatsoper. In 1933 Otto was forced to leave the country.

In Zurich he became stage designer at the Schauspielhaus and from 1938 to 1960 their chief scenic designer. It is due to Otto's stage designs that this theater became internationally famous. Among his most famous designs are sets for many plays by Brecht, for instance the first performance of *Mother Courage*. After the war he created many sets as a guest artist in Berlin, Frankfurt, Hamburg, Cologne, London, New York, Milan. From 1952 to 1957 Otto taught a class in the design of stage scenery at the Werkakademie in Kassel. In 1957 he was appointed to the Düsseldorf Kunstakademie as professor of theatrical art and he was elected a member of the German Academy of Arts in Berlin. Together with Eckhard Neumann and Wolfgang Schmidt, he undertook in 1964 the conceptual design of the exhibit "Bauhaus-Idee, Form, Zweck, Zeit," for the Göppinger Galerie, a private gallery that sought to further the relationship between commerce and culture. This was the first German post-war exhibition containing original works from all fields of the Bauhaus.

He has been awarded many prizes and decorations for his work as designer of stage scenery. Since 1927 it has been frequently shown in group exhibitions and one-man shows. A few days before his death an exhibition opened at the Frankfurt Operahouse displaying his artistic output. Otto died on June 7, 1968, in Frankfurt.

The history of the Bauhaus cannot be separated from the time of the industrial revolution, the social regrouping, the wars, and revolutions. The bourgeois world of security, rational certainty was destroyed. The accustomed, the familiar was shattered. Bourgeois culture and aesthetics were ruined. Everywhere was the will to find new artistic formations, new means of expression for pictorial art. Kindred souls of equal minds were found in the East as well as in the West, with the intention to strive for new aims on new paths. It was in the air. The disaster of the war, the misery of the masses, helped to expedite the process. Sects, reformers, world improvers, anthropologists, quacks, faith healers, apostles, theosophists, tramps, national Bolshevists, all joined in. All of them swam to new shores, preaching community and solidarity. All of them fought with each other, sang trooper's songs, and demanded equality, until the outstretched brotherly hands were taken by party membership, book and uniform. All of them appropriated arrogant, caste-group thinking, talked of "circle," "community," "spirit," of intolerantly destroying the self-willed, the good-for-nothing; all of them practiced flag-waving and loyalty to insignia and sang united in army *bel canto*, from right to left. . . . "and with us marches the new time."

Unemployed stood in line, soup kitchens fed upholders of culture, food-ration cards were objects of value. Everywhere was a shortage of coal. Members of secret groups made war at night with walking canes. There were rebellions in the Ruhr Valley, in Saxonia and Thuringia, inflation and political assasinations. This was the background for these many happy moments that made the Bauhaus possible and made it the crystallization point of similar thinking, which burst open in Europe and was scattered all over the world.

This is how the Bauhaus became the abode of future-directed realizations of the most beautiful impulses of the then-wounded Europe, the beaten Germany. The Bauhaus was an idea that reached beyond local limitations, that was an expression of a world-wide attitude. Its significant consequences could not be separated from its awareness of daily events.

Its work and creative processes were infiltrated daily by political cares, concerns about existence. The workaday world with its hardships equaled a test bench for the heights of the human spirit and its creative power.

It was miraculous that the danger of group thinking, of sectarian narrow-mindedness, art-sacerdotal intolerance, was mastered. Who did not want to improve the world at that time. Who did not want to win over for his cause somebody, sometime, at some place. If the situation of the Bauhaus was a particularly happy one, it was because splendor and misery, large and small matters, individuality and collectivism, counterbalanced each other. This polarity created the ferment of the effective liveliness far beyond its time, created the presupposition of continuous renewal of an idea. Active curiosity, aimful questioning, kept alive a presence that had to prove itself again and again and that was exposed to the hard blows of vulgar politics, a brutal lust for power.

Itten, for instance, can only be understood against the background of a disorganized world, resounding from the commands of the organizers, and the beginning soul-searching for new relations, new sources of the humanly possible. What could one do after misused order led to terror, became the death of liberty. They all collapsed under the shock of destruction. What was still valid? In the universities one served up the last remainders of military goods and chattel. The best asked themselves: "How can I help, serve?" Others: "Where lie the faults of our society?" Itten and Gropius differed in their views, differed in their questioning. Both endeavored in their own way to conquer sensibly the zero hour of that time after the chaos of the First World War.

The Bauhaus possessed geniuses of anticipation, possessed creators of world-wide reputation, each with his own view of life, each different. It was an enormous concentration of names — among them Feininger, Klee, Kandinsky — names of world-wide importance: Moholy, who tried to formulate anew taste, aesthetics, beauty; Schlemmer, who in his artistic capacity searched painting, sculpture, and stage for new possibilities of expression. Personalities such as Albers, Muche, and Hirschfeld, with their enduring impulses. Hannes Meyer, whose direction for functionalism and efficiency was not only dictated by the fact that in Germany there were 7 million and in America 10 million unemployed.

The life of the Bauhaus, its representatives and its students, was accompanied by a political drama which in its impact influenced the everyday life and every form of living. No wonder that Hannes Meyer, driven by responsibility in view of the economic misery of his time, gave priority to the important, the useful, the purposeful, over good taste, beauty, the aesthetic. The magnitude of an artistic action and the integrity of a concern becomes understandable in terms of the world around us. At that time the crime of tightening of the chin straps started, and the mob put on party uniforms. The great Mies van der Rohe headed the Bauhaus in its finishing phases. I do not regard it as an accident that fate assigned him this task, in view of the burning Reichstag and an upcoming apocalyptic time.

In the history of the Bauhaus everything happened; it could not have been otherwise considering the diversity of personalities that were assembled there. The works extended from the absurd to the visionary up to the concrete. It seemed incredible, very contradictory, and often confused in its diversity. But were these not various reflecting facets of the same thing? It remains for the future to show this. In a modest way, and to be regarded as an experiment, this effort is also the concern of this exhibition.

The Bauhaus became an idea due to the summing-up of human and artistic variety. If the Bauhaus was an idea, then this idea could not be bound by time and place; it belonged to the world. If, however, it was bound by locality, and thus a matter for the initiated, the appointed, then the guardians of the grail could have buried this idea. The aim of the exhibition is to be a forum, to question the usual outlook, to point toward its admirable variety, and to show associations. One cannot identify the Bauhaus Idea with expediency, squaring and geometrical treatment of the world, nor with industrial usage. A functionalism spent in mechanical superficiality is doubtful. Objectionable also is the simplicity that regards the colorful reflections of life in blue, red, and yellow, in the horizontal and the vertical. Polarity determined the Bauhaus. Black and white, dot and line, yes and no, order and liberty are expressions of infinity, are flashes of divine wealth, are positions of unbelievable variety. It is to the permanent credit of the Bauhaus that it has shown the way, in the midst of confusion — the eternal play between these poles.

Credits

Abbreviations:

Cat. GG.: Catalogue of the exhibition "Bauhaus — Idee — Form — Zweck — Zeit" (Bauhaus — Idea — Form — Purpose — Time) at the Göppinger Gallery in Frankfurt/Main, February 1 – March 28, 1964.

Zeit: Die Zeit ohne Eigenschaften — Eine Bilanz der zwanziger Jahre (Time Without Characteristics — An Account of the Twentieth Year), edited by Leonard Reinisch, Stuttgart, 1961. The book contains reports and contributing discussions of the Third Congress of the History of Ideas of the city of Munich, from November 21 – 25, 1960.

Walter Gropius: *Bauhaus Manifesto.* Published in April, 1919 in Weimar. (Translation by Alba Lorman.)

Walter Gropius: p. 15. Statement made by Gropius when he became *Ehrensenator* (honorary senator) of the Hochschule für Bildende Künste (College of Fine Arts) in Berlin, November 3, 1962. Published in *Schriftenreihe* (publications) of the Hochschule für Bildende Künste, Berlin, vol. 7, 1963. (Newly edited.)

Johannes Itten: p. 20. Published in Cat. GG., p. 20.

Bruno Adler: p. 22. Published in Cat. GG., p. 22.

Johannes Molzahn: p. 26. Published in Cat. GG., p. 26.

Gerhard Marcks: p. 27. Published in Cat. GG., p. 27.

Felix Klee: p. 37. First publication.

Paul Citroen: p. 44. Published in Cat. GG., p. 29.

Karl Peter Röhl: p. 51. Published in Cat. GG., p. 28.

Alfred Arndt: p. 53. Section reprinted in catalogue "Alfred Arndt," exhibition at the Bauhaus Archives, Darmstadt, November 30 – December 22, 1968. Published in Cat. GG., p. 28. (Original manuscript lower case.)

Robert Michel: p. 59. Published in Cat. GG., p. 45.

Herta Wescher: p. 63. First full-length publication. A brief version in Cat. GG., p. 47.

Hans Haffenrichter: p. 67. First publication.

Lothar Schreyer: p. 71. Published in Cat. GG., p. 48. (Former publications unknown.)

Werner Graeff: p. 73. Published in Cat. GG., p. 59.

Sigfried Giedion: p. 76. Section published in *Zeit*, p. 22. Reprint in Cat. GG., pp. 51 & 80.

Giula Pap: p. 77. First publication.

Alexander Bortnyik: p. 79. First publication.

Georg Muche: p. 83. Formal address in celebration of Johannes Itten's seventy-fifth birthday on November 11, 1963 in Zurich. Published in Cat. GG., p. 53.

————: p. 201. "Bauhaus Epitaph," newly edited version from *Zeit*, pp. 139 – 142.

Marianne Brandt: p. 97. First publication of letter to E. N., dated May 13, 1966.

Erich Lissner: p. 101. Reprint in *Frankfurter Rundscau*, February 1, 1964. Published in Cat. GG., p. 65.

Walter Dexel: p. 104. Published in Cat. GG., p. 62.

Walter Mehring: p. 108. Published in Cat. GG., p. 27.

Erich Buchholz: p. 109. First publication.

Lou Scheper: p. 112. Published in Cat. GG., p. 95. (Re-edited.)

Heinrich König: p. 118. Published in Cat. GG., p. 70. (Re-edited.)

Helene Schmidt-Nonne: p. 121. First publication. (Original manuscript in English.)

Gunta Stadler-Stölzl: p. 128. Published in Cat. GG., p. 110. (Translation by Beatrice Bruggmann. Re-edited.)

Herbert Bauer: p. 131. Poem presented by Wolfgang von Eckhart at Columbia University, New York, 1961. Published in Cat. GG., p. 98.

Fritz Hesse: p. 143. Published in Cat. GG., p. 74.

Xanti Schawinsky: p. 145. Published in Cat. GG., p. 93. (Original manuscript lower case. Translation by Bertrand Languages, Inc., New York.)

Tut Schlemmer: p. 152. Lecture published as a private print by the Kunstgewerbeschule (School of Fine Arts), Zurich, in 1962. (Revised.)

Ursula Schuh: p. 160. Published in Cat. GG., p. 76.

Will Grohmann: p. 163. Reprint from *Universitas*, vol. 12, Stuttgart, 1957, p. 1239. (Newly edited.)

Josef Albers: p. 169. Discussion published in *Zeit*, p. 150. (Newly edited.)

T. Lux Feininger: p. 172. Reprinted from *Criticisme*, vol. 2, no. 3, 1960, p. 260, by T. Lux Feininger by permission of the Wayne State University Press. (Original in English. Abridged.)

Hannes Beckmann: p. 195. First publication. (Original in English.)

Ludwig Grote: p. 205. Published in Cat. GG., p. 123.

Max Bill: p. 208. Published in Cat. GG., p. 120. (Original manuscript lower case. Revised.)

Emil Rasch: p. 209. Published in Cat. GG., p. 107.

Gustav Hassenpflug: p. 211. Published in Cat. GG., p. 96.

Howard Dearstyne: p. 212. Reprinted from catalogue of the exhibition "50 years of Bauhaus" in Chicago, 1969. (Original in English.)

Pius Pahl: p. 227. First publication. (Translation in collaboration with the author.)

Alfred Hoppe: p. 232. Published in Cat. GG., p. 113.

Richard Koppe: p. 234. First publication. (Original in English.)

Hubert Hoffmann: p. 242. Published in Cat. GG., p. 127. (Original manuscript lower case.)

Teo Otto: p. 248. Published in Cat. GG., p. 8.